What Kind of Democracy?
What Kind of Market?

What Kind of Democracy?
What Kind of Market?

Latin America in the Age of Neoliberalism

Edited by

Philip D. Oxhorn
and
Graciela Ducatenzeiler

The Pennsylvania State University Press
University Park, Pennsylvania

Library of Congress Cataloging-in-Publication Data

What kind of democracy? What kind of market? : Latin America in the
  age of neoliberalism / edited by Philip D. Oxhorn and Graciela
  Ducatenzeiler.

          p.   cm.
      Includes bibliographical references and index.
      ISBN 0-271-01799-6 (alk. paper)
      ISBN 0-271-01800-3 (pbk. : alk. paper)
      1. Latin America—Economic policy.   2. Latin America—Politics and
  government—1980–   3. Latin America—Economic conditions—1982–
  4. Democracy—Latin America.   I. Oxhorn, Philip.
  II. Ducatenzeiler, Graciela.
  HC125.W46   1998
  338.98—dc21   97-49899
                                                                           CIP

It is the policy of The Pennsylvania State University Press to use acid-free paper for
the first printing of all clothbound books. Publications on uncoated stock satisfy the
minimum requirements of American National Standard for Information Sciences—
Permanence of Paper for Printed Library Materials, ANSI Z39.48-1992.

Contents

List of Contributors   vii
Acknowledgments   ix

PART I: THEORETICAL AND COMPARATIVE ISSUES

1. Economic Reform and Democratization in Latin America   3
    Philip Oxhorn and Graciela Ducatenzeiler
2. The Missing Social Contract: Governability and
    Reform in Latin America   21
    Luiz Carlos Bresser Pereira and Yoshiaki Nakano
3. The Prospects for Open Regionalism in Latin America   43
    Juan Alberto Fuentes

PART II: COUNTRY CASE STUDIES: POLITICAL PARTIES AND SOCIAL FORCES

4. Economic Reform in Argentina:
    Which Social Forces for What Aims?   61
    Jorge Schvarzer
5. Brazil's Drifting Economy:
    Stagnation and Inflation During 1987–1996   89
    Werner Baer and Claudio Paiva
6. Macroeconomic Adjustment in Chile and
    the Politics of the Popular Sectors   127
    Manuel Barrera
7. Trade Unions and the Corporatist System in Mexico   151
    Francisco Zapata

8. Interest Representation and the Party System in Mexico   169
       Jean-François Prud'homme

        PART III: HYBRID REGIMES AND NEOPLURALIST POLITICS

9. Is the Century of Corporatism Over? Neoliberalism
       and the Rise of Neopluralism   195
       Philip Oxhorn
10. New Democracies and Economic Crisis in Latin America   219
       Francisco C. Weffort
11. Conclusions: What Kind of Democracy? What Kind of Market?   227
       Philip Oxhorn and Graciela Ducatenzeiler

References   241
Index   259

List of Contributors

Werner Baer is professor of economics at the University of Illinois at Urbana-Champaign. He has taught frequently in a number of Brazilian institutions, including the Fondaçao Getúlio Vargas and the University of São Paulo. His publications on the Brazilian economy include *The Brazilian Economy: Growth and Development*, which is now in its fourth edition.

Manuel Barrera has been a professor and researcher for several years at the Universidad de Chile and the Universidad Católica de Chile. He was also founder and director of the Centro de Estudios Sociales. A specialist in labor studies and the politics of the popular sectors, his publications include *Sindicatos bajo regímenes militares: Argentina, Brasil, Chile.*

Luiz Carlos Bresser Pereira is professor of economics at the Fondaçao Getúlio Vargas. Founding editor of the *Revista de Economia Política*, he has published numerous studies in the area of political economy, including *Economic Crisis and State Reform in Brazil.* He also has held several important positions in the government since Brazil's return to democracy and is currently minister of federal administration and state reform.

Graciela Ducatenzeiler is professor of political science and director of the Latin America Research Group at the Université de Montréal. Her publications have focused on organized labor, politics, and populism in Latin America, with an emphasis on Argentina. These include *Syndicats et politique en Argentine.*

Juan Alberto Fuentes is an adviser for the Economic Commission for Latin America and the Caribbean of the United Nations (ECLAC) and the United Nations Development Programs in Guatemala. He has worked with the ECLAC in Mexico and Chile and has published articles on trade and development issues in Latin America.

Yoshiaki Nakano is associate professor of economics at the Fondaçao Getúlio Vargas and has frequently taught at other Brazilian institutions. He is currently finance secretary for the state government of São Paulo. He has published widely in economics, business organization, and rural development.

Philip Oxhorn is associate professor of political science at McGill University and the author of *Organizing Civil Society: The Popular Sectors and the Struggle for Democracy in Chile*. He has published widely on civil society, social movements, and democratization.

Claudio Paiva is currently on the staff of the International Monetary Fund. Having received his Ph.D. in economics from the University of Illinois, he has specialized in and published articles on monetary economics, industrial organization, and economic development.

Jean-François Prud'homme is professor at the Centro de Estudios Sociólogicos of El Colegio de México. He specializes in the study of political parties and electoral reform in Mexico, as well as in the nature of political citizenship, and has published works on the Mexican political system.

Jorge Schvarzer is director of the Centro de Investigaciones Sobre el Estado y la Administración. He is also professor of the political-economic history of Argentina at the Universidad Nacional of Buenos Aires, and frequently teaches at the Institut d'études de l'Amérique Latine in Paris. His publications include *La industria que supimos conseguir. Una historia político social de la industria Argentina*.

Francisco C. Weffort is professor of political science at the Universidade de São Paulo, where he was director of the Contemporary Culture Studies Center. He has also taught in various European and American institutions, and has published widely on democracy, social development, and politics and government in Latin America, including *O Populismo na Política brasiliéra?* He is presently the minister of culture in Brazil.

Francisco Zapata has been professor at El Colegio de México since 1974, and is director of their Centro de Estudios Sociológicos. He is a specialist on organized labor in Latin America, particularly Chile and Mexico. His publications include *Autonomía y Subordinación en el Sindicalismo Latinoamericano*.

Acknowledgments

This book is the outgrowth of a conference held at McGill University, Montreal, in April 1994. The conference was made possible by generous grants from the Cooperative Security Competition Programme; External Affairs and International Trade Canada; the Faculties of Arts and Graduate Studies, McGill University; and the Faculté des Arts et des Sciences of the Université de Montréal. Original versions of the chapters included in the current volume were presented at the conference. The authors all benefited from the often lively discussion generated by the conference's other participants, whom we would like to thank (in alphabetical order): Normand Beaudet, Confédération des Syndicats Nationaux (CSN); Thomas Bruneau, Naval Post Graduate School; John Curtis, External Affairs and International Trade Canada; Jean Dominique LaFay, Université de Paris-Sorbonne; Edgar Dosman, Canadian Foundation for the Americas (FOCAL); Alonso de Gortari, minister for Economic Affairs, Mexican Consulate in Montreal; Frances Hagopian, Tufts University; John Hall, McGill University; Bernardo Kugler, World Bank; Laura MacDonald, Carleton University; Adriana Marshall, The National Research Council of Argentina; David Pollock, Carleton University; Jaime Ros, University of Notre Dame; Philippe Schmitter, Stanford University; Elizabeth Spehar, International Centre for Human Rights and Democratic Development (Montreal); Judith Teichman, University of Toronto; and Anne Weston, North-South Institute (Ottawa).

We would also like to give special thanks to Philippe Faucher of the Université de Montréal, who helped us organize the McGill conference. Special thanks are also in order for David Ainsworth, a doctoral student in the political science department at McGill, who did a superb job as an administrative assistant for the McGill conference.

Finally, we would like to thank Sandy Thatcher for his support, as well as Bill Smith and a second anonymous reader for Penn State, whose invaluable comments on the entire manuscript have helped make it a much better book.

I

Theoretical and Comparative Issues

1

Economic Reform and Democratization in Latin America

Philip Oxhorn and Graciela Ducatenzeiler

By now, it has become almost cliché to refer to the 1980s as Latin America's "lost decade." The resource drain caused by the servicing of excessive external debt and severe economic recession, frequently combined with escalating inflation, forced in almost every case difficult policy choices for national governments in Latin America. These policy choices not only have implications for the consolidation of democracy in the region but can also pose a significant threat to the governability of specific countries (Ducatenzeiler and Oxhorn 1994). They touch on many of the core problems affecting Latin American polities, including political, economic, social, and humanitarian issues. Yet we still know very little about the longer-term political and social impact of the policy choices being made today. This book attempts to fill this important void through a comparative study of the experiences of four countries: Argentina, Brazil, Chile, and Mexico.

Somewhat surprisingly, the severity of the situation has led to the emergence of a high degree of consensus among economic policy makers on how individual countries in the region should attempt to respond to the adverse economic trends. This is true even though the timing, pace, and extension of the reform process, as well as the actors that participate in the process, vary significantly. This policy consensus, whose prescriptions reach beyond Latin America to include other developing areas and the former Soviet bloc, stresses the need for more pragmatic economic policies of trade liberalization and the privatization of national economies with a limited role for the state (World Bank 1990; Williamson 1990, 1993). Old dogmas concerning economic nationalism and a large public sector as the motor for inward-looking development models seem to be dead or dying. A new outward-looking development model based firmly on market forces is being more or less rapidly put into place in virtually all Latin American countries, paving the way for renewed optimism that the 1990s will be a decade of growth.

After twenty years of experience in implementing such policies, starting with the now successful policies of neoliberal economic reform begun by the Pinochet military regime in Chile in the mid-1970s, there is an extensive body of literature that examines in some detail the various factors accounting for the "successful" implementation of liberalizing economic reforms.[1] This literature is still far from conclusive (Geddes 1995), at least in part because there is no single agreed upon gauge for measuring "success" (Bresser Pereira, Maravall, and Przeworski 1993), but it does seem to be unanimous in supporting one rather counterintuitive and paradoxical conclusion: regime type does not seem to play a central role in explaining the success of economic reforms.[2] This contrasts with earlier theories that suggested regime type is central by arguing that only authoritarian regimes have enjoyed the necessary insulation from those interests most likely to be hurt by what was considered to be painful economic medicine (Díaz Alejandro 1983; Sheahan 1980; Skidmore 1977). The failure of some authoritarian regimes to implement economic liberalization and the ability of a number of fragile new democracies to succeed where their authoritarian predecessors failed apparently fly in the face of such predictions, and have led a number of prominent

1. For example, see Haggard and Kaufman 1995, 1992; Smith, Acuña, and Gamarra 1994a, 1994b; Nelson et al. 1994, 1990; and Bates and Krueger 1993b. An excellent review of much of this literature is found in Geddes 1995.

2. An important exception to this conclusion is found in Bresser Pereira, Maravall, and Przeworski 1993. This is due to the specific definition of "successful" economic policies they adopt. Taking other authors to task for the uncritical approaches they use to gauge policy success, Bresser Pereira et al. argue that economic reforms should be considered successful only if they promote economic growth and support democratic institutions. The authors in this volume, including Bresser Pereira himself, would all agree.

researchers to abandon regime type altogether as a factor in explaining the outcomes of attempts at neoliberal economic reform. On the basis of what appears to be an overwhelming body of evidence from Latin America and elsewhere, a growing number of authors are now arguing for the need to move beyond the excessively broad categories of "democratic" and "authoritarian" regimes. Instead, this literature concludes that future research should focus on factors that appear to transcend regime type (Geddes 1995; Remmer 1990; Przeworski and Limongi 1993) or even completely reconceptualize what we mean by democracy in order to better reflect Latin American reality (O'Donnell 1994; Weffort, Chapter 10 of this volume).

Less surprisingly, this search for non-regime-specific factors to explain economic policy making has led to a corresponding de-emphasis on social forces and civil society in general. The earlier literature had framed the problem in terms of the state's accessibility to mass pressures: economic policy making in democracies was easily undermined by those interests that were adversely affected by economic liberalization, and only authoritarian regimes could provide policy makers with the needed insulation from societal pressures to get the job of economic reform done. The failures of brutal authoritarian regimes and the successes of weak democratic ones seemed to belie any problem of accessibility per se. If regime type was not a predictor of successful economic reform, then almost by definition neither was the degree of vulnerability to mass pressures. As Geddes concludes, "The reason economic reform has posed less of a threat to democratic government than expected is not that costs are unexpectedly light but that interests are unexpectedly weak. Societal interests hurt by liberalization, even when numerically large and well-organized (as labor is when compared with other groups), have often failed to force policy change" (1995: 205).

If the organization of interests (i.e., civil society) is weak, the literature seems to suggest that the analyst must look elsewhere to explain policy variation. The result has been a renewed interest in institutions, particularly state institutions, and the role that policy-making elites play in reform processes (Geddes 1995; Remmer 1990; Przeworski and Limongi 1993; O'Donnell 1994; Haggard and Kaufman 1992a). Few if any distinctions are drawn between what might be considered democratic institutions and those more closely associated with nondemocratic regimes. In particular, those institutions that provide for broad citizen participation and ensure governmental accountability are not seen as being particularly important or even relevant.[3] From a purely economic point of view, it seems to make little difference if a country is ruled by an elected government or not. Regime change per se appears more important than the transition to any particular type of regime simply because incumbents are removed and new elites are brought in (Geddes 1995; Malloy 1987). "Society-centered" theories are replaced by "state-centered" theories, leaving little room for a middle ground between the two. For it is precisely this "middle ground" that is the focus of the literature on regime type—the particular link between a given state and society. Moreover, society's capacity to influence reform policies depends on both the nature and size of its own power resources, and on the institutional setting of the state's decision-making processes. Political influence comprises not only interest-group power in terms of the type of organization and the resources at its disposal but also in terms of the relationship of these groups to the political system (Inmergut 1992). In other words, political influence depends also on the opportunities left to the society (labor and the popular sectors in general) to influence political decisions.

While state institutions are of central importance in explaining the success of any development strategy,[4] the current trend in the literature on economic reform in Latin America suffers from two critical problems. The first is actually an error of omission: more recent analyses of the success of economic reforms ignore the reasons *why* organized interests are so weak. The literature tends to abandon civil society as an explanatory variable without appreciating that civil society in fact was a major victim of the economic crisis that led to the need for economic reforms in the first place. Major societal actors are unable to resist or effectively express themselves. This is particularly true of organized labor in many countries, which has been ravaged by unemployment, hyperinflation,

3. One important exception deals with the institutions that provide for an appropriate relationship between key business interests and the state's economic policy-making apparatus (Evans 1995; Silva 1996). Here again, however, the nature of these relations are seen as transcending regime type. Indeed, in the Chilean case according to Silva, a major challenge facing the newly elected democratic regime was to retain the same positive relationship with the business community that had been established by the military dictatorship in the mid-1980s.

4. This is now quite clear from the abundant literature on the so-called South East Asian newly industrializing countries—South Korea, Taiwan, Singapore, and Hong Kong (see Deyo 1987; Amsden 1989; Haggard 1990; and Gereffi and Wyman 1990). It should be noted that much of this literature suggests that authoritarian institutions play an important role in explaining development successes. This is consistent with the earlier approach to understanding economic reform. For a somewhat different perspective that stresses the importance of both strong state institutions and political democracy, see ECLA 1990 and Bresser Pereira, Maravall, and Przeworski 1993.

and other economic maladies associated with the crisis (see Barrera, Chapter 6, Zapata, Chapter 7, and Oxhorn, Chapter 9 of this volume; Schneider 1995).[5] Moreover, interests are not only weak because of the weight of the crisis but also because of the lack of opportunities they have to influence political decisions. The new "rules of the game" provide, in most countries of the region, little space for popular influence.

The second, related problem is a normative one and concerns democracy itself: in de-emphasizing the importance of regime type, this literature seems to be taking political democracy for granted. It ignores the increasing tendency within Latin America for democratic institutions to become more authoritarian, or confuses the institutionalization of authoritarian political practices with democratization (Ducatenzeiler and Oxhorn 1994; O'Donnell 1993; Weffort 1991, 1992, and Chapter 10 of this volume; Oxhorn, Chapter 9 of this volume). The effects of dramatic changes in economic policy on Latin American politics are either taken for granted, on the assumption that renewed economic growth is almost a panacea for putting Latin America back on the path toward modernization, or simply ignored because growth is seen as a necessary (if not sufficient) condition for greater levels socioeconomic equity and the consolidation of still fragile democratic regimes. Criteria of efficiency, stability, or even simply "electoral mandate" (O'Donnell 1994) are emphasized over normative values such as accountability and citizen participation.

In a famous essay, Francis Fukuyama (1992) predicted "the end of history" with the collapse of socialist regimes in Eastern Europe. This collapse, together with the democratic transitions and the crises of reformist and populist states in Latin America, provided many intellectuals with the "proof" that Western democracy had become universalized and transformed into the only viable political alternative. Leaving aside more pessimistic arguments concerning democracy's future (Huntington 1989, 1991), this book takes as its point of departure the notion that the liberalism undergirding the current economic reforms is not synonymous with political democracy. On the contrary, liberalism appears to be compatible with different political regimes that include different levels of political competition and participation by citizens. Even

---

5. It should be pointed out that in a number of cases, repression was also a factor undermining the strength of civil society and particularly organized labor. This is most obviously true for the Chilean case, in which economic reforms were implemented by a military regime. It may also be part of the authoritarian legacy in other cases, in which similar reforms have been implemented by a democratic regime after a recent transition from authoritarian rule.

accepting a relatively minimalist definition of political democracy that emphasizes the institutions of the state and different forms of government to the detriment of the structure of civil society, the new Latin American democracies are clearly quite far removed from the mature democracies of North America and Western Europe. In particular, existing Latin American democracies possess low levels of governmental accountability to the citizenry. If we use a more demanding definition of democracy that combines both institutional aspects at the level of the state with aspects linked to the organization of civil society, such as the modes of organization of collective interests and the participation of the organizations of civil society in the elaboration and implementation of public policies, the differences between Latin American democracies and the liberal democracies of North America and Western Europe are even more significant. All of this serves to underscore the fact that, independently of the type of democracy that may actually be desired, there are many different types of democracy that are possible. Hence, the first question in the book's title: What are the characteristics of the new Latin American democracies?

In the same way that there is no single model of possible democratic regimes, the emerging market economies also appear to be far removed from the models of the early industrialized countries. The new neoliberal economic-reform policies presuppose the existence of a market that must regulate the behavior of all economic actors, a role played fundamentally up until now by the state. Markets, however, are essentially political creations (see Bresser Pereira and Nakano, Chapter 2 of this volume; Chaudhry 1993). The nature of the state and ruling coalition that creates them will, of necessity, reflect the relative distribution of power and interests of those groups most actively involved in its creation (or destruction). The destruction of economic autarchy did not necessarily give rise to the emergence of free markets to the extent that a lower level of microeconomic intervention was replaced by an active control of the macroeconomy (Canitrot and Sigal 1995). Yet the historical coincidence between economic liberalism and political democracy has allowed for certain facile conclusions concerning the consequences that this type of economic model would have for the political systems found in Latin America. The considerable evidence of a long-term correlation between economic development and political democracy has been used as a foundation for various attempts to demonstrate that the current wave of market-oriented economic reforms in Latin America will ultimately allow the various countries in the region to overcome historical problems of economic backwardness and political instability.[6] In this way, the well-known argument that capitalist development will create the necessary conditions for the construction of democracy reemerges. Democracy appears as a product (output) of the market, but what kind of market?

Even if the assumptions of the earlier literature on economic reform have been proven wrong, this literature did highlight the existence of alternative economic policies, the importance of power relations among different segments of society, and the significant role that repression has played in Latin American politics. With notable exceptions (e.g., Bresser Pereira, Maravall, and Przeworski 1993; Smith, Acuña, and Gamarra 1994a, 1994b; CEPAL 1990), the appropriate set of economic policies for reforming the moribund economies of the region has been taken as a given, with the possibility of alternative policies implicitly (or sometimes even explicitly) rejected. Democratic inputs are still often assumed to be obstacles to be overcome where they exist, the difference now being that they often do not exist—hence the weakness of interests noted by Geddes. The relative power of different social groups is generally overlooked, although some analysts have suggested that the effective power of business interests has been increased as a consequence of the severity of the economic crisis (Schneider 1995) and the mechanisms used to achieve a greater role for the market in economic activity. In effect, the fiscal crisis of the state provoked a process by which the protection of certain economic sectors provided by subsidies was replaced by other forms of political protection that have nothing to do with the regulation that is theoretically attributed to the market. The break with the old model of accumulation does not imply a drastic redefinition of the relationship between the state and economic agents. The most powerful economic groups appear to have achieved sufficient power to influence the application of the new model (Palermo and Novaro 1996; Silva 1996; see Schvarzer, Chapter 4 of this volume).

While the extremes of physical repression associated with the region's military regimes are (fortunately) largely now a thing of the past, the possible role that repression played in laying the foundations for subsequent economic reforms by limiting the capacity of specific interest groups in society to express their interests (particularly an organized

6. The correlation between economic development and democracy was first demonstrated in Lipset's famous essay, "Some Social Requisites of Democracy" (1959). That conclusion has been the subject of countless subsequent studies. For recent reviews of that work, see Diamond 1992; Rueschemeyer, Stephens, and Stephens 1992; and Lipset 1994. For a critical review of this literature, see Oxhorn and Ducatenzeiler 1998.

labor movement) are ignored. So too are the effects of other kinds of coercion, particularly economic, in undermining the strength of Latin America's civil societies (Oxhorn 1995b, Chapter 9 of this volume; Barrera, Chapter 6 of this volume).

Both of these problems have serious implications for understanding the future of democracy in Latin America. Even if regime type is unrelated to the success of economic reforms, economic-reform processes and the new economic model they embody do affect the type of democratic regimes that are possible. The literature on economic reform is correct in emphasizing that there are "losers" and "winners" in any economic-reform process of the dimensions characteristic of recent efforts in Latin America. The significance of this, however, has more to do with the relative possibilities for democratic participation that winners and losers enjoy than with the immediate success or failure of economic reforms. In other words, the causal relationship between economic reforms and regime type may be the reverse of what has been traditionally assumed. Although both authoritarian and democratic regimes can successfully adopt neoliberal economic reforms, *once they are implemented*, such reforms severely limit the potential level of citizen participation. While democratic regimes are obviously not ruled out, the resultant political regimes are characterized by a number of authoritarian aspects that can begin to blur the distinction between democratic and authoritarian regimes (Garretón 1989; Petras and Leiva 1994; Hagopian 1990, 1993; O'Donnell 1994, 1993; Smith, Acuña, and Gamarra 1994a, 1994b; Weffort, Chapter 10 of this volume). Indeed, it is this very blurring of the distinction between "democracy" and "authoritarianism" that is in part responsible for the ambiguous findings in the literature on economic reform.

Rather than abandon the concept of democracy entirely or redefine its fundamental meaning to conform to the Latin American reality, the various economic, social, and political trends in Latin America suggest the need to more closely analyze the *quality* of democracy in the region by examining its limitations and potential (Ducatenzeiler and Oxhorn 1994). As Schneider argues, researchers must begin to "disaggregate the composite concept of democratic regime and focus on the analysis of how the component parts operate" (1995: 220). This reflects similar conclusions drawn by several recent studies that have focused on democratic consolidation rather than economic reform per se (O'Donnell 1993, 1996a; Smith, Acuña, and Gamarra 1994a, 1994b; see also Oxhorn, Chapter 9, and Weffort, Chapter 10 of this volume).

The concept of the quality of democracy has two dimensions. One is explicitly normative and is manifested in part in the idea of "democratic autonomy" developed by Held (1987). Democratic autonomy implies a high degree of accountability on the part of the state and the democratic organization of civil society. Situating himself in the tradition of John Stuart Mill, Held argues that socioeconomic inequalities constitute obstacles to political equality. Above all, this is related to the idea of citizenship. Citizenship is a set of rights and obligations without which it is very difficult to talk about democracy (Schmitter 1983). As O'Donnell (1993) notes, however, Latin American political democracies are full of "brown zones" in which powers are created that recognize neither citizens nor accountability, and that reproduce themselves through procedures that deny both components of democracy.

The second dimension of the quality of democracy refers specifically to its institutional characteristics and how these both reflect and shape the particular contours of each country's civil society. The convergence of many social, economic, and political ills—high levels of poverty, income inequality, criminal violence, the growth of the informal sector, and so on—in the context of unprecedented levels of political democratization in the region presents a paradox that needs to be explained. The premise of this book is that the myriad social problems throughout much of Latin America are intimately linked both to the new economic development model (or at least the way it is being implemented) and the weaknesses of Latin American democracy. Renewed economic growth and further integration of Latin America into the world economy will undoubtedly generate new opportunities for development. Yet the relationship between an economic system based on free trade (with a reduced role for the state) and the economic policies required to create such a system, on the one hand, and democratic consolidation and governability, on the other, must be explored more systematically. Given the *kinds* of democracy that appear to be emerging, however, the concept of democratic consolidation may be a misnomer. More important, perhaps, is what type of democracy seems to be prevailing in the region and how stable it is likely to be—a theme we will return to in the volume's concluding chapter.

The essays in this book attempt to begin such a systematic study of the relationship between free trade and accompanying economic policies by comparing the experiences of different countries in Latin America. More specifically, this volume, which grew out of a conference held at McGill University in April 1994, examines how societies and politics have been affected by processes of economic change in Argentina, Brazil, Chile, and Mexico. The conference was organized around three sets of related questions:

First, despite growing agreement within academic and policy-making circles on the general policies that reform packages should include, we still know relatively little about the political and social factors that influence specific policy choices. In particular, we need to integrate our knowledge about economic-reform policies with what we also know about the problems of democratic consolidation in Latin America. While the historical record suggests that democratic regimes can successfully implement such policies, in a number of countries elected governments have attempted to do so by deliberately circumventing democratic institutions (Malloy 1991; Torre 1991; O'Donnell 1994). Is this just another example of "democracy by undemocratic means" (O'Donnell and Schmitter 1986)? Or will the long-term effects of how such policies are implemented be counterproductive for promoting democratic development in the region?

Second, the effects that adjustment policies have on the possibilities for collective action by Latin America's lower classes (or popular sectors) are not well understood. For example, although trade liberalization is associated with job creation in the region, we still do not have sufficient knowledge about the effects this has on organized labor, patterns of income distribution, and wage structures more generally. Similarly, the impact of macrolevel adjustment policies on the community-based self-help organizations founded on participation and solidarity that have emerged throughout the region over the past several decades has not been studied. These organizations may represent the beginnings of a process of the democratization of civil society that can help to strengthen otherwise fragile democracies in the region. A long tradition in democratic political theory, dating back at least to Tocqueville and John Stuart Mill, stresses the importance of a vibrant and well-organized civil society as a foundation for political democracy—a tradition that, interestingly enough, is part of the same liberal legacy that so clearly informs the new development model. The possibility that there could be a trade-off between the continued development of Latin American "civil societies" and economic liberalization should not be overlooked (Oxhorn 1995a, 1995b).

Finally, while Latin America's inefficient public sector and ingrained structures of economic protectionism need to be reformed, more serious attention must be given to understanding *how far* adjustment and economic liberalization should go. Is a system of free trade with only minimal state involvement in the economy realistic or even desirable? Are there alternatives to adjustment programs as they are currently conceived? If not, should existing programs be implemented differently?

The results of the Montreal conference are presented here in a series of case studies and in several more general chapters that detail the ways in which Latin American politics has been changed by both the economic crisis of the 1980s and the "remedy" of neoliberal economic reforms. It attempts to go beyond economics, even though several of the authors are themselves economists, by looking at the longer-term political and social dimensions of economic policy making. In this way, the book attempts to combine the strengths of both earlier and more recent approaches to the study of economic reform. Recognizing the importance of the recent literature's focus on the state, the various chapters attempt to examine the motives of the economic-policy-making elites, the nature of state institutions, and the effect that economic change has had on both. At the same time, the book endeavors to retrieve the earlier literature's emphasis on society. It looks specifically at the ways in which civil society has been weakened (as well as transformed) by the economic crisis, with the subsequent exacerbation of many of these negative trends by the economic reforms themselves.

Chapter 2 by Luiz Carlos Bresser Pereira and Yoshiaki Nakano examines the relations among politics, macroeconomic adjustment, and structural reforms. It raises crucial questions about the kinds of social consensus that undergird Latin America's current economic and political situation. According to the authors, markets are institutions that exist and function only insofar as they are regulated informally by society and formally by the state. This is not meant to imply that politics and economics are completely intertwined, only that political relations are not exogenous to the economic system. Looking specifically at the literature that suggests economic-reform programs are either not implemented or fail due to lack of political support, Bresser Pereira and Nakano argue this is only partially true: what much of the literature ignores is that such policies may be inefficient or the policy makers may be incompetent. The authors then conclude that the ability to govern depends on a basic social agreement concerning the economic regime. While such an agreement exists in established Western democracies, in Latin America there is no such agreement due to the tremendous social inequality. Bresser Pereira and Nakano suggest that Latin American governments face three different (but not mutually exclusive) alternatives for constructing a new social pact: short-term targeted social programs to compensate those hurt most by the implementation of economic reforms, long-term redistributive policies, and a developmental pact among elites, the middle class, and parts of the working class. The first alternative, which would be readily accepted by elites, would leave the underlying structural causes of poverty unchanged while possibly winning support for economic reform. The second alternative would address the structural causes of poverty, yet would face constant opposition from elite interests and therefore seems unlikely to come about by itself. Finally, the developmental pact holds out the promise of being a feasible compromise between the other two but will require the resumption of economic growth to be successful.

A defining characteristic of the markets that are emerging in Latin America today is that they increasingly are integrated with one another. The nature of this integration is examined in the chapter by Juan Alberto Fuentes. Fuentes argues that economic integration in Latin America has entered a new stage conditioned by economic strategies undertaken by democratically elected governments and by an international context forcing Latin American countries to increase their international competitiveness. Mercosur, in particular, marks the beginning of this new stage, which is characterized by more pragmatic and less ambitious integration efforts than in the past. Fuentes examines the reasons behind these trends, looking at two phenomena in particular. On the one hand, the unilateral liberalization, deregulation, and stabilization policies being implemented by national governments throughout the region drive what the author calls *de facto* integration. On the other hand, there are deliberate policies designed to build regional trade blocks, what Fuentes calls *policy-driven* integration. The interaction of de facto and policy-driven integration could lead to an open regionalism that would facilitate the development of Latin American economic competitiveness at the same time that it constitutes a building block for a more open international economic system. However, because integration is often adopted as an instrument intended to strengthen democracy by strengthening the links between democratically elected governments, Fuentes argues that there is often a gap between the declarations and concrete results of specific agreements. Fuentes analyzes the reasons for this gap and the obstacles to greater open regionalism that must be overcome. In Fuentes' view, the future of Latin American integration depends on the way countries in the region deal with two important problems: the differing rates of adjustment and stabilization in each country that wishes to integrate, as well as the tensions resulting from the existence of sectors that are more sensitive to trade liberalization than others, especially in the presence of under-developed markets or overvalued exchange rates.

The second part of the book examines specific-country cases beginning with Chapter 4 by Jorge Schvarzer that examines the social forces behind (and benefiting directly from) the economic reforms implemented in Argentina by the Peronist president Carlos Menem and his finance minister, Domingo Cavallo. It emphasizes the relationship between a particular social balance within civil society and the nature of Argentina's new democracy and newfound economic "success." According to Schvarzer these social forces represent a new alliance coming to power in Argentina that includes more traditional sectors of local economic power, external creditors, technocrats who believe in the new economic orthodoxy, and populist leaders. In other words, it is an alliance in which the most powerful sectors of civil society are represented. The newly elected leaders provide democratic legitimacy and retain for themselves control over those policies (e.g., social welfare) that will allow them to be reelected. The other members of the alliance, in turn, provide external contacts and their own economic power. The alliance now in power has accumulated tremendous decision-making authority, to the extent that it has been able to effectively nullify the opposition (real or latent) of a large part of society and diminish the capacity of democratic institutions to exercise a check on its power. At the same time, Schvarzer demonstrates how Argentina's new economic model, despite its similarity with the recommendations prescribed by the international financial community, has no strategy for creating a productive economic base. Rather, it is based on the hypertrophy of a financial order that has reaped tremendous benefits for those who are in strategic positions to obtain them. Thus, Schvarzer concludes, the retreat of the public sector from its old responsibilities was not compensated for by the emergence of a dynamic and efficient private sector.

Next, Chapter 5 by Werner Baer and Claudio Paiva examines how state institutions condition the behavior of important social actors based on a detailed history of the failures of successive economic stabilization policies by various Brazilian governments since 1987. Throughout, their analysis emphasizes the ways in which Brazilian state institutions (particularly after the adoption of the 1988 constitution) have undermined the emergence of the necessary political will to implement needed fiscal controls or even a consistent set of economic policies. Instead, economic actors (including politicians at all levels of government) have been encouraged to pursue their own short-term interests in what Baer and

Paiva describe as a "fight for shares" that provided the *political* foundation for hyperinflation in the midst of continued economic stagnation. Inflation became almost self-perpetuating as prices, governmental expenditures, and (to a much lesser extent) wages were pushed up to protect the relative position of individual actors. Politicians, unwilling to jeopardize their electoral ambitions after Brazil's return to political democracy in 1985, refused to enact needed institutional reform, much less budgetary restraint. This further intensified the fight for shares among economic actors, who viewed government economic policy as increasingly less credible. The authors conclude with an analysis of the 1993 Real Plan—what they see as the first economic stabilization plan that deliberately sought to break the political foundation of Brazil's stagflation and open the way for continued institutional reform and the possibility of renewed economic dynamism.

Turning to Chile, Chapter 6 by Manuel Barrera looks more specifically at the politics of the popular sectors, examining how economic-adjustment policies have affected their capacity to defend their historical interests in higher standards of living and greater social equity. Barrera demonstrates in the specific case of Chile, and Latin America more generally, how the nature of the new outward-oriented development policies has undermined the ability of the popular sectors, particularly organized labor, to engage in successful collective action. Organized labor has been seriously weakened by an economic development model that has fostered the growth of the informal sector and those segments of the formal economy which are historically the most difficult to organize (finance, agro-exports, small- and medium-scale enterprises, and so on). Similarly, legislation intended to increase labor market flexibility has eroded many of the previous institutional guarantees won by organized labor. Real wages have fallen dramatically, resulting in a rise in poverty rates and inequality. Thus, according to Barrera, the traditional role that even non-Marxist labor movements have played in promoting social change in Latin America has been reversed, with the fundamental role in the new development strategy now falling to employers. Trade unions no longer strive to represent the popular sectors as a whole, and instead have become increasingly concerned with their own corporate interests. While generally skeptical of the future potential for the popular sectors to overcome their current situation of social and economic marginalization without a fundamental change in development models, Barrera does hold out some room for optimism in the collective efforts to create self-employment opportunities among the popular sectors and the Chilean democratic government's efforts to reinvigorate the political and social role of organized labor.

The important case of Mexico is examined in the last two case studies. In Chapter 7, Francisco Zapata examines the impact that economic restructuring has had on organized labor, and corporatism more generally, in Mexico. He develops the hypothesis that workers, employers, and the state continue to interact through the same institutional structure that was established in the 1930s by Lázaro Cárdenas. For example, Zapata argues that the 1990 Pact for Stability and Economic Growth has not fundamentally changed the character of the relationship among Mexico's corporatist actors, particularly vis-à-vis the state. On the contrary, he demonstrates how business groups and unions recognized their subordination to the state while contributing to the implementation of the state's various policy objectives. This demonstrates how corporatism, after being institutionalized for a long period, can be used in times of crisis to attain aims very different from those for which it was originally created. The result, according to Zapata, is a situation in which the conditions for a new societal consensus may be emerging. Certain benefits for different corporate actors that are inconsistent with Mexico's current economic strategy are being eliminated as the various trade-offs supporting the earlier period of consensus from 1940 through the 1970s are reformulated. The old corporatist structure, however, is maintained and serves as the essential basis for successful concertation among business interests, organized labor, and the state.

In the last case study, Jean-François Prud'homme examines the broader issue of the relationship between development models and the system of interest representation in Mexico. He argues that in a situation of political and economic stability, both are self-reinforcing in a positive manner. Under such circumstances, an efficient and durable model of cooperation is consolidated between the principal actors. Prud'homme demonstrates how this was the case in Mexico until the end of the 1970s. He then analyzes the ways in which economic-adjustment policies and the pressures for liberalization of the system of interest representation have affected the political-party system. Specifically, Prud'homme looks at the relations among the three principal political parties in Mexico: the Institutional Revolutionary Party (PRI, *Partido Revolucionario Institucional*), the National Action Party (PAN, *Partido de Acción Nacional*), and the Democratic Revolutionary Party (PRD, *Partido de la Revolución Democrática*). He concludes that the relatively successful introduction of adjustment policies has not been accompanied by a model of efficient and durable cooperation between the principal political actors. On the contrary, the dynamic characterizing their interactions has been permeated by alternating strategies of cooperation and noncooperation in which negotiations over the rules of the political game were confused with strategies for attaining power. Only when an external threat to the survival of the party system as the central mechanism for political participation appeared at the beginning of 1994 (the Chiapas rebellion) did the political parties agree on a model of limited cooperation.

The book's final section attempts to develop more general theoretical concepts for understanding Latin America's current political and economic condition. It begins with Chapter 9 by Philip Oxhorn, who examines the intricate relationships between development models and modes of interest intermediation in order to understand the limits and future prospects of democracy in Latin America. Specifically, he argues that the gradual demise of import-substituting industrialization (ISI) as the region's predominant development model has led to the displacement of state corporatism as the dominant mode of interest intermediation in Latin America. It has been replaced by a new mode of interest intermediation, what he calls *neopluralism*, which better reflects the requirements for capital accumulation of the new, outward-oriented development model that has replaced ISI. As such, neopluralism reflects the extreme social fragmentation characteristic of most Latin American countries. Although neopluralism requires some form of electoral legitimation of executive authority, it exhibits a variety of authoritarian tendencies that reflect the cumulative nature of political resources in the region and contribute to the hollow character of many of the rights and freedoms associated with political democracy in the developed capitalist countries of the West. Oxhorn concludes by arguing that the long-term consequences of neopluralism can be mitigated by the presence of strong state institutions and representative political-party systems with strong ties to civil society. Mexico and Brazil are characterized as archetypical examples of most negative characteristics of neopluralism, while Chile is seen as representing the opposite extreme despite the high levels of social atomization among the popular sectors.

Many of the implications of the preceding chapters are summed up in Chapter 10 by Francisco Weffort. Weffort argues that the new democracies in Latin America are actually "hybrid regimes" which are being constructed with important political legacies from their authoritarian past in the context of an economic crisis that accentuates and creates great social inequalities. Under these conditions, democracy tends to be more delegative of political power than representative of societal interests. Among the political legacies of the past he considers first are the relative continuity of state structures, the armed forces and other institutions that allow for state intervention in the economy, and the assertion of executive primacy over Parliament. This preserves the subordination of the associations of civil society to the state apparatus. Second, he considers the relative persistence of leaders from the previous regime. The "democratic assumption" underlying these reflections is that leadership and related institutions matter in the consolidation of democracy, and Latin American leaders in the new democracies are not always "democratically self-conscious" but tend to form part of a diffuse amalgamation of individuals playing purely self-interested games. Turning to the problem of inequality, Weffort argues that most Latin American countries do not meet the minimal social conditions required to construct democratic systems according to political theory. There is a contradiction between a system based on the political equality of citizens and societies based on such extremes of inequality and social exclusion, what he calls "social apartheid." While political democracy is possible in such a context, democratic consolidation is not. Instead, the new democracies in the region are characterized by low political-party institutionalization, intermittent stalemates between the executive and legislative branches, and the persistence of the tendency to rule by decree (*decretismo*) as a way to overcome a permanent crisis of governability.

Finally, in a concluding chapter, we return specifically to the two questions in the book's title and attempt to provide tentative answers. After arguing that the literature must begin to move beyond the transitions/consolidation paradigm, we suggest that what is emerging in Latin America is a largely unregulated, *predatory* market capitalism. This kind of market, in turn, is reflected in and supports democratic regimes marked by hyper-presidentialism and only a shallow (at best) normative commitment to governmental accountability and broad citizen participation.

.

2

The Missing Social Contract

Governability and Reform in Latin America

Luiz Carlos Bresser Pereira and
Yoshiaki Nakano

The present conventional wisdom is that "economic problems have a political origin." An alternative way of approaching the same problem is to say that macroeconomic adjustment and structural reforms fail or are not completed for lack of political support. Finally, a safety net or targeted social policies are often presented as a strategy for overcoming the political support gap. This latter view corresponds to a real-world solution, yet it is imprecise and contradictory. It is plagued by ideological biases and often serves as an excuse for incompetent economic policy making.

In trying to clarify the different meanings and implications of the three related propositions presented above, we will discuss the hypothesis of the political origin of economic problems, the political support gap for adjustment and economic reforms, and compensatory social policies as means of overcoming political obstacles to economic reform. As an alternative to the "political-origin" and "political-obstacles" hypotheses that are dominant in the age of neoliberalism, we will suggest what could be called the "missing-social-contract hypothesis": the legitimacy of governments that assures governability and allows for effective economic reforms depends on the existence of a basic social contract. This contract is well institutionalized in advanced democratic societies. In developing countries, where it is weak and reflects limited social consensus, a development-oriented political pact is required as a substitute.

In Latin American societies, given their heterogeneity and deep income inequality, civil society is poorly structured. There is no broad political agreement on the prevailing economic regime, particularly on the pattern of income distribution. The long-term solution for this would be economic reforms that permanently reduce inequalities. Given that the local elites tend to oppose or procrastinate on distributional policies, an alternative is to promote development-oriented political pacts between the middle class and workers. This compromise has often been used in Latin America to secure governability, but its success depends on the resumption of the development process. Market-oriented reforms—particularly macroeconomic adjustment, price stabilization, and trade liberalization—are a necessary condition for this resumption. Such reforms, however, must also result in a stronger state that is able to implement social policies and promote economic growth. Otherwise, governability will not be achieved.

Our assumption is that given the crisis of the state that characterized Latin America more than anything else in the 1980s, the market-oriented reforms that have indiscriminately been identified with neoliberal reforms are necessary. Only through such reforms will it be possible to overcome the crisis of the state in Latin America, rebuild the state, and regain governability.[1] Yet it is quite clear today that these reforms are not enough to resume growth. Additional effective measures to rebuild the state and define its new roles in promoting economic growth and income distribution are required. At the same time, it is a mistake to assume that economists or policy makers know which reforms should be undertaken. It is very common for the content of economic reforms to be determined by dogmatism and ideological orthodoxy. Finally, it is inappropriate to blame economic problems and the obstacles to economic reform on politics. The recent increase in interest in political economy should be welcomed but should not serve as an excuse to give an exogenous rationale for economic-policy failures, as is implicit in the political-origin and political-obstacles hypotheses. And it should make us cautious

---

1. The Latin American crisis of 1980s was essentially a crisis of the state. This required a "crisis of the state interpretation" to understand it, and the adoption of social-democratic or social-liberal reforms to confront it. On the subject, see Bresser Pereira, Maravall, and Przeworski 1993 and Bresser Pereira 1996.

regarding simple solutions such as targeted social policies. The economy and politics are intrinsically linked. Economic problems and economic reforms always have a political content. In some cases, targeted social policies may represent a short-term answer but this should not lead to a disregard of more long-term economic and political reforms that could lead to a real social contract.

In the opening chapter of this book, Oxhorn and Ducatenzeiler state that the "more recent analyses of the success of economic reforms ignore the reasons *why* organized interests are so weak. The literature tends to abandon civil society as an explanatory variable" (6). In this chapter, while criticizing the naive political-origin and political-obstacles hypotheses, we will try to partially fill this gap by showing how in the faulty democracies of Latin America, broad political coalitions play a strategic role connecting civil society and the state, providing for governability, and making the required economic and political reforms feasible.

The Political-Origin Hypothesis

The political-origin hypothesis for understanding economic problems is often associated today with the same intellectual realm in which extremely abstract neoclassical economic models are developed. The reason is clear: since these models assume that markets are optimally able to allocate resources and maintain a balanced economy, economic problems must have an exogenous, nonmarket cause. This exogenous cause is power. In the past, the type of power that was emphasized was the monopoly power of big business. Today, political power—the power that comes from the state—is the focus of attention. If it were not for the expansionist policies populist administrations undertake and the rent-seeking activities that politicians are usually engaged in, economic problems would not exist or would be milder.

This approach loses most of its explanatory power when the assumption that markets are optimally able to coordinate the economy is dropped. In this case, economic crises cease to be just the outcomes of the wrong economic policies or of the pressure of interest groups. Instead, they become the inevitable result of the inner dynamics of the endogenous economic cycle. Additionally, if one adds externalities and increasing returns of scale to economic models (as is being increasingly done), multiple equilibriums will be found. Some of these are perverse and are consistent, for example, with economic stagnation or high inflation.[2]

The belief that economic problems have a political origin was an essential part of the views of classical and Marxian economists. Originally, they named their science "political economy." "Economics" was a word that was only adopted in the late nineteenth century by the rising neoclassical economists who wanted to rid the economic science from political influences and considerations. Today, "political economy" usually means an intermediate area between pure economics and political science, in which the political aspects of economic problems are taken into consideration. For the classical economists, this meant an economic science—a science that was not just a logical-deductive model whose microfoundations economists are supposed to discover and analyze but also an inductive and historical science in which market and power elements are intrinsically mixed.

After the crisis represented by the Keynesian revolution, neoclassical economics gained force and in the past twenty years recovered their hegemony. Yet, and paradoxically, the de facto political origin of economic problems gained weight in this century. The basic reason for this was the decisive, although complementary, role the state assumed in capitalist economies, either allocating resources or interfering in the distribution of income. Probably in reaction to this, mainstream economists, in line with the conventional wisdom, turned their attention to politics, which suddenly became the origin of all economic evils. The clearest manifestation of this fact was the emergence of the public-choice or rational-choice school—a neoliberal branch of neoclassical economics that aptly adopted in its research program a view of government action as an endogenous variable. The rational-choice school, whose leading representatives are James Buchanan, Gordon Tullock, William Niskanen, and Mancur Olson, borrows from neoclassical economics its methodological individualism. As economic agents rationally maximize their interests in the market, politicians do the same in the political arena, which is also seen as a kind of market. It is assumed that politicians are intrinsically selfish, and that there is no difference between the ethics of business, in which the exclusive pursuit of self-interest is legitimated, and the ethics of politics. The ideals of solidarity and collective action are also assumed to be unrealizable for large groups. As a result, the objective of politicians and governments is not the pursuit of

2. See Romer 1989, Grossman 1990, Krugman 1992, and Grossman and Helpman 1993.

the public interest but their own interests. These radical assumptions justify the rational-choice school's choice of a minimalist state as its utopian ideal.[3]

Thus, in a curious way, political economists, rational-choice adepts, and neoclassical traditional economists converge on the same and obvious view: politics matters. Yet their respective understanding of the problem is different. For the political economists, politics is an essential part of the economic system. For the adepts of rational-choice theory, government action is also seen as endogenous. Yet there is a substantial difference between the two schools: while political economists view the endogeneity of governments as a consequence of class and ideological struggles, rational-choice adepts view it as the outcome of individual preferences and strategies. Finally, for the more traditional neoclassical economists, politics is an exogenous (to the market) obstacle to market clearing and economic reform. The latter may also see politics as an obstacle to macroeconomic adjustment and structural economic reform, but an endogenous obstacle—an obstacle that comes from the dynamic interplay of economic and political factors in the real world.

The answer to the question about the political or economic origins of economic problems depends on how we define the economic and the political systems. If we define the economic system as just a self-regulating market system in which rational individuals make production and exchange decisions, while we view the political system as the domain of government power, economic problems will have primarily a political (or exogenous to the economic realm) origin. Conversely, if we define the economic system as a system of production and distribution of income and wealth through institutions, of which the market, money, and the state are the main ones, the conclusion will be the opposite. In the latter case, markets themselves are considered institutions that depend on other institutions, such as the property system, the legal-contract system, and the money system. They are institutions that exist and function as long as they are regulated informally by society and formally by the state. According to this view (which we share), individuals retain an essential role as economic agents in the market, but social classes are also crucial as they express their specific interests through social and state regulation.

3. For a survey of the public-choice school by one of its adepts, see Mueller 1976, whose article was later published in a book of readings (Buchanan and Tollison 1984) that, together with works by Buchanan and Tullock (1962) and Olson (1965), offers a general view of the school, which later became highly influential among American political scientists.

This does not mean that economics and political science are mixed. Economists remain basically concerned with production and distribution through the market and political scientists with power relations. But it does mean that the state is not exogenous to the economic system. On the contrary, it is an essential part of it. If the state is in crisis, the property and the contract systems will function poorly: Money (a manifestation of state sovereignty and credit) will be permanently endangered, entrepreneurs will ration investments, and the economy will also probably be in crisis.

The inverse of this is also true. Cyclical economic crises—particularly those associated with long waves—bring with them political crises. In the expansive phase, strong political coalitions are formed that break down in the downturn.[4] In this case, we have an economic origin for political crises. The economic crisis itself has its origin endogenously: short-term economic downturns are usually the consequence of a large and uncontrolled expansion, while long-term downturns are the result of the exhaustion of a cluster of Schumpeterian innovations.

Yet in some historical moments, the cause of a long-term economic crisis may not be purely economic but jointly economic and political. This is the present case in Latin America and Eastern Europe. If we look for a basic cause of this crisis, the best answer would probably be that it is a crisis of the state in several senses: (1) a fiscal crisis of the state; (2) a crisis of the mode of intervention (or the development strategy) of the state; and (3) a legitimation crisis, in which the role of the state in the economy is contested.[5] The fiscal crisis of the state is defined by the loss of public credit, while the crisis of the mode of state intervention is defined by the exhaustion of the import substitution strategy in Latin America and the statist strategy in Eastern Europe. The waning of state authority and prestige, caused by the fiscal crisis and the exhaustion of the mode of intervention and accentuated by the neoconservative wave that started in the 1970s, defines the legitimation crisis.[6]

The assumption behind this diagnosis is that the state has important economic roles that it is unable to perform well when it is paralyzed by the fiscal crisis, the lack of a clear intervention strategy, and lack of

4. Peter Gourevitch, in studying the 1873–96, 1929–49, and current crises, observes that, "In the prosperous years preceding the crisis, a policy approach and support coalition developed. Then came the crisis, challenging both the policy and the coalition" (1986: 21–22).

5. See Bresser Pereira 1988, 1990, 1993. In these texts, the author is trying to develop an explanation for the current crisis, its cyclical character, and its basic origin in a crisis of the state.

6. This neoconservative or neoliberal wave emerged in the 1970s, as a response to the excessive and distorted growth of the state over the previous fifty years. In the past three years, however, there are clear signals that this trend is slowing.

legitimacy of the government, its politicians, and public officials. Given the crisis, state capacity is reduced, the government is paralyzed or hampered, and political coalitions are shaky and unstable. Yet, the fact that the economic crisis derives from the crisis of the state does mean that it has just a political origin. It has an economic-political origin, since the state is a also a part of the economic system.

The corollary to this is that the solution to the problem is not the creation of a minimalist state, as neoliberals assume, but reform and rebuilding of the state. When people speak of "economic reforms" today, they are actually referring to reforms of the state. Fiscal adjustment, privatization, trade liberalization, and deregulation should be seen in this vein as strategies to rebuild a smaller but stronger state.

The Political Support Hypothesis

There is a second way of approaching the same theme. Instead of focusing on the origin of the crisis, one can focus on the reason why it has not been resolved. In this case, the standard assertion is that "required economic reforms are often not undertaken for lack of political support." Behind this affirmation is the belief that for all or for most economic problems, there is a set of economic policies that will solve them if there is political support. Political obstacles would explain the failure of economic reforms.

Concern with the political aspects of inflation may be viewed as an antecedent to the political-obstacles literature. Marxist economists always viewed inflation as a consequence of political conflict and monopoly power. In the 1930s, Gardiner Means, Michael Kalecki, and Joan Robinson analyzed the political cycle and cost-push inflation. In the 1950s, Aujac wrote about the influence of social groups on inflation (1950). The Latin American structuralist theory, initiated by Noyola (1956) and Sunkel (1960), and complemented by Rangel (1963) and Pinto (1973), has Keynesian and Marxian influences, in that it incorporates a sociological and institutional approach to inflation. Hirschman (1981b) wrote extensively on the subject. There also is an extensive literature on the political aspects of inflation and their relation to populism beginning with Canitrot (1975), O'Donnell (1978), and Hirschman (1981a). Only in the 1970s, however, did sociologists and political scientists start focusing their attention on inflation. The extensive literature began with three collections of essays: Hirsch and Goldthorpe 1978, Thorp and Whitehead 1979, and Lindberg and Maier 1985.

Up to this point, attention was concentrated on the political and social causes of inflation. In the 1980s, with the explosion of the debt crisis, which soon became a fiscal crisis, inflation rates accelerated in the highly indebted countries. The need for short-term fiscal adjustment and long-term structural reforms became evident. Pressures in this direction from the developed world mounted, and political scientists became particularly interested in the political dimension of policy making. The political-support-gap hypothesis was analyzed in a large number of books.[7]

Economists, on the other hand, became increasingly interested in the political aspects of adjustment and economic reform. Economic populism was revisited in two collections of essays, Bresser Pereira 1991b and Dornbusch and Edwards 1991, whereas the volume edited by Williamson (1994) focused on the political aspects of economic-policy reform. The concern with the political cycle in macroeconomic policy and political resistance to stabilization, which had been present since the 1970s, gained new strength, especially with the utilization of game theory (Alesina 1987; Alesina and Sachs 1988; Alesina and Tabellini 1988; Sachs 1989; Edwards and Tabellini 1990; and Alesina and Drazen 1991). The literature on economic development was also enriched by the "new political macroeconomics" (Cukierman, Hercowitz, and Leiderman 1992). Articles by Persson and Tabellini (1992) and Alesina and Rodrik (1992) showed the positive relations between distribution of income and growth.

All this literature is relevant and responds to a real problem—the political obstacles to much-needed, fiscal-adjustment policies and economic reforms. Yet most of it suffers from two limitations: (1) a technocratic bias—the idea that all economic problems have a policy solution; and (2) a naive assumption—that economists or policy makers are competent to adjust, stabilize, and reform the economy and do not succeed only because of faltering political support.[8] A more realistic approach was adopted by Williamson and Haggard (1994). After surveying several successful examples of economic reform, they concluded that prior

7. See Nelson 1989, 1990; Ethier 1990, Haggard and Kaufman 1995, 1992b; Przeworski 1991; Bresser Pereira, Maravall, and Przeworski 1993; Bates and Krueger 1993b; Smith, Acuña, and Gamarra 1994a; and Williamson 1994.

8. Bates and Krueger (1993a) were explicit on this assumption. After reviewing the experience in eight developing countries, they concluded that in no case were program design flaws crucial to the outcomes.

political consensus on the desirability of reforms is not required, at least to initiate them. In contrast, they found that a coherent economic team enjoying strong executive support was a prerequisite for successful reform.

Discussing the conditions for economic reform, Grindle and Thomas (1991: 4) took issue with "much of the literature in political science and political economy" that "narrowly focused on the analysis of obstacles to change," or assumed a "narrowly defined self interest as the basis of political action." Given these premises they asked, how could reforms have taken place in Latin America since the beginning of the debt crisis, as they obviously have? Grindle and Thomas' response was to credit a considerable autonomy to the policy elite (political leaders and bureaucratic officials). Our answer, however, is twofold. In the short run, we suggest that this will occur when the net transition cost of adjustment becomes negative or, in other words, when the costs of delaying adjustment and reform are higher than the expected costs of reforming.[9] In fact, in acute-crisis situations, the adoption of economic reforms that lack a political consensus behind them is common.[10] Only in the long run do reforms require substantial public support, that is, political support that will legitimize the government and ensure governability. In this regard, we later discuss the strategic role development-oriented political pacts play in replacing a missing social contract.

In the literature on the political obstacles to sound economic policies, the political-business-cycle theory has always received special attention. If a four-year political incumbency is assumed, politicians would adjust the economy in the first two years, opening room for engaging in expansionary policies during the last two years to get reelected. This theory is simple and its predictions have been repeatedly confirmed in the real world,[11] but it does not apply to economic reforms that often require a larger span of time, either to cause pain or to induce favorable outcomes. It also does not apply in abnormal times, such as when the fiscal crisis turns acute and results in high inflation. During such moments, economic expansion does not win votes, and we see a reversal of the political cycle: the recommended political strategy to facilitate

---

9. This usually happens when the economic crisis is so acute that the state's treasury is empty and the economic crisis entails unbearable costs. Then, the net transition costs, that is, the costs of adjustment and reform minus the costs of delaying them, become negative. We will not discuss the theme in this chapter but refer the reader to Bresser Pereira and Abud 1994.

10. This point was made strongly by Sachs (1994).

11. See, among others, Nordhaus 1975; Soh 1986; and Alesina and Sachs 1988.

reelection is to adjust and control inflation. As a matter of fact, during such a period an expansionary fiscal and monetary policy tends to be ineffective in promoting growth, given faltering government credibility. The expectations of economic agents are that expansionary policies will be short lived, and thus they do not invest or consume as they would in normal times if given the same policy incentives.

A False Assumption

Successful economic reforms depend both on a consistent economic program and on long-term political support, and yet the political economy of economic reforms tends to emphasize the second prerequisite, when the essential one is the first. An economic program based on false premises, that adopts mistaken economic policies, is doomed to fail. When Washington policy makers write or speak about economic reforms that would be appropriate for Latin America, they usually start from the assumption that the economic programs they are offering are consistent and efficient. Accepting this premise, political scientists in the First World ask themselves why reforms are delayed or take place in an incomplete way. They often fail to consider that these policies may be simply wrong or inadequate.

An example of this is the recent experience of Latin America, and particularly Brazil, in fighting high inflation. Economic policy as a pervasive economic and political phenomenon is a new historical fact that dates from this century, specifically from the Keynesian revolution. Before that time, economic theory denied the need for economic policy and did not offer a relevant set of policy tools, and political science ignored the problem. After Keynes, while governments in developed and developing countries made extensive use of economic policy to achieve full employment and growth, neoclassical economists denied that they had any real effects. Instead, they insisted on the need for permanent and credible policy rules. Yet this did not prevent mainstream economics from assuming the full effectiveness of conventional stabilization policies in a technocratic and optimistic way when often this was not the case.

In a first phase, the assumption behind the macroeconomic models was that governments were exogenous and all-powerful entities. More recently (given its obvious lack of realism), this assumption has been dropped and given rise, among economists and political scientists, to the political-obstacles literature. The technocratic bias still remains as reflected in the idea that if conventional economic policies designed to avoid economic imbalances are consistently followed, if permanent rules endowed with credibility are adopted and enforced, stabilization and growth will follow. Thus, if an economy gets out of balance, it is a problem of political will, since it is only a question of adopting the required corrective economic policies. Because the possibility that imbalances might originate in the economic realm itself is ignored, the chance that the failure of the economy to stabilize and grow is due to an incorrect economic diagnosis and poor policy making is overlooked.

Stagflation in the 1970s, and inertial inflation in the 1980s, challenged this view. Particularly in Latin America, where the neostructuralist theory of inertial inflation was initially developed, economists challenged the conventional stabilization policies.[12] Later, a new Keynesian school followed the same line of thought,[13] when in many Latin American and Eastern European countries it became evident, as inertial inflation became hyperinflation, that they were experiencing abnormal or exceptional times—times in which conventional monetary and fiscal policies alone are unable to control inflation.[14]

When political scientists became interested in the politics of economic reform, they often recognized the unique character of inertial inflation and the exceptional nature of hyperinflation and the fiscal crisis of the state. Yet they ignored the neostructuralist and new Keynesian critiques of conventional policy making, and assumed that orthodox or conventional economists knew how to stabilize the economy. They adopted this stand either because they shared the orthodox and technocratic views or because they preferred not to intrude in an alien domain. In doing so, they unwittingly offered an alibi for incompetent and weak policy makers who adopted a kind of contented political determinism: it is useless to design and implement bold economic reforms, since there is no political support for them.[15]

12. On the Latin American theory of inertial inflation, see Pazos 1972; Bresser Pereira and Nakano 1987; Arida and Resende 1984; and Lopes 1984.

13. See Bruno et al. 1991, and Mankiw and Romer 1991.

14. For a critique of conventional stabilization policies in Brazil, see Bresser Pereira and Nakano 1987, 1991, and Bresser Pereira 1996: chap. 14.

15. This happened, for instance, in Brazil in 1991–92, when the International Monetary Fund (IMF) approved a gradualist and conventional stabilization program instead of demanding that the 25 percent a month inflation be controlled abruptly through the combination of orthodox and heterodox policies (see Bresser Pereira 1996: chap. 15).

As a matter of fact, in abnormal times when a fiscal crisis of the state critically undermines public credit and hyperinflation or a hyper-inflationary process prevails, only bold shock policies (usually including monetary reforms) can succeed in stabilizing the economy. If these policies are skillfully designed and courageously implemented, they may readily produce positive economic results, and thus garner wide political support. This was what happened when inertial inflation was brought under control in Israel (1985), Mexico (1987), and Brazil (1994), or when hyperinflation was defeated in Bolivia (1985), Poland (1990), Peru (1990), and Argentina (1991). The shocks that controlled inflation and neutral-ized inertia were "heterodox," while those that ended hyperinflation were "orthodox" shocks.[16] Obviously, policy makers took into account and tried to circumvent political obstacles in the design and imple-mentation of the shock policies, but the essential factor in the positive outcome was the efficiency and consistency of the economic reforms.

In some cases, stabilization policies fail simply because they are wrong and therefore unable to achieve their announced goals. In most cases, however, they hypothetically may achieve those goals but are inefficient because they involve unnecessary transition costs that eventually make the stabilization program unviable in political terms.

The Strategy of Social Compensation

Summing up the previous discussion, economic crises may have a political origin, but it is basically a mistake to adopt the implicit assump-tion that markets efficiently coordinate the economy and attribute all or most economic problems to politics. Market failures and the consequent endogenous character of economic cycles probably remain the basic cause behind economic problems. At the same time, the existence of political obstacles to adjustment and structural reforms, although a fact, has a more limited scope than present conventional wisdom allows,

16. In Israel and Mexico inertial inflation was brought under control through a price freeze combined with conversion tables that neutralized inertia; in Brazil, an original mechanism was adopted to neutralize inertia. These mechanisms are called "heterodox" due to neutralization of the inertial inflation involved. In Bolivia, Poland, Peru, and Argentina, inflation had already turned into hyperinflation, which was defeated by an exchange-rate anchor. Since this policy has long been a part of mainstream economic policy, it may be called "orthodox." In all the countries mentioned, conventional fiscal adjustment and tight monetary policies were required to consolidate stabilization.

given that the implicit assumption that the economic policies being proposed and which face political resistance are always consistent and efficient is at least disputable.

To the extent that a political support gap does exist, however, compensatory targeted social policies have became a favorite strategy recently, particularly within the realm of the Washington consensus.[17] Through such policies, the specific social groups hit hardest by fiscal adjustment or structural reform would be partially compensated. Aside from the important humanitarian value of this strategy, it is also a short-term or pragmatic means of overcoming or circumventing the political obstacles to reform or of winning political support for the administration.

The World Bank (1990: 3) has asserted that the basic strategies to fight poverty are (1) to promote the productive use of the poor's most abundant asset, labor; and (2) to provide basic social services: education, health care, nutrition, and family planning. But it added that when an adverse macroeconomic shock takes place, "a comprehensive approach to poverty reduction calls for a program of well targeted transfers and safety nets as an essential complement to the basic strategy." This view is essentially correct. The compensatory social policies are a temporary complement to job creation and the supply of basic social services. Or, in other words, to long-term distributive policies. Yet there is the permanent risk that such temporary social policies will be adopted as a substitute for longer-term policies. Populist and authoritarian governments alike often tend to see targeted assistance as a cheap way to gain or conserve short-term political support, at the moment when economic reforms are being implemented.

Oxhorn and Ducatenzeiler (1994) observed that the market-oriented reforms that were adopted recently in Latin America were often the outcome of authoritarian or technocratic political coalitions. In order to compensate the losers, targeted-assistance programs focused on helping *individuals* to escape poverty, thus encouraging state paternalism, which serves to undermine long-term prospects for the full incorporation of the popular sectors. Yet it is possible to identify cases that would require targeted compensatory social expenditures. When some groups are

---

17. One of the authors of this chapter was among the first to criticize the Washington consensus for its neoliberal bias (Bresser Pereira 1990, 1993). It should be noted, however, that this critique was not directed at the recommendations entailed in the consensus—basically the insistence on observing macroeconomic fundamentals and adopting market-oriented reforms—but at the failure to devise a positive role for the state in promoting economic growth and income distribution.

particularly hard hit, there is an obvious case for them, particularly if the losses are transitory and targeted social expenditures have a corresponding limited duration. When reforms are introduced at a very slow pace or take too much time to produce positive outcomes, compensatory social expenditures may also be recommended. It is important, however, to ensure that this situation is not simply the result of inefficient economic reform. In other words, it is important to explore alternative economic policies that might produce positive outcomes more rapidly. A third and related situation is the one in which there is a permanent reform process, with one economic reform following another. In this case, the social costs involved in each reform may be quite transitory, but the total losses may be large, given the succession of reforms. In such a case, the reform process is long not because reforms are incomplete or partially unsuccessful but because there are many required reforms. If reforms are not producing the expected results, we have a case of inefficiency that requires a change in the design of the reforms rather than targeted social expenditures.

It is not realistic, however, to believe either that compensatory social policies will really compensate the losses involved or that they will not be used as a substitute for more long-term income distribution. The World Bank's pro-poor policies, which in the 1970s were intended to be permanent and implied an effective redistribution of income, were never really implemented on a large scale because of the resistance of privileged groups in each country. With the debt crisis and the fiscal crisis, they were abandoned for some time. Pro-poor policies reappeared at the end of the 1980s in the form of targeted social expenditures that were supposed to involve limited resources and play a political role: winning support for reforms. Under these circumstances, it is clear that they were intended to replace more long-term distributive policies.

In her survey of compensatory social programs, Joan Nelson observed that they are often criticized as "Band-Aids" applied to relieve some of the damage caused by depression and adjustment. She added that, "A longer term and more enduring approach to protecting and promoting the poorer groups in the course of adjustment is reorienting the structure of public social sector programs. Such reorientation is a major theme in present adjustment dialogue because it addresses both poverty problems and the acute fiscal crisis likely to continue in many countries into the 1990s" (1989: 105). By the mid-1990s, this reorientation has not yet taken place. Instead, targeted social expenditures, as found in Chile, Bolivia, and Costa Rica in the 1980s and, more recently in the National Solidarity

Program (PRONASOL, *Programa Nacional de Solidaridad*) in Mexico, continue to be popular in Washington.[18]

This fact may be explained in several ways. First, they are often the only alternative left, given the political weakness of the poor in Latin America in the aftermath of the crisis that began in the early 1980s and was magnified by an excess supply of unskilled labor. In reality, long-term distributive policies are unlikely when they depend on the solidarity of the rich, rather than a demand from the poor. A second reason for the popularity of targeted-assistance programs, in this case not in Washington but among politicians in Latin America, is that, if well administered, they may create support, if not directly for economic adjustment, for the government (Graham 1992).[19] Still, the basic rationale behind their attractiveness is their relatively low cost and immediate results—if the programs do not become victims of partisan interests.

The popularity of compensatory social policies in Washington does not mean that they are neoliberal or conservative programs. As Draibe (1993) observes, that social programs assume a targeted or limited scope, and that they adopt decentralization as a strategy, does not necessarily mean that they are conservative or neoliberal. In Brazil, for example, when an IMF-approved adjustment program was nationally imple-mented in 1983, the progressive Montoro administration in São Paulo successfully adopted targeted social policies.

The criterion to distinguish progressive from conservative social policies is not if they are targeted but if the selective programs are seen as a substitute for long-term, income-distribution policies. Conservatives usually see poverty and inequality as consequences of individual differ-ences, rather than of the existing economic structures and institutional framework. Another way to approach the same problem is to ask if the political obstacles that these policies are supposed to overcome are specific problems that require clearly defined solutions, in which case targeted policies are recommended, or if they are structural ones, such as those relating to the property system, the structure of overall state

---

18. The Brazilian program "*Comunidade Solidária*," which began in 1995, is targeted but not compensatory in nature. And its target is broad, including the poorest municipalities in the country.

19. Carol Graham studied Bolivia's Emergency Social Fund adopted by the Paz Estensoro administration between 1985 and 1990. Her evaluation was highly positive. She attributed the good results to the fact that "the ESF managed to remain remarkably free of political constraints and influences, and to deserve its reputation for conducting the vast majority of its operations in an efficient and transparent manner" (1992: 1246).

expenditures, the distribution of income, and the quality of the political institutions, which require a broader approach.

The Missing-Social-Contract Hypothesis

The last phrase brings us back to the central problem of this chapter: the political origin of economic problems. There is no doubt about the close relation between the economic and the political systems, between economic policy and politics. The critique of neoclassical economics by Marxist, Keynesian, structuralist, and institutionalist economists is based on its ignorance or underestimation of power relations prevailing in the market. As we saw earlier, in the past ten years mainstream economics has become increasingly interested in politics, but the emphasis has been placed on short-term analysis of the political obstacles to the proper functioning of markets.

The alternative is to assume that the economic and the political spheres are intrinsically and dynamically interrelated (Sola 1994), and not only because markets are themselves political institutions that must be regulated by the state, although this type of analysis is beyond the scope of this chapter. It is also because governability—the support governments have in civil society based on political institutions that adequately mediate interests—is a central political variable that intrinsically depends on the economic regime.[20] From this assumption, we can develop a "social-contract hypothesis" to explain the governability problems Latin American countries face and to clarify why development-oriented political pacts or class coalitions are so crucial in these countries.

Since Hobbes, it has been clear that to be governed, capitalist societies require that a state and its respective government be legitimated by a social contract. Hobbes came to this conclusion and established the basis for the contractual theory of the state. The power of the prince ceased to be a divine right or a historical fact but was seen as the outcome of a contract. Hobbes applied a logical-deductive method to arrive at this theory, but in fact he was reflecting on the emergence of capitalism and the separation between civil society and the state, between the private and the public domains.[21] If this observation was true in Hobbes's times, when a mercantilist economy prevailed, it is more so in the complex and

20. Governability—the effective power to govern—does not assure governance, the quality and effectiveness of government action. In this chapter, we are not dealing with governance, not withstanding the relevance of the problem.
21. On this subject, see Bobbio 1979.

democratically advanced capitalist societies of today. In these societies, there is a basic agreement on the prevailing economic regime, that is, on the property system and the distribution of income between individuals and social classes.[22] Przeworski and Wallerstein (1985: 182) gave the classical social contract a specific and more rigorous economic and class content when they argued that, "Given the uncertainty whether and how capitalists would invest profits, any class compromise must consist of the following elements: workers consent to profit as an institution, that is, they behave in such a manner as to make positive rates of profit possible; and capitalists commit themselves to some rate of transformation of profits into wage increases and some rate of investment out of profits."

Thus the class compromise, or the basic social contract, behind all capitalist societies is based not only on an agreement between a government and citizens and a trade-off between order and personal freedom, as Hobbes proposed. It is also based on an agreement between capitalists and workers and on a trade-off between profit legitimation, on the one hand, and investment and wage increases on the other. This basic agreement also involves a third party, the state, that presides over the second-best choices made by capitalists and workers in its role as intermediary. In the words of Paul Buchanan (1995: 16), "The strategic interaction between the state, labor, and capital under democratic capitalism is fueled by a triple logic of collective action. . . . What labor wants from the state in terms of public goods it cannot get from capital; what the state wants from capital in terms of investment it cannot get from labor; and so on. The overall need for systemic reproduction leads to overlapping and complementary strategies of accommodation based on a belief in compromise and mutually beneficial exchanges resulting in second-best choices for all sides." It is this agreement, this basic social contract, apart from a complex institutional system, that legitimates governments, assures governability, and guarantees the effectiveness of economic policies. This does not mean that the distributive conflict has been eliminated. It just means that it is under control, not only because differences in wealth and income are not so great but also because civil society is well structured and effectively connected to the state such that there is a complex and well-structured institutional system of interest representation and intermediation (Putnam 1993).

22. An interesting question is whether the concentration of income that took place in the developed countries, particularly in the United States, over the past twenty-five years is endangering this basic social contract.

When civil society is weak and this basic agreement is lacking or incomplete, as is the case in most developing countries, the political obstacles to economic policy making become evident. Although opposition to the capitalist system in these countries became irrelevant with the collapse of communism, disagreement over the pattern of income distribution has remained extremely high, particularly in Latin America where income concentration is a major problem. The political response to this problem has been either to resort to authoritarianism or, in the realm of democracy, to compensate for the weakness of the basic social contract by welcoming broad but exclusionary development-oriented political pacts that give a positive role to the working class.

The literature on political pacts in Latin America is extensive. Political pacts are usually understood as specific agreements between workers and businessmen mediated by unions and political parties,[23] but we are not using the term in this sense. Development-oriented political pacts are defined here as broad and informal class coalitions that tend to be formed to legitimize a set of interpretations and strategies adopted by the political elite. They may be united in and represented by a political party, a group of associated political parties, or even a group of competing political parties that share common beliefs. Our hypothesis is that in Latin America, political pacts are a surrogate for the social contract that characterizes developed capitalist societies.

These political pacts or class coalitions are exclusionary because they do not involve the whole society. Since the 1930s, these pacts in Latin America were in the form of the "national-developmentalist and populist pacts" that Vargas, Perón, and many others led in the 1940s and 1950s. Urban workers were included, while rural workers and urban informal workers were excluded from this class coalition. The economic distortions brought about by populism led, in the 1960s and 1970s, to the "authoritarian capitalist-bureaucratic regimes" that were even more exclusionary. The authoritarian pacts were not populist, but in spite of their alleged modern character deepened the protectionist and statist policies that characterized national developmentalism.

---

23. This is, for example, what Paul Buchanan eventually does. His book begins with a broad concept of class coalitions, such as the one quoted above, but continues by identifying class compromise with several attempts involving Latin American governments to reach a formal agreement between labor and capital. In his words, "Democratic class compromise is a product of institutionalized strategic interaction between the state, labor, and capital" (1995: 27–28). Only in a few cases do formal agreements become relevant, while the informal, development-oriented political pacts we are referring to are of overwhelming importance.

In Brazil, this authoritarian pact started to break down in the mid-1970s, when the business class began to reconsider its alliance with the civil and military bureaucracy, giving rise to a "democratic political pact" that resulted in redemocratization in 1985. Yet the populist aspects of this pact led to the failure of the Cruzado Plan and the collapse of the democratic pact itself in 1987. Between then and 1994, Brazil experienced a political vacuum and serious governability crisis, since no political pact was in place. Only in 1994, after the Real Plan stabilized inflation, did the election of Fernando Henrique Cardoso involve the formation of a "pragmatic and social-democratic political pact." As is the case with all hegemonic political pacts, it occupied the ideological center. If it can be consolidated as a class compromise, it may well represent the beginning of a new stage of economic development for the country.[24]

In the absence of development-oriented political pacts, the democratic regimes in Latin America face to different degrees a permanent governability crisis aggravated by the fact that we live in times of structural adjustment and state reform. This governability crisis will only be overcome when stabilization is achieved and growth resumed. Stabilization was achieved in most countries in the early 1990s due to severe fiscal adjustment, combined either with heterodox shocks that neutralized inertia or orthodox shocks when straightforward hyperinflation was taking place. Growth, however, has remained weak and uncertain as fiscal adjustment, trade liberalization, and privatizations were not enough to rebuild state capacity, and they were not followed by development-oriented political pacts that defined a new and positive role for the state in the social and economic realm.

Acuña and Smith (1994: 53), in exploring the future paths that may spring from current politicoeconomic tendencies, concluded that "full-blown neoliberal restructuring with the consolidation of democratic rule is not a likely future for most Latin American societies." We would say this is true for all of them, since the neoliberal insistence on a minimum state is not realistic. According to these two authors, "The most probable scenario seems to be dualist democracies. In this scenario state elites establish an alliance with a strategic minority of the opposition for the purpose of excluding the majority of the remaining social actors by disarticulating and neutralizing their capacity for collective action."

24. The analysis of political pacts in Brazil and Latin America presented here is a "heroic" summary of two books (Bresser Pereira 1985 and 1996). In the later book, the relationship between the lack of a basic social contract and the need for development-oriented political pacts is discussed extensively (chaps. 11 and 17).

This is a pessimistic view, probably modeled on Argentina's recent experience. Whether it is a realistic perspective or not is difficult to say. Yet it has the merit of requiring a political pact to legitimize the governing elite. The question is how can we know whether or not this pact will have to be as exclusionary as Acuña and Smith predict? A realistic development-oriented political pact that rejects the minimum state ideology, strengthens the state, and defines a clear role for it in the coming century will not necessarily be exclusionary. It will always imply a certain degree of capitalist exclusion—this is how political pacts are distinguishable from basic social contracts—but not such a radical exclusion as the one implicit in Acuña and Smith's "dualist democracies." We would rather suggest that political pacts will be social-democratic or social-liberal in nature and thus will be able to engage an increasing share of the Latin American population. Here, however, is not the place for predicting the future.

Conclusion

The conventional wisdom that economic problems have a political origin must be qualified in many ways. Many economic problems have a strict economic origin, deriving from the dynamics of the economic cycle and the imperfections of the market. At the same time, the belief that stabilization programs and structural economic reforms are not implemented or fail for lack of political support is only partially true. In many cases, the inefficiency of the reforms and the sheer incompetence of policy makers also plays a part in the explanation of the negative outcomes.

A more fruitful approach to the question of the origin of economic problems is to consider that governability, the effective power to implement required economic reforms, depends not only on institutional and personal considerations but essentially on a basic social agreement on the prevailing economic and political regime. When civil society is poorly structured, when this agreement is weak, when the property system and particularly the pattern of income distribution are being strongly contested, governments lack legitimacy and face increasing problems in implementing economic reforms.

In such a case, the strategy of securing political support for economic reforms through a transitory social safety net may be effective, provided that targeted social programs are well and transparently managed. But the limits of such a strategy are clear. A better alternative is to promote economic and political reforms that will not only provide for a return to state solvency, assure a more efficient allocation of resources, and build an adequate institutional framework but will also guarantee a permanent reduction in income inequalities. Yet this is an "expensive" alternative in the sense that it means income will be transferred to the poor from the rich and the middle class, whose permanent opposition must be confronted. A third alternative is the promotion of development-oriented political pacts that legitimize the political elite in government. This alternative, however, involves a chicken and egg problem. It is only viable when economic development is resumed, which depends on the implementation of the reforms that require political legitimation.

Thus, at certain times we have to rely on the convergence of several economic and political factors so that stabilization can be achieved, growth can be resumed, and a political pact can be created ensuring governability. Among these factors may be the exhaustion of populist policies provoked by the crisis, the adoption of bold and innovative economic policies to control inflation, the ability to build political institutions that mediate group interests, and the capacity to rebuild state finances and restore state governance.

This approach is quite different from the one assumed in the political-origin and political-obstacles hypotheses. They assume that stabilization and growth are automatically guaranteed by market-oriented reforms but are not adopted only because of the opposition of politicians. This is a neoliberal approach that ignores the relations between the economic and the political spheres, and adopts a linear cause-and-effect approach. In place of this, we stress that the economic reforms will only make sense if they are able to overcome the fiscal crisis of the state and rebuild the state. We suggest that this kind of reform will be adopted when the economic and the political spheres work together, when economic reforms and a development-oriented political pact assure governability.

3

The Prospects for Open Regionalism in Latin America

Juan Alberto Fuentes

Economic integration in Latin America has entered a new phase, conditioned by new development strategies implemented mainly by democratically elected governments. These strategies are aimed at adjusting to a changed and increasingly demanding world economy, while simultaneously attempting to increase the economic competitiveness of Latin American countries. The "stylized facts" of this new phase of economic integration are briefly reviewed in the first part of this chapter, followed by an explanation of the main determinants of the significant growth of reciprocal trade and investment flows within the region during the 1990s. A third section explores the meaning of "open regionalism," a current proposal by the United Nations Economic Commission for Latin America and the Caribbean (ECLAC) for economic integration in the region (ECLAC 1994a). A final section identifies some of the obstacles to further economic integration in the future, taking into account the eventual establishment of a Free Trade Area for the Americas (FTAA).

The Stylized Facts of Economic Integration in Latin America

Two phenomena characterize the process of economic integration in the 1990s: first, the proliferation of free trade agreements, originally mostly at the bilateral level, and second, a significant expansion of reciprocal trade and investment within the region.

The Characteristics of Recent Trade Agreements

More than fifteen bilateral free trade agreements were signed between 1990 and 1996. This was in addition to fourteen agreements signed between 1982 and 1990 (ECLAC 1994a, Table 2-5), which expanded even further as new bilateral agreements between Mexico and Bolivia, Mexico and Costa Rica, and Canada and Chile were signed. In addition to these bilateral agreements, Mercosur was formed in 1991, an integration agreement that includes Argentina, Brazil, Paraguay, and Uruguay; these countries as a group concluded free trade agreements with Bolivia and with Chile.[1] All of these agreements share five characteristics.

First, the areas covered by liberalization in the new agreements of the 1990s tend to be greater than in the past, although they are still limited. Specifically, there are an increasing number of new treaties that include "negative" lists of products excluded from free trade, thereby granting free trade to all remaining products. This contrasts with more restrictive "positive" lists contained in past treaties, which limited free trade to those products included in the list. This trend compares favorably to the recent past, since all but one of fourteen bilateral free trade agreements signed during the 1980s had a negative list. Moreover, Mercosur includes a commitment to gradually eliminate all exceptions included in its negative lists.

Second, more recent agreements involve greater preferential tariff reductions than in the past. Whereas past tariff reductions were often only partial, current preferences normally involve a complete elimination of tariffs.

Third, restrictive sectoral agreements are not very important (with the notable exception of automobiles). This is a significant departure with respect to the older integration agreements such as the Central American

---

1. More general integration commitments, including the association of groups of countries (Central America and Mexico, the Caribbean Community [CARICOM], and Venezuela, as well as the group of three formed by Colombia, Mexico and Venezuela), have also been made.

Common Market and, in particular, the Andean Group, which included industrial programming efforts at a subregional level.

Fourth, services are not usually covered by these agreements (with the partial exception of maritime and air transport). However, there are a growing number of agreements that include clauses on reciprocal investment granting most favored nation or national treatment to investment originating in partner countries. Since trade in services often involves foreign investment, these clauses in fact favor reciprocal trade in services.

Finally, the building or renewal of common institutions generally has not, until recently, been part of this new wave of integration. Even though there has been a proliferation of agreements, including ambitious ones like Mercosur, a common trait has been the reluctance of governments to create new permanent supranational institutions that would be in charge of promoting or monitoring integration agreements. Greater informal contact between various actors (government officials, political parties, nongovernmental organizations, and private enterprises) at a regional level, as well as greater realism concerning the role of institutions, appear to be behind this phenomenon. More specifically, the greater skepticism concerning regional institutions appears to reflect a certain frustration with regional institutions in the past, as well as the need to avoid premature institutionalization of a process of integration that is still in a state of flux.

The Expansion of Intraregional Trade and Investment

With the expansion of the number of integration agreements, there has been a significant expansion of intraregional trade and investment. Intraregional exports in Latin America as a proportion of total exports grew from approximately 12 percent in 1990 to about 18 percent in 1996. During this period intraregional exports increased from 16 to 20 percent in Central America, and from 12 to 13 percent in the Caribbean. Most intraregional exports consist of industrial products, but agricultural products traded within the region as a proportion of total agricultural products exported also increased significantly during the late 1980s and early 1990s (ECLAC 1994a, Table 2-2).

Although information on intraregional investment is difficult to come by, there is some evidence that it has increased significantly, shifting from the short-term capital flows of the past to more permanent direct investment today, with a growing proportion of foreign regional investment in services (ECLAC 1994a). Larger Latin American firms seem to be going through a process of mergers and acquisitions, in addition to forming strategic alliances with foreign firms in order to have access to new technologies (CEPAL 1996). There are also indications of a gradual process of rationalization of the activities of subsidiaries of transnational enterprises as they gradually adopt subregional or regional goals and perspectives. This replaces an older national approach that was the result of producing for relatively closed national markets in which an import-substituting strategy had made itself felt.

The Sources of Greater Economic Interdependence

The contribution of integration agreements, particularly bilateral ones, to the expansion of intraregional trade and investment was initially unclear. First, a large, though falling, number of bilateral agreements were still based on positive lists, in which reciprocal free trade was granted for only a limited number of products. This limited the coverage of products subject to the liberalization of trade. Second, many pairs of countries without bilateral free trade agreements experienced high-growth rates in their bilateral trade, higher than among those countries that had integration agreements. For example, in 1992 Brazil and Colombia, Brazil and Mexico, and Mexico and Venezuela experienced higher-growth rates of reciprocal trade than many other countries that had signed bilateral or subregional integration agreements (ECLAC 1994a). Nevertheless, the impact of newer, less restrictive agreements has been greater.

A closer evaluation of trade patterns in the region leads to the identification of other, possibly complementary, explanations for the significant expansion of intraregional trade. First, the region's total imports have grown dramatically, increasing from less than US$100 billion in 1990 to more than US$250 billion in 1996. Second, the significant increase in imports can be attributed to lower levels of protection, stabilized economies that are experiencing signs of reactivation, and, in an increasing number of cases, appreciating exchange rates. Intraregional trade has grown as part of this phenomenon. Specifically, it can be associated with more or less simultaneous unilateral liberalization processes that have allowed geographical proximity to become an important determinant of trade flows. Thus, neighboring countries that have proceeded with unilateral liberalization, sometimes reinforced by integration agreements, have become major poles of dynamic intraregional trade expansion. These poles include Argentina and Chile, Brazil and Argentina, Colombia and Venezuela, and El Salvador and Guatemala.

Furthermore, in addition to privatization, especially in the telecommunications and transport sectors (Devlin 1993), most countries in the region have gradually reduced the number of sectors reserved for state ownership and national investors and adopted rules that do not discriminate against foreign investors (Calderón 1993). Moreover, just as unilateral liberalization has contributed to greater intraregional trade expansion, deregulation and privatization have contributed to greater intraregional flows of investment. This is particularly true in services, for which not only geographical proximity but also cultural affinity are important explanatory variables for such flows (UN 1993). In addition to these factors, the process of economic restructuring in Latin America and the growing globalization of some of the most successful firms in the region have meant that these firms have begun to invest abroad, both in Latin America and beyond (Peres 1993).

Toward Open Regionalism

Two phenomena would thus appear to be promoting integration in Latin America. On the one hand, unilateral liberalization, deregulation, and stabilization have created conditions that "naturally" or spontaneously favor greater economic interdependence between countries sharing a geographical space and certain cultural characteristics. On the other hand, there are additional policies of a preferential nature that can further strengthen interdependence. Open regionalism consists of strengthening the links between both elements, de facto integration and policy-driven integration, in such a way as to enhance the competitiveness of the countries of the region and, in so far as possible, constitute a building block for a more open and transparent international economy (ECLAC 1994a).

For integration agreements to be consistent with open regionalism, they should do the following (ECLAC 1994a):

1. Provide for an extensive liberalization of markets in terms of sectors, including both goods and services, without excluding different transition periods that would allow for gradual adjustment;

2. Involve a broad liberalization of markets in terms of countries, which implies that the entry of new members should be facilitated;

3. Be governed by stable, transparent rules, favoring those trade rules that are consistent with the General Agreement on Tariffs and Trade and harmonize standards in accordance with international agreements;

4. Take place among countries that have managed to stabilize their economies, while strengthening regional institutions that provide balance of payments financing in order to minimize the possibility of macroeconomic disequilibria;

5. Apply moderate levels of protection against third-party competitors and favor the use of common external tariffs, phased in gradually if necessary;

6. Eliminate or harmonize institutional arrangements (regulations, norms), facilitate the convertibility of currencies or other adequate payments arrangements, and build infrastructure, all to minimize transaction costs both within and between countries;

7. Adopt flexible and open sectoral agreements that will favor the international transfer of technology;

8. Include special measures to favor the adjustment of the relatively less-developed countries or regions, including the *gradual* reduction of protection, while granting fiscal incentives to favor intraregional investment; and

9. Favor flexible institutional arrangements, promoting widespread participation of the countries' different social sectors.

The justification for the first five conditions is quite orthodox. The first two conditions would facilitate the realization of economies as a result of scale and specialization. Together with stable multilateral rules (3) and stabilized economies (4), they would help to create favorable expectations for investment, both national and foreign. Multilateral rules and harmonized standards (3) would also reduce administrative costs and waste. The rationale for having wide membership is equivalent to the one favoring "natural" partners (i.e., partners with a high proportion of reciprocal trade). It would reduce the probability of having to purchase imports from more costly producers, while facilitating imports offered by least-cost producers—an outcome that would also be aided by low levels of protection against third-party competitors (5). Larger markets also promote greater investment. Common external tariffs (5) would discourage triangulation and contraband and avoid the need for strict rules of origin, which are increasingly being used as disguised instruments of protection.

The justification for the remaining conditions may be less well known or more controversial. The reduction of transaction costs (6) may eliminate trade diversion resulting from preferences completely, since it can reduce the price of regionally produced goods and services below those of imports obtained from outside the region (Reynolds, Thuomi, and Wettmann 1993). Meeting this condition may require sizable investments or substantial institutional reforms, which in turn need careful cost-benefit evaluations. Flexible sectoral agreements favoring the transfer of technology (7) are part and parcel of a new division of labor in which there is a growing deverticalization of larger firms, geographical decentralization, and subcontracting of productive activities, as well as a continued need for innovation and the diffusion of technology. These are also part of what can be considered an innovation-led process of integration.

Allowing for gradual adjustment processes (8) is based on the presumption that markets do not respond immediately to changing relative prices. This is particularly true of imperfect and incomplete markets (both in factors and final goods and services), especially in underdeveloped countries. Subsidies favoring intraregional investment in less-developed countries (8) assume that the countries that gain the most can compensate those which gain less or experience losses, and that the success of integration agreements can be undermined by member countries that do not benefit significantly from the integration process. Flexible institutional arrangements (9) presume a process of integration that is still relatively "shallow" and in a state of flux, while greater participation of different social sectors is in accordance with the democratic spirit prevailing in the region.

Obstacles to Furthering Integration

Renewed interest in integration has been partly motivated by the recent wave of democratically elected governments in the region. The group of Rio, which is a forum of dialogue and coordination that includes South American countries and Mexico, was created in this context. Integration, correctly or not, has been adopted as an instrument intended to strengthen democracy and the links between democratically elected governments. This has often led to a gap between general declarations about the merits of integration and specific integration agreements, but there is no doubt that recent economic integration efforts are widely perceived as part and parcel of a new ethos associated with democracy at a regional level. Further impetus was provided by the Miami Summit in December 1994, when all heads of state of the Western Hemisphere, with the notable exception of Cuba, agreed to establish an FTAA by the year 2005. In fact, trade and the creation of an FTAA emerged as the basic centerpiece of the process of inter-American cooperation launched by the summit. In what follows, some of the obstacles faced by economic integration in this new context and the possible reasons for the gap between intentions and actions are identified.

Differing Patterns of Stabilization and Adjustment

Macroeconomic imbalances have been an important source of friction and have created obstacles to achieving integration agreements with a wide geographical coverage. Specifically, tensions are likely to arise when countries with very different rates of inflation try to integrate, since there will be continually changing relative prices at the bilateral level. For example, bilateral-exchange-rate variations have been a bone of contention between Brazil and Argentina within Mercosur, and the strong devaluation of the Mexican peso in December 1994 was also a major source of conflict with some of its trading partners in the region. The Mexican crisis clearly illustrates how macroeconomic risks may arise from uncertain prospects regarding capital flows to Latin America, which in recent years have served to cover growing trade deficits while appreciating each country's exchange rates. Economic integration accompanied by highly appreciated exchange rates could give rise to all kinds of protectionist pressures and eventually lead to a spiral of competitive devaluations. To the extent that stabilization processes are not consolidated in the region, there is always the danger that integration could exacerbate intraregional conflict rather than promote cooperation.

Moreover, varying rates of progress in stabilization and adjustment have led to the establishment of separate categories of relatively more successful and relatively less successful groups of countries. These do not necessarily coincide with the traditional integration groupings, in which geographical proximity appeared to be the determining criterion for association. In fact, differing degrees of progress in adjusting have become a divisive issue, which in recent years has led to the possibility of creating new integration agreements as alternatives to those that existed in the past.

To begin with, the conditions attached to entering the North American Free Trade Agreement (NAFTA) (even though not yet explicitly stated) tend to coincide with the so-called "Washington consensus" and with the conditions existing in those countries, such as Chile, that have advanced most in terms of adjustment (IDB-ECLAC 1993). This leads these countries to seek their own individual accession to NAFTA, rather than waiting for the remaining countries that are members of older and more traditional Latin American integration agreements. Thus, in the past representatives of Costa Rica, Jamaica, and Colombia expressed the desire to accede to NAFTA individually, without having to wait for other members of the Central American Common Market, the CARICOM, or the Andean Pact.

Within Latin America, the countries that have advanced most in terms of controlling macroeconomic imbalances (especially inflation) have been those most prone to engage in integration agreements. This partly explains Chile's and Mexico's (less successful) initiatives to enter into bilateral or trilateral agreements with other countries in Latin America, as well as the fact that Brazil was one of the countries with the least number of bilateral trade agreements in the region. Other countries, like Colombia, Venezuela, and Costa Rica that belonged to subregional agreements like the Andean Pact or the Central American Common Market and appeared to have advanced most in terms of stabilization and adjustment, also entered into negotiations to reach bilateral agreements with third countries. This led to resentment and criticism on the part of the rest of the member countries and also favored the multiplication of overlapping preferential agreements, in which older "historical" agreements—often kept alive mostly by political and geographical considerations—coexisted with newer bilateral or trilateral agreements that reflected greater affinity among participating countries in terms of economic policies.

An example of conflicting arrangements involves Mexico, which was forced to break one of the Latin American Integration Association (ALADI) rules as a result of its membership in NAFTA. Article 44 of ALADI establishes that any preference granted by a member to a third country must be extended to all ALADI members. This means that Mexico would have to extend the same treatment that it gives to U.S. exports to its imports originating in ALADI countries. The Mexican government requested an ex post facto waiver, which was initially rejected by Brazil. This led to a drawn-out period of painful negotiations in order for a new relationship between Mexico and ALADI to be defined.

The different degrees of progress in terms of stabilization and adjustment have made it difficult to reach integration agreements that are both
deeper *and* wider, as Mercosur pretends to be. Furthermore, these
different rates of progress in adjusting may also be a source of a growing
gap between those countries that would enter NAFTA early and those
that would not, since the latter would be more affected by trade and
investment diversion.

Divergent macroeconomic performance in the region, however, has
recently had quite unexpected results. On the one hand, once the
progress in Brazilian stabilization became evident, Mercosur's credibility
as one of the dynamos of hemispheric integration grew. On the other
hand, the Mexican crisis weakened the credibility of NAFTA, both as a
result of the Mexican economy's vulnerability and because of growing
protectionist sentiment in the United States that was fueled by the
Mexican crisis. This relative strengthening of Mercosur vis-à-vis NAFTA
has been further reinforced by a general agreement of economic cooperation signed by Mercosur and the European Community, and by the fact
that Mercosur's members decided to replace each country's bilateral free
trade agreements with ones jointly negotiated by Mercosur as a whole.
On a smaller scale, final peace agreements in three Central American
countries (Nicaragua, El Salvador, and Guatemala), combined with the
significant progress they have made toward stabilization (in contrast to
Costa Rica's difficulties in consolidating its stabilization), have also
strengthened the credibility of the Central American, traditional subregional integration scheme, albeit as conceived in terms of open
regionalism.

Going Beyond "Shallow" Integration

The overall adjustment costs of Latin American integration have not, at
least until recently, been a major policy issue in most of the region's
countries nor, therefore, a major obstacle to furthering integration in the
region. On the one hand, unilateral trade liberalization generally took
place before the new integration agreements were put in place.
Adjustment costs were mostly associated with opening up vis-à-vis the
rest of the world, rather than with trade liberalization at a regional level.
On the other hand, intraregional trade liberalization has advanced
gradually, mostly through bilateral trade agreements among countries
that historically have not been major trade partners, while the expansion
of intraregional trade has been, to a considerable extent, the result of

unilateral liberalization. This would suggest that a rather "shallow" form of integration has predominated.

Furthermore, with the unilateral trade liberalization that has taken place, there is a danger that newer instruments of protection will be used to avoid some of the effects of an expansion of intraregional trade, especially when overvalued or appreciating exchange rates exist. Specifically, there is evidence of a growing use of antidumping duties to block or reduce competition arising from greater intraregional imports, as the application of antidumping duties in Mexico against fish meal from Chile illustrates (*El Financiero*, 14 February 1994) and in Guatemala against cement exported by Mexico in 1996.

An indicator of the difficulty in *deepening* integration in Latin America, and of going beyond "product integration" to "policy integration," is the existence of productive sectors that are not subject to (reciprocal) liberalization. A specific source of difficulty has arisen from varying degrees of earlier unilateral trade liberalization associated with the processes of adjustment, with differences largely of a sectoral nature. For example, in early 1994, Mercosur members were not able to reach an agreement on a Common External Tariff (CET). This was mainly because Brazil favored higher protection in certain sectors (e.g., capital goods) in which it had higher average tariffs than the other Mercosur members. Furthermore, there could be a trend toward including sectoral arrangements in other bilateral (e.g., Mexico-Chile) or wider (Mexico-Colombia-Venezuela, Chile-Mercosur) integration agreements, including special rules of origin, very long transition periods (for agriculture in particular), and safeguards (such as already occurs in the case of automobiles) postponing reciprocal trade liberalization. Different domestic prices for oil and oil derivatives have also been a source of friction, since they may have effects similar to those of a subsidy.

In general, different sectoral priorities and the desire to keep open the option of bargaining bilaterally with other parties has meant that most integration agreements do not involve establishing common external tariffs. Keeping individual bargaining options open has been an obstacle to reaching a CET in Central America, even though each country's structural adjustment agreements with the World Bank have led to a convergence of tariff levels that has created the basic conditions required to apply one.

Furthermore, as indicated earlier, most integration agreements in the region do not yet involve significant progress in terms of the coverage of services, investment, and intellectual property. For instance, Chile's bilateral integration agreements have mainly consisted of agreements liberalizing the trade of goods. When other themes, such as investment and certain services (mostly transport), have been considered, these have usually taken the form of clauses of a general nature, and potential agreements on more specific issues have been left for discussions to take place in the future. Alternatively (as Mexico has discovered), the inclusion of issues such as intellectual property and government procurement has led to prolonged negotiations. This probably explains the greater number of bilateral integration agreements signed by Chile than by Mexico.

Still, prospects for further progress are promising. By 1997, the preparatory stage of negotiations to establish an FTAA had almost been concluded, after the creation of twelve working groups,[2] and agreement had been reached by the hemisphere's governments based on those principles that would guide future negotiations. Indeed, with the actual beginning of negotiations on an FTAA, it is hoped the bilateral stage of integration agreements will end, giving way to a multilateral and more balanced process of negotiations in the hemisphere.

In general, the preparatory stage of negotiations has had open regionalism as its basic frame of reference, along with the need to reach agreements consistent with the World Trade Organization's norms. This is indeed one of the principles of future negotiations agreed upon by Western Hemisphere governments, in addition to consideration of the special needs of smaller economies. Other principles agreed upon include more operational matters (similar to those accepted as part of the Uruguay Round of Multilateral Trade Negotiations) such as conceiving of the FTAA as a single undertaking, allowing countries to negotiate individually or in groups, establishing a secretariat to support negotiations, and concluding negotiations by the year 2005 (IDB 1997).

Equity Among and Within Nations and Institutional Requirements

Agreements that *implicitly* discriminate against smaller, less-developed countries by using demanding rules of origin or by restricting the liberalization of trade in agricultural products could become an important obstacle to integration. Specifically, the application of rules of origin with

---

2. Working groups were established to deal with the following issues: market access, customs procedures and rules of origin, investment, standards and technical barriers to trade, sanitary and phyto-sanitary measures, subsidies, antidumping and counterveiling duties, small economies, government procurement, intellectual property, services, competition policy, and dispute settlement.

higher local content requirements favors more developed countries and discriminates against the manufactured exports of smaller economies, which usually have industrial sectors that are highly import intensive. It also discriminates against those countries with a high proportion of foreign firms that use imported inputs. In addition, the preference for liberalizing trade in industrial rather than agricultural goods further discriminates against the relatively less-industrialized countries. Both themes are likely to be major negotiating issues in Latin America in the future.

In general, it appears that the degree to which the smaller countries are "ready" to participate in the FTAA is lower than is the case with the larger countries (ECLAC 1996). Although the smaller countries in the region have usually had more favorable macroeconomic performance (with lower rates of inflation and more moderate exchange-rate fluctuations) than larger countries, they face other institutional and economic problems that place them in a situation of relative weakness. Thus, smaller countries have made less progress in making international commitments in the areas of labor, the environment, and intellectual property. They are more dependent on foreign trade for their fiscal revenues, maintain a lower percentage of international reserves, and have wider tariff spreads. For smaller countries there is also less diversification of exports, with vulnerable products such as textiles making up a high proportion of exportable goods, and in some small countries education and infrastructure conditions are appalling. Overcoming these problems will require both new domestic policies and international support (ECLAC 1996).

Furthermore, while there is growing recognition of the fact that nonreciprocity is no longer a very useful trade negotiating strategy, the smaller and relatively less-developed countries in the region continue to request some kind of special and differentiated treatment. More specifically, they want longer adjustment periods in cases of reciprocal trade liberalization commitments. This is not an unreasonable demand, although it applies to all cases in which product and factor markets are imperfect or incomplete, and it is not restricted to the relatively less-developed countries of the region.

Thus, although both the identification of Latin American integration with common cultural and historical traits and the unilateral trade liberalization that has already taken place tend to reduce opposition to integration agreements, the question of adjustment costs remains. Adjustment and transition issues that emerge as a result of economic integration can also be seen as part of a process leading to the reduction of transaction costs at a national level, which favors the vertical integration of markets in each country and the horizontal integration of markets of different countries. This involves a challenge of an institutional nature, since reformed and liberalized product and factor markets require new forms of regulation and supervision. It also requires building a consensus to ensure effective implementation, one of the weak spots of adjustment policies applied in Latin America (Naím 1993).

At a regional, Latin American level, this institutional challenge is less urgent, since it involves responding to conditions of integration that are only beginning to develop. Three trends regarding the institutional development of integration agreements are apparent. First, increased attention is being given to the participation of nongovernmental actors, specifically business groups. This is achieved mostly through the creation of forums that assign them a consultative role. Second, older institutional arrangements created to respond to a more interventionist integration strategy are in the process of being reformed, with a view to simplifying procedures and focusing on core integration responsibilities. As part of this process, for instance, in 1997, Central American presidents agreed to reform Central American regional institutions so as to concentrate in one organization all major integration-policy decisions. Finally, newer integration agreements, especially Mercosur, have so far favored a minimalist institutional strategy with very small or nonexistent supranational institutions. Decisions are made by consensus in intergovernmental forums. One weakness of this approach is that dispute-settlement procedures have not been institutionalized and therefore tend to become a source of high-level political frictions, usually at the level of ministers or presidents. This minimalist approach has also been manifest in the preparatory stage of negotiations to establish an FTAA, since a tripartite committee (formed by the Organization of American States, Inter-American Development Bank, and ECLAC) was established to provide technical support without creating any new institutional arrangements. To facilitate the actual process of negotiation, governments have agreed to establish a mostly administrative secretariat with few or no substantive responsibilities.

Conclusions

A series of bilateral agreements and a new subregional agreement (Mercosur) mark the beginning of a new stage of integration in Latin

America. It is characterized by more pragmatic and less ambitious integration efforts than those in the past. Actual integration is also being fueled by nondiscriminatory policies, such as unilateral trade liberalization and deregulation, which have favored the growth of reciprocal trade and investment within the region.

Open regionalism, as proposed by the ECLAC, involves the interaction of both policy-led and de facto integration. This should be encouraged by nondiscriminatory policies in order to facilitate the development of Latin American countries' competitiveness and will serve as a building block for a more open international economic system. The prospects for open regionalism in Latin America will depend on how different obstacles facing integration are dealt with, especially as part of the process for creating an FTAA. These include problems arising from the existence of different degrees of stabilization and adjustment in those countries wishing to integrate. They also include the tensions resulting from the existence of sectors that are more sensitive to trade liberalization than others, especially in the presence of underdeveloped markets, overvalued exchange rates, and different degrees of readiness.

To the extent that stabilization and adjustment processes advance, some of these problems may become less important. Overcoming them will require significant progress in terms of institutional reform, mostly at a national level, while the still relatively "shallow" and ad hoc process of integration currently underway does not appear to require the creation of ambitious institutions for the time being. However, minimum institutional arrangements could facilitate the settlement of disputes, and will require further strengthening once the process of negotiation and implementation of an FTAA is undertaken.

II

Country Case Studies
Political Parties and Social Forces

4

Economic Reform in Argentina

Which Social Forces for What Aims?

Jorge Schvarzer

After the "lost decade" of the 1980s, Argentina has anchored its economic policy on the path of orthodoxy. The opening up of the economy, the privatization of almost all public enterprises, Argentina's efforts to achieve fiscal equilibrium, and other measures favoring the rules of the market have reshaped the economy and society in a very short time. The stabilization of prices following hyperinflation and economic recovery (1991–94) were recognized as the crucial outcomes of these policies.

This reform was applied, beginning in July 1989, by a democratic government. The populist origin of this government was another sign of the vitality of democracy. The reform demonstrated a change in the president's opinions about the problems faced by the Argentine economy and their solutions. These facts help explain the optimism in several circles about the future of the country.

A complete analysis of the new economic policy and its outcomes is beyond the scope of this chapter. For this reason, as well as for the sake

Translated by Philip Oxhorn with the assistance of Carmen Sorger.

of clarity, there will be little mention of earlier political and economic events, and no references to other social subjects, even though several of them were important to the current evolution of Argentine policy. Instead, the focus will be on certain aspects of economic policy in order to expose the restrictions imposed upon them by structural factors, specifically the external debt. These were expressed in the demands of creditors, which skewed the decisions made by the government. I will attempt to demonstrate how stabilization, privatization, and the opening up of the economy were carried out in a way that produced outcomes different from those predicted by orthodox theory.

However, here I will discuss not orthodox theory but its applications and the policy options that are marked by this approach, as well as the interests of pressure groups as determined by their strategic positions. The balance is clear. Instead of competitive markets, economic policy has built up several big monopolies, while the local market has been opened wider for flows of financial capital than for merchandise (and more for merchandise than for services). In fact, the kinds of markets created by this policy respond to pressure groups that are now leading the economy in ways that are different from what had been expected in earlier analyses.

I will emphasize those aspects of economic policy most relevant to this argument, even though there have been several policy changes that cannot be analyzed in this chapter. Some of the changes already carried through in the Argentine economy are worthwhile, even if they are the object of general criticism here. In reality, the concrete logic of economic policy has run deeper than simply resolving certain problems. Although the social forces behind the economic reform were able to change the economic landscape, they are not going to be able to push Argentina into a true process of economic development and social progress. The new economic model, born of the interplay of the economy and politics, is based on one kind of democracy and the construction of one kind of market. The concrete explanation of this process is one way to evaluate the application of theory on society.

An Unexpected Change

The first change of government in Argentina's new democratic period brought about a deep change in the direction of its political economy. Carlos Menem's ascension to the presidency, in July 1989, ushered in a new economic project that was completely contrary to what had been expected: having been viewed until that time as the representative and heir of a classic populist party (called Peronist or "justicialist"), he became a role model for orthodox international economics. Because of his strong desire to carry out a program of structural reform, specialists portrayed him as an example of success.

The political tradition of the party that won the elections was tightly linked to the statist policies of Perón's first presidency (1946–55). This tradition favored internal markets and unions, and the entire electoral campaign was marked by Perón's memory. Yet as soon as the first electoral results ensured a Peronist triumph, the victorious candidate announced his decision to ally himself with sectors of Argentina's traditional Right—the same sectors to which he had allegedly been politically opposed. On the very night of 14 May 1989, the press published the agreement that had been reached with Bunge and Born, one of the biggest national business enterprises: the elected president offered them the strategic post of minister of economy, in which position Bunge and Born planned to place one of its managers. That news was still being confirmed when it became known that the victorious candidate was meeting with A. Alsogaray, a prominent representative of the economic Right. These dealings had more than a symbolic value for the new alliance: Alsogaray had been a minister under various governments, and he was known for his orthodox beliefs and open opposition to Peronism.

On 8 July 1989, the government took office with a cabinet containing many members who were well-known for being traditional foes of the Peronists. The Ministry of the Economy was headed by a manager from Bunge and Born (who was replaced by another man from the same firm after his sudden death a week later); Alsogaray was named special advisor for foreign debt negotiations; Alsogaray's daughter, María Julia, was named president of Entel (the state telephone company, which the government had promised to privatize); the presidency of the Central Bank was offered to a technocrat who had worked as a financial consultant and who confessed (as did several of his colleagues) that he did not vote for Perónism; and D. Cavallo was sworn in as minister of Foreign Affairs. Cavallo thus benefited from his previous relationship with Peronism (although it was with a different faction than that of Menem) and gained new political support for the application of programs that he had already tried out while a member of the military government. Several political and social posts were given to classical Peronists. In this way, the distribution of tasks and responsibilities was clearly defined: the economy would be handled by representatives of economic orthodoxy in its various forms, and political and social areas would be the responsibility of the victorious political party.

The new alliance in power was not as stable as one might have at first expected. During its first two years, intense conflicts arose within the heart of the government. This resulted in a constant shuffling of posts and changes in short-term policies. There were four ministers of economy and seven presidents of the Central Bank during this period. An uncountable number of other ministers, secretaries of state, and directors of public enterprises were also replaced. Only at the beginning of 1991, with the shift of Cavallo to the Ministry of the Economy and the launching of the so-called Convertibility Plan, did government instability tend to decrease (although it did not stop).

The changes mentioned so far offered a clear indication of the degree of conflict that was occurring within the center of power. There were other indicators as well, and an analysis of the policies put into effect in specific areas demonstrated the same thing. These conflicts reflected ideological struggles, competing interests, and sometimes both. The conflicts were hidden, although they were intense. The consolidation of the final structure of this alliance, when viewed over time, makes it possible to identify the winners and their concrete logic. This is what I will try to outline in the course of this chapter, although I will not examine the details of the specific conflicts.

Achieving Power

Schematically, one could say that the new alliance brought together traditional sectors of national economic power (in which commercial and financial interests predominate), foreign lenders (international institutions and banks that share a similar outlook), technocrats representing the new economic orthodoxy, and political leaders with populist backgrounds. The first two groups offered the alliance their capacity to influence the entire power structure from the vantage point of their hegemony over the financial market.[1] The technocrat group offered its knowledge and ability to design policies, as well as its foreign contacts and its capacity to lobby,

1. Elsewhere, I have analyzed these groups, which I call the "establishment," in terms of both their internal composition and their political logic. See Schvarzer 1986, which deals with the establishment's policies during the 1976–80 period. These policies created the conditions that led to the changes in the current period. On a more general level, see Sábato and Schvarzer 1988, in which the history of the establishment's positions is described.

and finally, the political leaders took advantage of the government's legitimacy, which came from their electoral victory and the expectation that they would remain in power for a long time if they could ensure the permanence of the new policies.

The alliance achieved a degree of political stability that had been impossible to attain during the entire period beginning with the coup that brought down the first Peronist government in 1955. Each successive government had to face contradictions within the center of the power structure that ended up nullifying its own power to act. As O'Donnell wrote (with surprise and concern) at the beginning of the 1970s, for nearly two decades the country had tried all imaginable alliances and yet all had failed.[2] Elected governments were thrown out by military coups. The succeeding governments, in turn, became embroiled in their own internal conflicts and finally were forced to call new elections. The experiences of the 1970s and the 1980s were not very different.

Until July 1989—thirty-four years after the fall of Peronism—only one government managed to reach the end of its planned term, whether it was a constitutionally established term or one previously fixed during military rule. The succession of coups had appeared to consolidate a new alliance in 1976 under the economic direction of J. A. Martínez de Hoz, who remained minister of economy for five years and led Argentina along new development paths.[3] The alliance broke down soon after his departure, as a result of internal political and military contradictions that led to the Falklands War. The military then withdrew from power in what has become the classic way of calling elections. The subsequent democratic government, headed by Raúl Alfonsín, tried to overcome these difficulties in order to consolidate a democratic system. Alfonsín's project, which had to confront a difficult economic situation inherited as a result of earlier policies and the foreign debt crisis, ended up inextricably involved in an inflationary explosion that forced Alfonsín to hand power over to Menem six months early. In other words, Argentina's first democratic change of government arrived "on crutches," barely maintaining the system's apparent "normalcy."[4]

2. See O'Donnell 1972. For later analyses by the same author, with a similar perspective, see O'Donnell 1978 and 1982.

3. My analysis of the nature of this alliance and its policies, which has important elements for understanding later events in the country, is in Schvarzer 1986.

4. The slogan that it was necessary to "go to the elections even if it is on crutches" was used at the beginning of 1976, by the main opposition leader, R. Balbin, in the face of the inflationary and political crises that affected the government of Isabel Perón. The coup in March of that year aborted this hope of achieving, at any cost, the replacement of the government in power through legal means.

The stability that ensued can be explained by several key factors. First, through their accumulated experience, various actors discovered both the need for and the convenience of making an alliance that could overcome the problems caused by earlier conflicts. This conclusion coincided with the collapse of the Alfonsín government at a time when all the participants in the power structure could recognize the veto power that large private interests had already achieved over official economic policies. In this sense, the hyperinflationary explosion sent an obvious message: the Argentine economic crisis could be overcome only with the close collaboration of sectors within the power structure. The Radical Party government had tried to negotiate with these sectors in the belief that its democratic legitimacy would give it enough power to counterbalance its weakness in other areas. The result was that different agreements were successful at certain points during the radical period, but they were not able to avoid the final disaster. This outcome was made more acute by the attitude of open confrontation between the parties to those agreements. Menem expressed this idea repeatedly, stating that Alfonsín had failed because he confronted all the elements of the power structure (economic, military, trade union, and church sectors). He concluded that the time had come to negotiate with them, assimilating them into the government.

The other members of the alliance had no problem with such collaboration, as long as their presence in the power structure was recognized under the conditions they desired. Many of the leaders from the economic right in the Peronist government had been active members of several military regimes and had no scruples about the military's actions. Accusations about human rights violations, which grew in strength after the 1976 coup, were viewed as something that did not affect them, as if they had not been part of the same government. Why should they reject an alliance with Peronism (that they had hated and despised), as long as the Peronists accepted their terms? For them, political power was and is a "natural" consequence of their social and economic power, and they assume such power is a part of the conditions that emerged in the complicated life of Argentina.[5]

The alliance cannot be understood without recognizing its limits and possibilities for both sides. The newly elected leaders could offer their

5. Various members of the government's economic team insisted that they are not Peronists and thus feel no obligation to support certain policies with which they do not agree, as if their presence in the government alone was worthwhile and did not demand any political solidarity. The majority of them participated in the previous military government and had adopted a similar attitude.

electoral legitimacy, which is valuable both internally and abroad given the broad recognition of the virtues of democracy. This allowed them to retain their ability to maneuver in those spheres, such as social policy, which had strategic value during electoral periods. The other members of the alliance could offer their foreign contacts and their economic power (including restraint on the use of their veto to stop any policy they disagreed with), in exchange for direct participation in economic decision making. One can logically assume that the negotiations were not this explicit (at least not at first), and that a good number of the initial conflicts arose from the exploration of the limits that each of the internal factions was willing to accept.[6]

The real power of this alliance cannot be understood without reference to the hegemony it established over society. That the alliance consolidated itself in the midst of the hyperinflationary chaos of the second trimester of 1989 and the political defeat of the Radical Party administration was a decisive factor in its victory. The first price shock began in February and peaked just prior to the elections, with a 50 percent increase in price indices for April. After the triumph of the Peronists, and while the new government team was negotiating its alliance, the price of the dollar began a rapid upward spiral that dragged national prices along with it and ended by bringing down the political system itself. During the first week after the elections, the price of the dollar doubled, generating an 80 percent increase in prices for the month of May. During the next month, the price index increased 100 percent as the exchange market went mad. In barely fifty days (from 14 May to 8 July, the day government power was transferred), the price of the dollar shot up from a hundred to seven hundred pesos, creating a hyperinflationary spiral. This situation forced Alfonsín's government to accelerate its departure from power (which had been legally scheduled for 10 December of that year). Handing over the reins of power appeared to be the only way to recover the open ungovernability of the entire economic system.

The inflationary crisis precipitated the urgent replacement of a government that had lost the confidence of society. It also provoked a series of economic and social changes, whose consequences are still not understood years after their explosion. The crisis compressed the purchasing

6. Conflicts also occurred within each one of the individual groups, which obviously did not have a homogenous composition. The individual interests of some members of these groups ended up generating more than one specific (and acute) conflict during this period. Some of them are analyzed in a more general context in Acuña 1995 and, in more specific cases, in Schvarzer 1993a.

power of salaries to 24 percent of their average in the ominous month of May 1989. Their value later returned to close to 70 percent of the average purchasing power during the first five years of the Radical Party government, and has oscillated around this level since. Hyperinflation created a sharp break with past tendencies. Its effect prevented wage earners from thinking in terms of the relative normalcy of previous periods. The persistent fear of a new inflationary outbreak (and the brutal fall of income that accompanied it) became the chief factor limiting labor movement activity. One member of the local establishment pointed out (correctly) during the crisis that even if hyperinflation did not last long, its effects would: the collective memory has been so shocked, he said, "that we will avoid falling once more into situations like inflation, the bankruptcy of the state, or the non-payment of taxes."[7] The same conclusions were also reached by John Williamson in January 1993.[8]

This inflationary memory endured over time, and although it evolved as new problems arose, it conditioned all social action. Even as late as mid-1993, a well-known journalist said that the enormous social costs borne by workers as a result of the economic policies introduced by Menem (in terms of the fall in real wages and the large increase in unemployment) were "lamentable but understandable." "With inflation," she added, "we would have the same social cost or maybe even a greater one. We were living with increasing inflation. We have already seen what happened during the time of the Alfonsín government with the [looting of] supermarkets."[9] Four years after the economic chaos of hyperinflation, the images of hunger and the looting of supermarkets justified continuing with the same economic policies that had brought it to an end. This argument, it seemed, was accepted by a large part of society.

The consolidation of the alliance required an additional component in the political realm: the concentration of decision-making power in the executive branch in order to facilitate the achievement of the objectives being sought. For years, Alsogaray had insisted on this. It is necessary, he said as a deputy in Congress, "that the Minister of the Economy be given

7. Statement by R. Alemann to the newspaper *Cronista Comercial*, 9 June 1989. This period is discussed in greater detail in Schvarzer 1993. Alemann was the minister of the economy in 1981, during the military government and was offered the presidency of the Central Bank in 1991.

8. Fiori (1994) cites Williamson's paper "In Search of a Manual for Technopols," presented at the conference entitled "The Political Economy of Policy Reform," sponsored by the Institute For International Economics, Washington, January 1993.

9. Statements made by Magdalena Ruiz Guinazú and published in the magazine *Arca del Sur* (Buenos Aires, April 1993).

full power for a term of two or three years, after which he should appear before Congress for approval of what had been done." He felt that this would be the only way to overcome the crisis democratically, and in fact this was precisely one of the demands that the Peronists made before "accepting" the early transfer of power: the Radical Party deputies would have to approve two "emergency" laws, the Economic Emergency Law and the Reform of the State Law, which concentrated decision-making power in the executive branch for a period of two years, and even allowed it to dictate laws by decree in several decision-making areas. These laws, giving wide discretionary powers to the executive in a variety of areas, were approved without discussion only a few days after the installation of the new government.

The hyperinflation accentuated the urgency of making decisions quickly. It was thus functional for this concentration of power, which was maintained for a long time. The president continued to use decree laws after the period in which emergency laws were to remain in effect, claiming he needed to do so given the urgency of the demands he faced. It has been estimated that he signed 160 decrees of this sort during his first term, not counting those that were permitted by the above-mentioned laws. Even today, the executive resorts to threatening to decree laws when Congress does not respond with the necessary urgency to its projects.

In sum, the new alliance in power has accumulated so much decision-making authority that it has been able to suppress any opposition (real or latent) from within society, limiting the ability of various institutions to exercise control over the government in the democratic system. This concentration of decision-making power has allowed the executive to negotiate with all the structures of power and adopt measures that obeyed this relationship of power, whose logic may be imagined (but not known) when observed from a distance. This is why the alleged strategies that will be discussed in what follows can only serve as a reference point for the hypothesis to be presented about the formation of the alliance and its objectives.

Basic Goals and Their Instruments

In the official discourse beginning the day after the elections, it was argued that embracing a structural reform of the Argentine economy along traditional orthodox lines was necessary. The best excuse for this policy was based on the urgency of overcoming the chaos that inflation had inflicted on society; a complete break with the past emerged as the only way to resolve the problem. This argument was accepted by large segments of the population, even though it contradicted the classic Peronist discourse. Inflation was linked to the budget deficit, which in turn was linked to the way public enterprises were run; their privatization became one of the pillars of the new policy.

Reform of the state, privatization, and fiscal balance became not only means to reach stability but ends in themselves. The political discourse also included other objectives considered to be no less important, such as budgetary reform, the renegotiation of the foreign debt, and changes in the rules that regulated industrial and agricultural policy (tariffs, industrial protection, investment subsidies, and so on). All of these policies were included in the wave of structural transformations that produced, without a doubt, the greatest change in the way the Argentine economy functioned since the crisis of 1930. A complete analysis of this is beyond the scope of this chapter. I will concentrate on some key aspects of this policy, with a focus on the logic of the alliance in power and its main objectives.

My argument is that priority was given to everything related to payment of the foreign debt, which was considered to be the main obstacle to Argentina's economy taking off. This decision became a strategic one, given that it implied pushing all political decisions toward that end. As a consequence, the entire economy was oriented toward achieving this goal, which created new restrictions on its future evolution. Examples of this abound, although the analysis here will concentrate only on some of the most important: privatization of public enterprises, which was partially used to pay off the foreign debt and reduce obligations to banks; the exchange rate that was adopted (or accepted) for stabilization, which served to reduce the weight of the debt on the Argentine economy; and, finally, the swift opening up of the financial sector, which allowed for the inflow of external funds that also helped resolve the debt problem. Each one of these policies reflected the global logic of economic orthodoxy, but they did not correspond to it exactly. What must be emphasized is that in each case, the policy options chosen were subordinated to the priority of reducing the weight of the debt (and the demands of creditors). This conditioned the results being sought. Behind the formal appearance of orthodoxy, there was a strategy that in many key aspects was different from what would have been done had other priorities and goals been adopted. A review of this phenom-enon will serve as the basis for confirming these hypotheses in the chapter's conclusion.

The Problem of External Debt

The foreign debt reached such a magnitude that by the beginning of the 1980s, it was impossible to meet the obligations it entailed. The high interest rates that dominated the world market during this period made it nearly impossible to pay even the service charges. In the case of Argentina, the figures are most eloquent. The country faced a principal debt of $50 billion by the mid-1980s, and yet its gross domestic product was US$75 billion. Interest payments alone amounted to $6 billion per year, which represented 8 percent of the gross domestic product (GDP), 35 percent of the national budget, and close to 80 percent of export earnings.[10] These three variables were critical. Interest payments threw the economy off balance because of their effect on production. They were enormous with respect to the state's fiscal capacity, and could absorb almost all the foreign exchange earned by commercial activity. In order to continue repaying the debt, these three gaps had to be resolved simultaneously, and soon it became evident that this was practically impossible under the conditions in which the Argentine economy (and Latin America as a whole) functioned.

It is well known that these problems were not recognized as such in orthodox economic theory, which emphasized that the problem was a liquidity crisis and ignored the structural problems associated with debt service payments. The pressure to pay these obligations distorted Argentina's economic balance and stimulated the high rate of inflation that characterized the country and the whole region during this period. The refusal of creditors to recognize these inconveniences was slowly softened, as they started to solve their most urgent problems. In any case, reality demonstrated the impossibility of repeating the old pattern. Prescriptions to pay the debt by generating a positive commercial balance had negative effects on the national budget, because the govern-ment had to buy foreign exchange with domestic currency. Subsequent

10. Data on the macroeconomic conditions in Argentina changed with the evolution of the system and the related statistical analyses. Here I can present only general information in order to highlight the size of the problem. Its characteristics can be found in the literature on the debt.

prescriptions for capitalizing the debt by exchanging it for productive assets (debt-equity swaps) also demanded recourse to the national budget or printing domestic currency, and both created the same problem. For each of these alternatives, obstacles were created by one or more of three key variables: budget limitations, the availability of foreign exchange, and the global economic balance.[11] In turn, these phenomena stimulated capital flight, tax evasion, and other responses that were no less perverse from the private sector, aggravating the tendency toward disequilibrium.

Slowly, the creditors began recognizing these problems, particularly after they began resolving their own crises by adopting new measures. First the Baker Plan, and later the Brady Plan, paved the way for a different diagnosis that emphasized the urgency of structural reforms in the indebted countries, although at the same time they recognized the need to reduce the stock of debt. In these measures, the debt had to be reduced through the use of "market" methods or concessions from creditors. The illusion of a liquidity crisis gave way to recognition of a crisis of insolvency, which could not be seen in the critical moments when many large international private banks were on the verge of bankruptcy as a result of their previous lending policies.[12]

This recognition was not always explicit, but it can be seen in the new policy proposals for solving the debt problem that arose, one after another, both in international financial centers and in Argentina. Toward the end of the 1980s, the local "establishment" had become convinced that the only way to pay the debt was to apply a range of measures that included several successive steps. The first was to reduce the level of debt by offering public enterprises as part of the payment. This was particularly important because this kind of capitalization did not generate budgetary or monetary problems as did earlier alternatives. The second was to profit from the above measure to gain access to the Brady Plan in order to further reduce the level of debt and the annual flow of debt service to creditors. The third was to encourage all types of external financial flows in order to facilitate debt repayment and avoid relying on

11. I made these points in an earlier article (Schvarzer 1984), which I mention here simply because its conclusions contrast with the hegemonic thought of the period that refused to accept these arguments.

12. Within the already voluminous literature on the debt, a summary of the predominant arguments at each stage in its evolution can be found in the report by Sullivan (1991) for the United States Congress. Bailey (1990) explains the logic of power that prevented Washington from debating the theme while dismissing realistic diagnoses and relying on the fictions created by creditor interests.

the foreign currency earned by the export of goods and services. A key component of these projects was the hope of recovering Argentine capital that had fled out of the country.

These ideas are found throughout "establishment" publications during the period and were brought together in a collection published in July 1989, under the title *Argentine External Finances in the Decade of the 1990s* (CARI 1989).[13] This document emphasizes the decisive importance of recuperating Argentina's external credit as a matter of national prestige, as well as improving relations with private creditors who are seen as indispensable to the future of the country. The text highlights the national interest in associating with "the main creditors of Argentina who are among the 20 major international banks [and] also have more power and influence than many sovereign countries" (CARI 1989).

This relationship was reflected in the above-mentioned publication, which included several contributions from representatives of creditors, and it would be repeated in the composition of the alliance in power. The directors and representatives of the major creditor banks participated in the power alliance, whether through official posts in the government or through private organizations that had been established in recent years to consult and cooperate with the government. In this manner, entities with "more power and influence than many sovereign countries" participated in the power structure of Argentina, making decisions that affect the whole society and national sovereignty.

Privatization and the Debt

Before assuming power, the government had already announced its decision to privatize public enterprises and to start with two that had a key role to play in the first stage: Entel (the telephone company) and Aerolíneas Argentinas (the national airline). Menem named María Julia

13. This book was published by the Argentine Council for Foreign Relations (CARI), an establishment think tank that toward the end of the 1980s decided to prepare it as a contribution to the strategies that should be followed by Argentina's next elected government. Several of the experts who collaborated on this work later held positions in that government, and their proposals traced the path that domestic economic policy would follow. The differences among the contributors (and there are some) offer an excellent basis for a study (which still remains to be done) of the changes in this group's ideas and the effect of different pressures on the power structure.

Alsogaray, daughter of Alvaro and a militant promoter of privatization, as the person in charge of the privatization of Entel. This can be taken as a first sign, *urbi et orbi*, of the decision to move toward privatization. It is likely that her nomination was part of an agreement with Alsogaray, who believed it indispensable and urgent that public enterprises be handed over as payment of the debt (a topic that became his responsibility as presidential advisor). These decisions permitted father and daughter to work together toward this objective, which the privatization measures taken make clear.[14]

The first measure concerning the privatization of Entel established a fixed time period to hand it over to new private owners. The date that was chosen required a veritable marathon to meet the deadline. Although this measure can be explained by the urgency to find solutions to the crisis and the concern to reduce the ability of possible opposition forces to block it, this official political commitment increased the leverage of foreign creditors in the process. These creditors waited until the last moment to grant the required waiver, which had become essential for the sale in that during negotiations over the debt, public enterprises had been offered as guarantees of repayment. As a result, the creditors would have to agree to each sale (privatization) beforehand. The delay in conceding the waiver generated political polemics in the country, but it was never explained to the public why the government had not asked for it earlier. There is little doubt that the delay was a powerful tool for exercising control over the entire process. The creditors granted waivers, both for Entel and for Aerolíneas, after the auctions and once all formal decisions about how to hand over these enterprises to the final winners had been made. The capacity of the creditors to control the process through this tool is obvious, even though evidence of it is hidden and difficult to confirm in a conclusive manner.

The guidelines for the sale of Entel stimulated the entry of business associations composed of telephone companies (to guarantee its effective operation), creditors (in order to exchange it for debt), and national partners. The formal requirements required that telephone operators hold only minority participation in the association to be formed (which was later reduced to 5 percent in order to meet U.S. rules on the subject). No conditions were placed on national partners, and there was not even an attempt to avoid potential conflicts of interest. This laxity helps

14. In an earlier publication (Schvarzer 1993b), I dealt with the privatization of Entel and Aerolíneas in detail.

explain why building contractors and other suppliers were present in each association. The creditors were included implicitly, because it was established that the payment for Entel would be made by transferring debt certificates, a decision that favored whoever offered the largest quantity of such titles. In other words, to buy Entel it was necessary to own debt certificates, either through previous ownership or through purchases made in the secondary market that had emerged in the international financial system.

By basing the auction on debt certificates, any attempt to establish the value of the enterprise in more concrete terms was nullified. The winning consortia offered certificates for $5 billion at face value, which at that moment had a market value of only 15 percent of their nominal price in the international market. In this way, the enterprise whose worth had not been officially established was handed over in exchange for ownership of debt certificates whose nominal value differed greatly from their market value, leaving a large margin of doubt about the sum actually paid for Entel.[15]

Entel was divided into two smaller enterprises covering different geographical areas, with the objective being to compare the efficiency of the new operations with each other. The $5 billion price represented payment for the control of both. The new owners received 60 percent of the capital of the company (enough to ensure control), while the remaining 40 percent was divided into one part (30 percent) to be placed on the stock market and the rest (10 percent) to be handed over to the sector's labor unions. The winners also received a concession on telephone services, which included a monopoly for ten years and rates high enough to ensure good profits on the operation from the beginning. In fact, creditors exchanged their claims on debt, whose repayment was doubtful (as was evident from their low price in the secondary market), for shares in a monopolistic enterprise whose returns were guaranteed. From then on they would receive a constant flow of dividends instead of the interest on the debt. This was the main difference: the interest that was to be paid by the Argentine state became, through privatization, profits that would come from paid user fees. In order to accomplish this, it was necessary to maintain a monopoly over the service and high user fees.

The strategy of handing over Entel in exchange for ownership of the debt was prominent in the official logic. María Julia Alsogaray, in the

---

15. To be precise, additional payments of $212 million in cash were made, but these are not mentioned to avoid complicating the discussion. This does not, however, change the central argument that is being explained. For more details, see Schvarzer 1993b.

middle of a polemical exchange, stated that it could "save" the delicate situation of the Manufacturer's Hannover Bank, one of Argentina's main foreign creditors, which was on the edge of bankruptcy.[16] This willingness to help creditors and the desire to become associated with them guided the logic of privatization toward objectives that were distinct from the search for efficiency that the orthodox model presumed.

Only three business associations presented bids for the two parts of Entel, each one comprising telephone operators, creditors, and national business partners. The decision in favor of two of these consortia excluded the third operator (Bell Atlantic) but did not prevent the regrouping of the winners. These later included the bank associated with the consortium that came in third (Manufacturer's Hannover Bank) which, through undisclosed transactions, brought in its share of the debt. In other words, the selection of operators for the privatized telephone companies allowed Argentina's three main creditors to participate in the new business, together with other financial institutions that managed to obtain debt certificates in the secondary market at profitable prices. The creditors, who were the largest partners in each one of the consortium that bought Entel, thus became the true winners in the process. The press tended to point to foreign operators as the final arbitrators of the winning bids in the auction, without noticing that the exit of one of these (as a loser) did not prevent the bank associated with it from participating with the winning operators. The bidding chose the operators before the buyers.

The monopoly conditions guaranteed to the telephone companies, added to the high user rates accorded to them, placed a heavy burden on private agents in Argentina. The protests of large companies, especially those with intense contact abroad that saw their costs rise because of this measure, helped to stop attempts to repeat this practice in later privatizations. Otherwise, the fees for the use of key services such as gas and electricity would have severely limited the potential competitiveness of the whole national productive sector.

These user rates also affected the same official budget that was to be made "healthy." In fact, the state no longer had a deficit as owner of the company but found itself with a large bill it had to pay as a consumer of these services. Furthermore, experience suggests that most of the deficit of the former Entel that could be accounted for was due to the nonpayment of bills by many public offices; in this way, they passed on

16. Statements to the newspaper *Página* 12 (16 February 1990), cited in Schvarzer 1993b.

their funding problems to the service enterprise. After privatization, these offices were forced to pay for (or else lose) the service, and to pay a much higher price than they were used to.

By not recognizing the role of the state as a consumer of the services provided by public companies that are being privatized, most studies on the economic impact of this process have ignored this phenomenon, but it is nevertheless relevant. The increase in costs paid by the public sector as a consumer are in addition to the costs generated by its withdrawal as owner of the enterprise.[17] Because it is likely that the increased costs were greater than the supposed savings, this sale increased the overall level of expenditures of the entire public sector.

The privatization of Aerolíneas followed a similar route with regard to the establishment of a fixed time frame for its sale and withholding of the waiver until the end of the entire decision-making process. Payment with debt certificates, the requirement for a foreign operator, and the possibility that national partners could participate without conditions also applied in this case. The only consortium that finally presented a bid consisted of Iberia as the operator, three large creditor banks, and an Argentine group that owned the domestic airline company that competed with Aerolíneas in the national market. The presence of this last group implied the rebuilding of a monopoly in domestic air travel (culminating in the later sale of the national airline company to Iberia), and the authorities did not object. The sale of Aerolíneas took place in the midst of a confusing process that included changes in many earlier regulations and led to a guarantee that the new enterprise would retain its status as the country's flagship airline. This meant that half of all seats offered on the country's incoming and outgoing flights would be reserved for it.

In this case, while it was more difficult to guarantee high returns on international traffic (due to the competition with other companies), it was done for domestic traffic (which resulted in very high costs). The state also discovered that it was such a large consumer of the airline's services that the price increases were more significant than its potential savings as the former owner of the company that had been sold. Moreover, a significant portion of the price that was to have been paid in cash was subsequently paid in services to the government (with the new fares applied that had been established for the privatizations).

17. In order to sell the enterprise under favorable conditions for the buyers, the state also assumed the enterprise's outstanding debts with its suppliers. These amounted to a significant sum, on the order of $2 billion. This amount continues to weigh heavily on the national budget, as does that of other enterprises handed over free of debt.

The great struggle unleashed by the privatization of Aerolíneas culminated in a private meeting between the minister of public works and the Senate committee in charge of following the process. In that meeting, according to what all the media published and that was never denied, the minister said that there was no room for negotiation: "Every document has a nonwritten clause, which we have not written down out of national shame, that is the degree of dependence that our country has, that it does not even have dignity, in order to be able to sell what must be sold. A country that has no control over its riches, a country that is internationally inhibited, on bended knee, in shame. . . . We are being monitored in absolutely everything."[18]

The privatization of Entel and Aerolíneas, which in fact was a form of payment ("capitalization") of the debt, served as a first step for negotiating with the country's major creditors. This system was useful for reducing the debt level rapidly and for calming creditors' demands while conditions were being prepared for entering into the Brady Plan in order to regulate future payments. The privatization served as a signal of the Argentine government's new disposition toward orthodox policies and as an argument for attracting overseas capital and negotiating with international credit institutions. It did not, however, have the desired effect of creating an ideal market (competitive and transparent) capable of conditioning business decisions in a dynamic way.

The process of bidding on a case-by-case basis was presented as a way of encouraging competition among bidders. This contrasted with the negotiations among the small number of creditors and national business partners who ended up with majority control of these enterprises.[19] The back room dealings confirmed the need to award monopoly conditions and assured profits, and this is reflected in the results of the privatization process. The logic of these operations would not lead to an optimization of the productive functioning of the national economy.

Experiences like this led World Bank experts to conclude that "selling for cash is preferable to accepting debt," as well as it "is better to eliminate monopoly power and to unleash potentially competitive activities than to maximize revenues from sales into protected markets. And it is better to construct appropriate regulatory frameworks to protect con-

---

18. This notable statement was published in *Página* 12 (4 September 1990).

19. One study (Gerchunoff 1992) of the privatizations found that there was "collusion" between private bidders during the process because there were so few of them given the large number of assets being offered by the public sector.

sumer welfare than to increase revenue by selling into an unregulated market" (Kikery, Nellis, and Shirley 1992).

The embarrassments that arose early in these two cases led to slight modifications in some of the later decisions regarding the privatization of other public enterprises. Alsogaray proposed selling several public enterprises together in one pack in order to reduce the debt, but this idea was rejected. The official strategy after 1992 was to build systems that worked more like markets through the division of activities and attempts to create competition among the private enterprises created in the privatization process.

The problems in the first cases could not be corrected, because they were already protected by legal decisions. Yet the results from later cases of privatization were not much better. The strategy being pursued did not prevent the consolidation of a relatively perverse system, given its most obvious characteristics: the system itself is largely oligopolistic (such that there is no assurance of normal market pressures for efficiency); ownership associations exist in which conflicts of interest arise between some of the business partners and the enterprise that has been sold; there are costs for users (who pay rates that ensure profits for the service providers) and costs for the public treasury (which is a consumer of these same services); there are demands for profit remittance abroad (which affects long-term trends in the balance of payments); and so on.

The Financial Opening

Payment of the foreign debt required, as an almost inevitable corollary, the unrestricted opening up of the country to international financial flows. To begin with, the mere limitation of any flow meant a potential restriction on the remittance of profits abroad from companies that were being privatized. This risk would have reduced the interest that creditors had in capitalizing on the debt and was eliminated by a series of measures that ensured the unrestricted entry and exit of funds into the country. This opening also was necessary in order to pay the debt according to the logic of recycling foreign exchange funds, whether through the return of flight capital or new foreign credits.

Recourse to returned flight capital was part of the plan of the national establishment's economists and creditors, who expected that the government would be able to use such funds as a source of the foreign exchange needed to take care of the debt.[20] Financial maneuvering toward this end began in early 1990, with a monetary strategy that managed to raise $5 billion in external reserves for the Central Bank that same year by manipulating the exchange-rate policy and interest rates. Part of this foreign currency had been accumulated by private individuals to protect their purchasing power during the period of hyperinflation (from April through June 1989) at a real price three to four times higher than that fixed by government policy during 1990. The recovery of flight capital was limited to acquiring what was available from the stock of domestic savings. The second phase required moving on to the recycling of credits from abroad.

The stability achieved with the Convertibility Plan and the Brady Accords opened the way to acquiring new credits in the international market, which would help to pay debt flows. Strictly speaking, the credits would also be used to cover the entire deficit in the balance of payments made up of the commercial deficit and the deficit in other services. Issuing bonds abroad became, after 1991, a decisive tool for generating foreign exchange that would be used to cover the deficit and pay creditors. Privatized companies, as well as the public sector, some large banks, and national enterprises, are issuing foreign currency bonds in international markets. The foreign funds are recycled to repay previous debt (in addition to new debt that is generated by the very program of stabilization). Issuing bonds amounts to several billions of dollars that help postpone the need to balance the country's external accounts.[21]

These financial movements were consolidated by the stimulus given to the national stock exchange, which was chosen to play a decisive role in attracting new foreign and national capital into the system. The stock exchange became one of the most attractive "emerging markets" beginning in the middle of 1991 as a result of the growth in trading. Measures adopted by the government included the sale of minority shares in the enterprises that were being privatized, which increased the

20. J. González Fraga (who later became president of the Central Bank during 1989 and 1990) said, "The return of part of the capital that Argentines keep abroad is a necessary condition for being able to meet foreign obligations" (CARI 1989).

21. It is not possible to calculate their accumulated value from the published information because some short-term bonds become due before new ones are issued, although they appear on the same listing. From the perspective of microeconomics, it is interesting to note that what is happening is a change of actors: new creditors (the owners of bonds) and new debtors (the issuers of bonds) emerge, at the same time that these actors collect (banks and others) or pay (the state). But from the point of view of macroeconomics, the country's foreign debt continues to grow and can only be resolved in the short run by this recycling of credits.

amount of capital marketed in the stock exchange. The entry into the market of 40 percent of the shares of the two telephone companies, plus that of two hydroelectric plants and part of the capital of the state petroleum company (YPF), multiplied the size and the activity of the stock exchange, allowing for the entry of large quantities of foreign funds. The market value of shares rose from $4 billion in 1990, to $28 billion in 1993, thanks to the increase in prices and the trading of these new enterprises on the stock exchange.

The size of the stock exchange, in absolute value as well as relative to the national product, gave it an important role to play in attracting foreign funds. The sale of shares of public enterprises, the issuing of debt certificates by private companies and the increase in trading attracted a lot of financial capital that entered the national market (as happens in other emerging stock exchanges). The entry of this capital offers another means for generating foreign exchange, allowing for the recycling of debt payments.

A recent report by the Morgan Bank (1994) pointed out that the issuing of bonds and other forms of financing changed the composition of the actors involved with the debt. Now, the report notes, the vulnerability of the debtors has been reduced: "the investors are more diversified; there are more of them, and for this reason it is probable that they will not all move in the same direction and at the same time, as happened with the commercial banks at the beginning of the 1980's." The report assumes that the conditions of the debt improved, not so much because their absolute value was reduced (a phenomenon that is not significant in most cases) but rather because its ratio to each country's total exports improved. In the case of Argentina, this result has been neutralized because the country is experiencing a period of commercial deficit as a result of its exchange-rate policies (which will be dealt with below).

In this sense, the impulse behind the financial opening, the liberalization of all movement of capital and the re-creation of the national stock exchange, came from decisions based on the central objective of resolving the debt problem. All other decisions were subordinated to this. The complexity of the new financial system (internal and external) makes it impossible to know the actual movements through which creditors not only are paid but are also replaced by other lenders. Even so, available information is illustrative of the general tendencies.

The creditor banks that capitalized their debt into shares in Aerolíneas sold these shares to Spanish banks, which are now part of the parent company that owns the airline. These operations allowed the banks to convert the debt into a source of cash income at an unknown price, while Iberia has become the main shareholder and exercises control over the enterprise.

The entry of minority shares of the telephone companies into the stock exchange generated a price per share that was much higher than the one paid originally by the winning consortia. This market price has allowed some minor national business partners of these consortia to sell their shares at a price that multiplied their original capital. It is probable that some banks are carrying out the same kind of activities within the limits and rules established for privatization when the firms were originally sold to the consortia.[22]

The most visible case is that of Citibank, Argentina's largest individual foreign creditor and one of the most active in the process of debt capitalization. Citibank entered as a business partner of the one of the two new telephone companies (and later increased its role by buying additional shares on the stock exchange). In addition, it participated in the purchase of electric companies, gas companies, a medium-sized steel mill, public hotels, and shares in YPF. In its strategy to capitalize on the debt, Citibank bought several private enterprises that were indebted to the state, giving the state debt certificates in exchange for shares. The sum of these activities made Citibank one of the major holding companies in Argentina. Later, in order to comply with U.S. Federal Reserve Bank regulations, Citibank created a special holding company to own these shares (Citicorp Equity Investment or CEI), which in turn was traded on the Argentine stock exchange. In 1992, CEI had a capital value of $700 million. This rose to $1,500 million when it entered the stock exchange, and climbed to $2,300 million in early 1994, when it announced net profits for 1993 of $135 million.[23] Citicorp Equity Investment is currently selling its shares on the stock exchange in a way that allows its controlling company, Citicorp, to make an appreciable profit on its debt capitalization. In fact, the financial decisions based on new rules governing the functioning of Argentina's economy were better for Citicorp than the actual effort to pay off the debt.

22. One national group that was a minority partner in the purchase of one of the telephone companies sold its shares in 1993, at a price four times higher than its original dollar investment (which was in addition to the profits it had received in the interim). This "excellent" transaction, according to a national magazine, spurred criticism of privatization, which was characterized as the "distribution of booty" that the beneficiaries were now selling on the market. See *Panorama*, February 1994.

23. See, for example, the statements made by the president of CEI in the newspaper *La Nación* (13 March 1994), which summarize the company's evolution.

The above description suggests that the close relationship between privatization, the opening of the economy, and the restructuring of the financial markets and stock exchange formed part of an indivisible single "solution" for the debt problem. It must be noted that these operations also required an overvalued peso, as was created, beginning in 1990, and consolidated with the Convertibility Plan.

The Revaluation of the Peso

The rise in the price of the dollar during the period of hyperinflation coincided with the expectation that a "super high" value would be imposed on the dollar (as was confirmed by one of the proposed candidates for an economic-policy-making post) as soon as the new government was installed. This strategy was seen as the only one that could encourage exports in order to generate a positive commercial balance and provide foreign exchange to pay the debt. This idea was present in several proposals and, in reality, was put into effect in the first period of the government. The policy was quickly abandoned after a silent struggle among different power holders (which led to the departure from the government of the Bunge and Born group) and in the face of accumulating evidence supporting an alternative policy.

Toward the middle of the 1980s, experts in the economic-policy-making apparatus began to debate the problem of exchange-rate policy. From a commercial point of view, a devaluation was necessary to achieve a positive commercial balance (given that devaluation encouraged exports and discouraged imports), but from a financial point of view, the requirements were the opposite. A devaluation would make it more expensive for the Central Bank to acquire the foreign exchange needed to pay the debt. The "commercial dollars" generated by the private sector became an extra burden on the budget as the price of foreign currency rose. As a result, government bureaucrats began looking for a difficult balance between commercial requirements and the requirements of the debt.[24]

---

24. This problem, known as the transfer problem, distinguishes nations in which the private sector exports (like Argentina and Brazil) from those where the public sector is the main exporter (like Chile, Venezuela, and Mexico). In the latter cases, the state receives the foreign currency it needs for the payment of the debt directly through its sales of petroleum or copper. It is not a coincidence that budgetary problems and inflation are much worse in nations where

The alternative consisted of generating "financial dollars" that would enter the country through mechanisms such as those mentioned above under conditions of an overvalued currency. The Central Bank's experience during 1990 had demonstrated that it was possible in a single year to obtain five billion financial dollars at local prices below those that would have been paid for "commercial dollars." The decision was thus made, and it was consolidated beginning in 1991, with the stabilization plan that created an overvalued peso that was freely convertible into dollars.

The overvaluation of the currency changed all the variables related to the debt in a positive way. It reduced the ratio of debt to GDP, the cost in pesos of annual payments, and the portion of the national budget corresponding to debt. These effects were obvious. Due to the new exchange rate applied under the Convertibility Plan, the ratio between debt and GDP fell from 99 percent, in 1989, to 40 percent in 1992.[25] A similar trend occurred with interest payments, which fell from 8 percent of GDP in the mid-1980s to less than 2 percent in 1993. This contraction of costs in national currency had a significant positive effect, which cannot be scoffed at, on the advance toward balancing the budget that had begun with stabilization. Given that the national budget is approximately 24 percent of production, interest payments fell from 25 percent of total expenditures to 8 percent as a result of this change.[26] It is difficult to imagine another method that would have yielded so effective a result in such a short time.

The overvaluation of the peso had another important effect on the economic program: it contributed to the control of the evolution of internal prices for national goods, as was required by the Convertibility Plan. Opening up the country to imports, with a reduction of import duties, resulted in the importation of goods that competed with national production. This threatened the traditional price behavior of businesses

---

the government must buy foreign currency to pay the debt, compared with those where state enterprises exist that operate in the world market (although economic orthodoxy continues to refuse to accept this phenomenon, which contradicts some of its policy prescriptions, such as maximum privatization, in Latin America).

25. These estimates, which must only be taken as an indication of the order of magnitude of the decrease, are found in Damill, Frenkel, and Rozenwucel 1993.

26. Part of this reduction was the result of the fall of international interest rates during the interim, as well as a consequence of the Brady Plan, but there is as yet no detailed analysis that would identify the relative weight of each variable in the outcomes that are being discussed. In any case, the role of the overvaluation of the peso will always be decisive, as can be seen from the data presented.

that used to control the protected local market. This phenomenon is one of the main elements that explain the containment of prices after the implementation of the Convertibility Plan. It also explains the distortion between industrial prices (that could not rise because of foreign competition) and the prices of services (that could rise with greater freedom because they did not have to face such competition).

Total imports rose from $4.1 billion in 1990 to $15 billion in 1992: that is, they tripled in only two years spurred on by the reactivation of the economy and the exchange-rate policy. The overvaluation of the peso, nevertheless, did not affect exports as much as might have been expected: the level of exports remained at approximately $12 billion during this period due to the great rigidity over the short term of the available supply, whether agricultural or industrial.[27] As a result of these changes, the commercial balance changed from a surplus of $8 billion, in 1990, to a deficit of $3.5 billion in 1993. This commercial deficit was financed through new debt.

The revaluation of the peso has played a decisive role in a model that prioritizes the payment of the debt. Its effects in terms of reducing the relative magnitude of the pressures placed on the budget and the productive system (in addition to those already mentioned for the stability of prices) became more important for economic policy than the presumed negative effects on the export sector and the dynamics of economic growth. The official discourse expected that potential exporters would be able to function with the existing exchange-rate policy (which is difficult to change without affecting stability and, even more so, the system of financial flows in foreign currency that are freely convertible into pesos and vice versa). In other words, it had moved beyond the logic of stimulus to the expectation of the spontaneous emergence of needed dynamic businesses.

The commercial deficit of $3.5 billion per year becomes an overall deficit of $11 billion when one includes other foreign accounts (the remittance of interest payments and profits to foreign countries, plus tourism and services). This difference is covered by financial flows

27. Seventy percent of Argentine sales abroad consist of raw materials that have a delayed response to price signals from the international market, for reasons that have to do with the business cycle and the alternatives available to landowners. These goods depend, in addition, on the evolution of the prices of each one of the products, which do not always follow the same tendencies as the exchange rate. The other 30 percent for the most part corresponds to goods from industries that export any excess that cannot be sold on the national market, given the need for industrial plants to operate continuously for technical reasons. I have analyzed this phenomenon in an earlier publication (Schvarzer 1993c).

coming into the country, which are the only means of maintaining this precarious equilibrium that has no foreseeable solution in the medium term. The system that was adopted to resolve the problem of financial flows arising from the debt was based on the multiplication of those same flows in order to postpone any resolution of the problem.

The already-mentioned report by the Morgan Bank (1994) pointed out that the newly available foreign financing offers indebted countries the "opportunity to develop competitive sectors" for export. If this does not occur, it adds, "at some point the countries could again become vulnerable to a sudden change in the preferences of investors."[28] It can clearly be deduced from this that the debt crisis has not ended for countries like Argentina, and that a new crisis could occur if the time gained is not used to transform the productive structure.

These are the same conclusions reached by other authors, like Gerchunoff and Machinea (1994), who analyzed the relationship among the main variables of the Convertibility Plan. According to these authors, the Argentine economy faces a "twin impossibility": it is not possible to continue with the current exchange rate, but neither is it possible for it to be devalued.

Conclusion

The Argentine strategy is portrayed in world forums as a model of a policy of successful adaptation to orthodox policy prescriptions. These prescriptions were based on the creation of a market that must regulate the behavior of all the economic actors, in place of the state, which is considered incapable of performing this task. This ideal market must give adequate signals, among which is the exchange rate, and contribute to the regulation of the conduct of actors in search of their desired conditions of dynamic equilibrium.

Even leaving aside arguments about the actual validity of this orthodox project, it is important to point out that the Argentine strategy did not follow these theoretical postulates. The formal or less important similar-

28. It is worth pointing out that this chapter was originally written in early 1994, before the unleashing of an economic crisis in Mexico in the aftermath of a peso devaluation that in fact led "to a sudden change in the preferences of investors." After the crisis, even the IMF (1995) recognized "the risks (for the indebted countries) of the great dependence on the financial flows being able to quickly change their orientation."

ities disguise central differences in the strategy that was applied. Adapting the strategy to the requirements of the debt led to the prioritization of policies that in essence had results contrary to the logical postulates of the model. The strengthening of oligopolies in the internal-service market (protected from foreign competition), as well as measures that generated a strong disequilibrium in the balance of payments, are examples of "systemic" defects created by the established priorities. The "model" was not based on the development of productive activities but instead on the hypertrophy of a financial order that provides great benefits to those who are in strategic positions to capture them. The correlation between this logic and the criteria and aims of the alliance in power allows one to understand the phenomenon.

These affirmations stand in contrast to figures suggesting that the GDP has grown in the period beginning in 1991. These statistical presentations have their origins in two convergent factors. First, the recovery in economic activity beginning with the achievement of stability made it possible to reach the production levels of 1987 (the last year before the price rise). The increase was as great as the fall in economic activity during the period of hyperinflationary crisis (and as a consequence of the first recessive measures adopted by the government). Second, an opportune change in the methods of measuring the GDP gave preference to the service sector (and evaluated the activity of this sector using indicators whose "optimistic" slant is notable). Actually, the activity of the productive sector has not gone beyond a stage of recovery. The effect that this will have on the evolution of the Convertibility Plan will only begin to be visible at the end of this stage, which began in 1994, and can only be evaluated with the passage of time. For now, opinions are divided between those who expect the reactivation to continue in a process of sustained growth and those who believe that there must be changes in the model to achieve this.

My hypothesis is that the priority given to financial activity creates conditions that make it difficult to forge a productive base oriented toward development. This priority is reflected in the sequence in which the financial opening won over the commercial opening. This is the opposite of what took place in all of the countries that have exhibited a successful development process in recent times. As a result, a financial logic can establish conditions contrary to the natural needs of productive activity. This problem merited the analysis of several experts and was taken up by McKinnon (1993), although no consensus was reached regarding solutions.

The combination of the financial opening and revaluation of domestic currency expresses the goals of producers of goods that are not tradable internationally, as well as the goals of international operators and investors. This was expressed well by Jeffrey Frieden (1991) in an article that combines social and economic analysis. The exchange-rate policy generates distributive effects of the same magnitude as the interplay of interest rates (although not with the same effects), and it can be explained by the orientation of the groups that predominate in the system.

In essence, the preference for the financial recycling of the debt gave rise to a sequential order according to which the requirements of these groups predominate over any other demands from the productive system. The withdrawal of the public sector from its former investment responsibility has still not been replaced by a dynamic and efficient private sector (except in a few rare cases). The revaluation of the peso diminished the potential role of external demand as a basis for development. The penetration of imported goods has limited the capacity of the internal market to become a factor in expansion, and the distribution of income (regressive as a result of exchange-rate policies and financial movements) created a small favored nucleus that is able to direct its demand to the international market.

Argentina has managed to stabilize prices after a genuine record level of inflation. It has also managed to put its public accounts in order, as well as its relationship with the so-called international financial community. But the cost of these successes was very high. Wage earners lost 30 percent of their income, unemployment rose, and worse still, nothing suggests that the country has found a path that leads toward development. Until now, the alliance in power has been satisfied because it has resolved the problems of its members. The problems of the rest of society raise a different question.

5

Brazil's Drifting Economy

Stagnation and Inflation During 1987–1996

Werner Baer and Claudio Paiva

The return of civil society to Brazil in 1985 and the gradual evolution of fully democratic institutions over the following ten years was accompanied by a long period of mediocre economic leadership and years of little growth and economic instability. Only gradually did the democratic governments fashion a new framework within which to conduct economic policy. By the 1990s, they had adopted policies of trade liberalization and deregulation, but only in 1994 were they able to introduce a successful stabilization program. Although this chapter concentrates on Brazil's economic performance, it also attempts to account for some of the political reasons for economic policies adopted.

From the collapse of the Cruzado Plan in late 1986, until the ouster of President Collor in late 1992, Brazil's economy stagnated (real GDP grew at an annual rate of 0.6 percent), with inflation at the three-digit level for two years and at the four-digit level for four years. As will be argued in this chapter, these problems can be interpreted as resulting from the malfunctioning of the public sector. Ironically, although Brazil's public sector had been a crucial force in bringing about the country's industrialization and growth, by the second half of the 1980s, it had become a barrier to further growth and development.

The General Setting

José Sarney was president from 1985 until March 1990. The basic problem during his administration after the Cruzado experience was that he did not have a long-term vision or project for the Brazilian economy. In addition, a lack of sociopolitical cohesion made it difficult even to effectively develop and implement short-term reforms. One reflection of this is that Sarney had three finance ministers and three different stabilization programs after 1986 (see Table 5.1).

Sarney was a president without a well-defined term of office. It was up to the Congress, elected in November 1986, to set the length of that term, since the Congress was also to serve as a constituent assembly in 1988.

Table 5.1 Policy Makers and Policies in Brazil (1985–1996)

President/Finance Minister	Year	Major Economic Policy	Major Political Event
José Sarney			
F. Dornelles	1985	Orthodoxy	Election of governors and
D. Funaro	1986	Cruzado Plan	constituent assembly (Nov. 1986)
L. C. Bresser Pereira	1987	Bresser Plan	Constituent assembly
M. da Nobrega	1988	Rice and beans	Presidential
	1989	*Plano Verão*	elections (Nov. 1989)
F. Collor			
Z. Cardosa de Melo	1990–91	Collor I	—
		Collor II	—
M. Marques Moreira	1991	Orthodoxy	Impeachment
Itamar Franco			process
G. Krause	1992	Undetermined	
P. Haddad	1993	Undetermined	—
E. Rezende	1993	Undetermined	—
F. H. Cardoso	1993–94		Election of F. H.
R. Ricupero	1994	*Plano Real*	Cardoso, governors, and
C. Gomez	1994	*Plano Real*	Congress (Oct. 1994)
F. H. Cardoso			
P. Malan	1995–96	*Plano Real*	—

Sarney was anxious to have his term lengthened from four to five years. With the failure of the Cruzado Plan, he had lost a considerable amount of public support. This, in turn, weakened his political power. The decision on the length of his mandate was dependent on good relations with Congress, since he was unable to muster any popular support. Thus Sarney bowed to the preferences of Congress in his economic-policy moves.

Upon assuming the presidency in March 1990, Collor presented the country with a well-defined plan for the economy. He introduced what seemed to be a unique way of dealing with inflation (which was close to being hyperinflation when he took office) and of modernizing the country's economy through drastic liberalization moves. Despite the approval of the initial set of measures that constituted the stabilization plan, Collor's minority position in the political sphere and his imperious personal style made it difficult to attract the congressional support necessary for some of the structural reforms.[1] The most important consequence of this political weakness was the impossibility of implementing a definitive fiscal adjustment, as this required changes in the constitution.

With the failure of stabilization attempts and accusations of widespread corruption ultimately resulting in an impeachment process in Congress, Collor's government lost its economic and political leadership capacity. An increasingly desperate administration sacrificed monetary and fiscal stabilization and industrial policies to short-term measures designed to halt the impeachment process. The absence of economic leadership continued with the assumption of the presidency by Vice President Itamar Franco and his continuous disagreements with the four different economic staffs he had during his first year in office.

Sarney After the Cruzado Collapse

A General Overview

Unlike their position during the Cruzado Plan, Sarney's policy makers, in the period 1987–89, seemed to have recognized the importance of controlling the government budget deficit in order to achieve lasting stabilization. This did not mean that drastic austerity measures were implemented. Promises to enact greater fiscal controls were officially

1. Although most of the members of Congress approved Collor's initial plan, this did not mean that they supported the government in general. Since the plan had been decreed and was therefore already being executed, it was almost impossible for Congress to stop it. Legally it

made, and some minor ones were actually achieved. For political reasons, however, a true fiscal adjustment was not carried out: the executive lacked determination due to its desire to have Congress vote in favor of a five-year term and most members of Congress had never sympathized with fiscal restraints. By the time a fifth year had been approved, the government had no prestige left with Congress, as most politicians had their eyes on the next elections. This meant that they were more interested in receiving funds for local projects, and the government's attempts to cut expenditures were undermined. Only minor expenditure cuts were made in some fields, mainly investments.

The continuing government budget deficits led to a rapid growth of the government's domestic debt and an acceleration of inflation. The rising debt also undermined the credibility of government debt papers, which necessitated the rapid rise of interest rates. The worsening inflation also led to a shortening of the terms of government papers. Thus the ratio M1/M4 fell continuously in the second half of the 1980s, from 31.7 percent in December 1986, to 8.4 percent in 1989. As interest rates were rising and the terms of the debt were falling (most of it being placed into the overnight market), a situation arose in which the growing deficit was mainly due to the government's financial condition.[2]

Besides the negative impact on the budget, the debt had an additional negative effect on monetary control due to the characteristics of its financing. On top of the high returns and short terms of government bonds, the government (through the Central Bank) was committed to "buy back" from the intermediary financial institutions those bonds that did not find buyers in the market. This automatic repurchase of government debt instruments caused a loss of control over monetary policy, in that the withdrawal of funds from the overnight market resulted in an automatic increase in the money supply, and such withdrawals were increasing due to inflationary expectations. In other words, the public debt in this context was increasingly the major cause of the lack of fiscal (financial deficit) and monetary control.

The large fiscal deficit and high interest rates also had a profound effect on resource allocation. There was an increasing allocation of credit to the

could overturn it, but this would have created such a confusing situation that most members thought it better to let it stand. For illustrations of these general remarks, see various issues of *Latin American Regional Reports: Brazil Report* (published by Latin American Newsletters Ltd., London) from the years 1990–92.

2. This is clear from Table 5.7. It should be noted that interest payments on the domestic debt rose dramatically in 1988 and 1989.

government, as the financial system became less and less an intermediator of resources to the private sector and increasingly a facilitator of the transfer of savings to the public sector.[3] The rising amount of funds placed in the financial rather than the productive sector implied a decline in economic activity.[4] In the years 1981–90, the average growth rate of the financial sector was 5 percent per year, which was double the growth rate of the GDP. As a result, the share of the financial sector in the GDP rose from 8.56 percent in 1980 to more than 19 percent in 1989 (von Doellinger 1991).[5]

The Bresser Plan

After the collapse of the Cruzado Plan, the monthly inflation rate increased dramatically, from 1.4 percent in October 1986, to 27.7 percent in May 1987.[6] With this renewed upsurge of inflation, the official indexation of financial contracts was reintroduced, which represented an admission by the government that its policy had failed. The inflationary resurgence was related to the realignment of prices that had lagged behind during the Cruzado Plan price freeze, speculative price increases in anticipation of another freeze, and other cost pressures provoked by the automatic wage increases that resulted from the trigger mechanism instituted during the Cruzado Plan. The public-sector deficit, which rose from 3.7 percent of GDP in 1986, to 5.4 percent in 1987, and the declaration of a moratorium on the foreign debt in February 1987, which worsened inflationary expectations and caused investments to decline, further contributed to uncertainty and instability.

3. This can be illustrated by considering that the investment to GDP ratio fell from 22.9 percent in 1980 to 16.7 percent in 1989, while the net domestic debt of the public sector rose from 5 to 22.2 percent of GDP. Other evidence is the change in the composition of internal credit allocation: in 1980, the private sector received 74 percent of total credit, with the rest going to the public sector. In 1990, this composition changed significantly, as the private sector received only 47 percent and the public sector 53 percent. See IPEA 1992b.

4. The high real interest rates in the financial sector, especially the overnight market, induced many firms to place a growing proportion of their resources into financial markets. Thus, many firms showed profits due to their financial dealings rather than to their fundamental productive activities. Da Costa (1993) estimated that the share of gains from the financial market made up about 37 percent of the profits of enterprises in 1989.

5. Von Doellinger (1991) supplies data showing that between 1980 and 1988, the net worth of the financial sector rose by 187 percent in real terms (283).

6. Much of the information in this section is based on various February issues of *Conjuntura Econômica*, which give extensive reviews of economic events in the previous year.

In May 1987, Dilson Funaro, who was finance minister during the Cruzado Plan and in the chaotic months following its collapse, was replaced by Luiz Carlos Bresser Pereira. In June 1987, the latter introduced a Plan for Economic Stabilization, more popularly known as the "Bresser Plan." Although it involved the freezing of prices and wages, it differed from the Cruzado Plan in that these freezes were to be applied in a flexible manner lasting 90 days, allowing for periodic price and wage readjustments. This flexibility was also applied to public-sector prices and the exchange rate, in order to avoid two of the major problems of the Cruzado Plan: the deficits of public enterprises and the overvaluation of the currency, which had hurt the competitiveness of the country's exports. Of great importance was Bresser Pereira's stress on controlling the public deficit as a major anti-inflationary tool. His aim was to reduce this deficit to 2 percent of GDP by the end of that year. Finally, the Bresser Plan also aimed to keep interest rates above the rate of inflation so as to prevent the type of excess consumption that had contributed to the fall of the Cruzado Plan.

The Bresser Plan showed some promise for a short period as the monthly inflation rate declined from 27.7 percent in May to 4.5 percent in August. After that, however, it rose again and reached double digits by October. Along with the intensification of the distributive conflict that resulted from the demand for the recuperation of wages and the rise of public utility and other controlled-sector prices prior to the introduction of the plan (Bonelli and Landau 1990: 17), the basic problem was the failure to control the budget deficit. Government spending grew as a result of salary increases of government employees amounting to 26 percent in real terms, the need to transfer resources to state and municipal governments whose combined deficits had increased by 41 percent, and growing subsidies to state enterprises. This lack of fiscal control reflected the political priorities of Sarney—that is, to win congressional support for including a fifth year for his presidency in the new constitution. As a result of this attitude, the Bresser Plan failed and its author resigned in December.

From Gradualism to Shocks and Back Again

Mailson da Nobrega was the finance minister and chief policy maker for the rest of the Sarney administration. He initially refused to use any type of shock treatment, stressing only the need for austerity measures to combat inflation. Mailson did not introduce any program of structural adjustment, limiting himself to a tighter administration of the treasury's cash flow. Among the major measures implemented were the prohibition of new hirings of public servants, freezing of the real value of financial sector loans to the public sector, and the temporary suspension of an indexing mechanism to readjust the salaries of public-sector employees. With the absence of deeper structural reforms, Mailson complemented his strategy of cash-flow controls with some artificial short-term measures to slow down inflation. The rate of increase of the prices of public utilities and of other state-controlled firms was slowed down,[7] contradicting his intention to reduce the public deficit, as was the devaluation of the exchange rate. This meant, in fact, that attempts to fight inflation were made at the expense of the public services and export sectors. These gradualist anti-inflationary policies came to be known as the "rice with beans" (*arroz com feijão*) strategy, due to its lack of any strong structural content.

Not surprisingly, this strategy was incapable of controlling inflation, as the average monthly inflation rate rose from about 18 percent in the first quarter to about 28 percent in the last quarter of 1988. The social unrest provoked by this situation led union leaders and employers, sub-sequently joined by the government, to attempt a Brazilian version of the successful Mexican "social accord." Such an accord would set future adjustment of wages and prices at a decreasing rate. Bonelli and Landau (1990) observed that this attempt failed because of the difficulties in reconciling conflicting interests, which had been exacerbated by the great dispersion of relative prices and a lack of political support (21).

As the situation was made worse by preventive price readjustments (due to expectations of a new shock program), policy makers felt it necessary again to resort to price controls. At the beginning of 1989, the Sarney administration tried once more to cope with inflation through a special program called "*Plano Verão*" (Summer Plan). Among its prin-cipal measures were (1) a new price and wage freeze; (2) abolition of indexing, except for savings deposit accounts; (3) introduction of a new currency, the *cruzado novo*, equivalent to 1,000 cruzados; (4) attempts to restrain monetary and credit expansion (increasing reserve requirements to 80 percent, reducing the length of consumer loans from 36 to 12

7. For example, the index of real prices (using 1984 as the base year equaling 100) of gasoline fell from 107 in 1987, to 82 in 1988, and 56 in 1989; of telephone fell from 77 in 1987, to 76 in 1988, and 55 in 1989; and of basic steel fell from 74 in 1987, to 60 in 1989. See Instituto de Economia do Setor Público, FUNDAP, *Indicatores IESP*.

months, and suspending debt-equity swap operations); and (5) a 17.73 percent devaluation of the exchange rate.

The impact of the *Plano Verão* was even shorter than the previous heterodox plans. From a monthly rate of 36.6 percent in January 1989, the general price index fell to a low of 4.2 percent in March, thereafter rising steadily to reach 37.9 percent in July, 49.4 percent in December, and 81 percent in March 1990.[8] The reason for this early collapse was not hard to find. The earlier failures of heterodox policies to control inflation made official decrees to freeze and de-index prices impotent. The low credibility of these policy instruments and the negative expectations of economic agents resulted in the use of extralegal measures to raise prices.

The economic crisis worsened in the last months of the Sarney government. Lacking an effective fiscal adjustment and thus facing persistent high budget deficits, the government was forced to maintain a high interest rate, which significantly raised the cost of the public debt. As a result, financial expenditures in 1989 rose 158 percent and were the major cause of the government deficit.[9] The deterioration of public finances was by that time reflected not only in the difficulty in placing new government debt papers but also in a tendency toward the monetization of the government debt.[10] The authorities feared the flight of resources from the overnight market into real assets,[11] and this was perceived by many as an imminent detonator of an open hyperinflation process.

The Fiscal Impact of the 1988 Constitution

The 1988 constitution had a negative impact on Brazil's public finances. It exacerbated an already-increasing trend of transferring fiscal resources from the federal to the state and municipal governments. Since the middle

8. The consumer price index behaved in an even more dramatic way. Its monthly increase of 70.3 percent in January 1989, fell to 3.6 percent in February. From March on, it began to rise again, reaching 84.3 percent in March 1990.

9. See *Conjuntura Econômica*, February 1990. The burden of the federal debt payments rose from 1.8 percent of the federal government's expenditures in 1987 to 11.6 percent in 1988 and 31.7 percent in 1989 (various issues of *Conjuntura Econômica*).

10. Attention should be called to the fact that the expansion of the monetary base, which amounted to NCr$63.8 billion in 1989, resulted from the NCr$10.6 billion needed to finance the government's primary budget deficit and the NCr$53.2 billion required by the "buy-back" operation mechanism.

11. As Zini pointed out, the stock of M4 decreased by 45.4 percent between April 1989 and January 1990. He attributed this to "political uncertainty and the escalation of inflation [which]

of the 1970s, the latter were increasing their share of tax revenues. In 1975, the share income tax and the tax on manufactured goods amounted to 5 percent each, and by 1980, these shares had increased to 14 and 17 percent, respectively. The constitution of 1988 made it a requirement of the federal government to transfer 21.5 percent of income tax and manufactured goods tax revenues to the states and municipal governments by 1993. As the decreased resources of the federal government were not matched by decreases in its obligations, the constitution worsened the structural disequilibrium of the federal budget. Also, as a 1989 study warned, there was a risk (later to be fully realized) that "the states and municipalities—with their additional receipts and without any new obligations—would fully use the new receipts by increasing their activities, thus making a future decentralization of government obligations unviable."[12]

The Collor Period

Collor-I

When Fernando Collor de Mello assumed the presidency in March 1990, inflation had reached a monthly rate of 81 percent. Facing runaway hyperinflation, Collor immediately introduced a dramatic new anti-inflation program that consisted of the following measures:

1. A new currency was introduced. The cruzeiro (Cr) was substituted for the cruzado novo (Cr$1.00 = NCr$1.00).
2. Of deposits in the overnight market, transaction, and savings accounts that exceeded Cr$50,000 (equivalent to US$1,300 at the then prevailing exchange rate), 80 percent were frozen for 18 months, which resulted during this period in a return equal to the prevailing rate of inflation plus 6 percent a year.
3. An extraordinary, once-and-for-all tax on financial transactions (IOF) was charged on the stock of financial assets, on transactions in gold and stocks, and on withdrawals from savings accounts.

resulted in a significant portfolio shift to dollars, gold and capital flight. Acquisitions of gold and dollars help to reduce the stock of M4 by the inflation tax on cash holdings of dollar vendors and of domestic residents employed in the extraction of gold" (1992: 226).

12. See Rezende et al. 1989: 554. These authors also note that besides new social security expenditures for public employees, the constitution also "created the potential for raising expenditures on public employees by increasing their social benefits by guaranteeing wage adjustments, equiparacão." See also Afonso et al. 1989: 585–609.

4. An initial price and wage freeze was implemented, with posterior adjustments following governmental determination based on expected inflation.
5. Various types of fiscal incentives were eliminated for imports, exports, agriculture, the North and Northeastern regions, and the computer industry; income tax was applied to profits from stock market operations, agricultural activities and exports; and a tax on wealth was created.
6. Taxes (on income and on manufactured products) were immediately indexed, forcing their adjustment to inflation the day after the transaction was made.
7. Disciplinary measures and new regulatory laws were implemented on financial operations in an effort to substantially reduce tax evasion.[13]
8. An increase in the price of public goods was instituted (e.g., a 57.8 percent increase in the price of gas, 83.5 percent in postal services, 32 percent for electricity and telephones, and 72.28 percent for wages).
9. The exchange rate was liberalized and various measures to promote a gradual opening of the Brazilian economy to external competition.
10. A number of federal government institutes were eliminated and the government announced its intention to lay off about 360,000 public-sector workers.
11. Preliminary measures were enacted to institute a process of privatization.

Later, the government adopted an important complementary measure to Collor I. It consisted of a change in the automatic buy-back mechanism in the overnight market. This operation had formerly been done at no cost to financial institutions. With the new measure, however, a payment was required for each transaction.

The Impact of Collor I

The immediate impact of the plan was to dramatically reduce the country's liquidity, as the money supply (M4) as a percent of GDP fell from about 30 to 9 percent.[14] Within a month, inflation declined to a

13. For instance, checks for more than the equivalent of US$100 made out to the bearer (*cheques ao portador*) were no longer permitted. This reduced fiscal anonymity and was thus supposed to reduce tax evasion.

14. See C. de Faro 1990. See also Table 5.4 for further illustrations of quarterly changes in monetary assets.

single-digit monthly rate (5 or 9 percent depending on the index used). The sharp decrease in liquidity led to a pronounced fall in economic activity, as revealed by the negative growth of the GDP of 7.8 percent in the second quarter of 1990.[15] The fear of a recession and pressure from various economic groups led the government to release many blocked financial assets ahead of schedule. This was done in an ad hoc fashion without well-defined rules.[16] The many concessions that were made, the impact of the surplus in the balance of payments, and the public-sector budgetary process (whose taxes could be paid in old blocked currency, even though its expenditures were in the new currency) led to a rapid remonetization process. After 45 days, there had been a 62.5 percent expansion of the money supply, raising it to 14 percent of the GDP (Nakano 1990: 146).

One of the main purposes of the Collor Plan was to reduce the primary deficit from 8 percent of GDP to a surplus of 2 percent; the actual surplus achieved for 1990 as a whole was 1.2 percent. This result, however, was mostly due to artificial or temporary measures, such as the once-and-for-all tax on financial assets and reductions in debt servicing accomplished by the assets freeze.[17]

The temporary decline in the financial component of the deficit created a situation in which government expenditures on personnel and related social changes amounted to 37 percent of total expenditures, while transfers to states and municipalities (instituted by the 1988 constitution) represented 23 percent. The government's attempts to lay workers off was constrained by the 1988 constitution, which stated that all government employees who were employed for longer than five years could not be laid off.[18] Further reforms aimed at permanently improving the government's fiscal situation would now be dependent on modifications in the

15. Table 5.5 shows that industrial production declined by 15.4 percent. The manufacturing index (1981 = 100) declined from 106.8 percent in March to 92.2 percent in April, capital goods from 90.4 to 73.1 percent, intermediate goods from 116.9 to 98.4 percent, and durable consumer goods from 122.8 to 115.6 percent. See IPEA 1991: Table 1.1, p. A1.

16. For example, in April a US$500 million line of credit was made available to the construction sector, and shortly thereafter credit lines of US$1.8 billion and US$1.1 billion were opened to the heavy machinery and agricultural sectors.

17. Also helpful was the lateness of government payments to suppliers. *Conjuntura Econômica*, February 1991: 20.

18. Under prevailing laws, most government workers could only be suspended, during which time they received a slightly reduced salary. In the first four months of the Collor Plan, only 30,000 government workers were laid off or suspended, compared with the initial goal of 360,000.

constitution. These, in turn, required the approval of two-thirds of the Congress. Collor could not count on this kind of support.

The Collor Plan froze all prices for 45 days. After that, maximum percentage adjustments were fixed by the government each month based on the (officially) expected inflation during the period. Another percentage was to be determined on the fifteenth of each month for fixing increases in the minimum wage.[19] Wage adjustments exceeding that percentage were allowed to be negotiated between employers and employees but could not lead to further price increases by the firm since these were subject to government monitoring. As actual price increases in April surpassed the predetermined rate of zero percent, the government faced political problems. The rule for wages was dropped after April, and wage adjustments were to be determined through free negotiations between employers and employees thereafter.

The plan had a strong recessive impact on the economy due to the dramatic decline in the stock of liquid assets. Also, as observed by Zini, "some recessive impact was unavoidable because of the defensive stockpiling of raw materials and finished goods and the artificial level of activity provoked by the previous hyperinflation" (1992: 223). Real GDP declined by 7.8 percent in the second quarter of 1990. With the unblocking of a number of frozen assets within the following months, economic activity rebounded, producing a 7.4 percent growth of GDP in the third quarter (see Table 5.2), while in the last quarter there was again a decline of 3.4 percent.[20] For 1990 as a whole, the GDP decline of 4.4 percent cannot be attributed exclusively to the Collor Plan. In the first quarter, prior to the plan, a decline of 2.5 percent had already occurred. The contractionary gradualist policies adopted after June (which resulted in the decline in the last quarter) also contributed to the final result.

On the external side, the Collor government began a process of liberalization that continued throughout the early 1990s. A gradual reduction of tariffs was initiated and the exchange rate was allowed to fluctuate. With the acceleration of inflation in the second half of 1990, the real exchange rate began to appreciate again. This led the government to enter the exchange market in order to prevent a severe overvaluation of the cruzeiro. The overvaluation in the middle of the year, combined with

19. The initial effect of the plan on wages was a controversial issue. Significantly different results were reached, depending on the methodology and price index used. Bresser Pereira (1990) estimated a real increase of 23 percent in March, based on the 72.3 percent nominal adjustment, and an inflation rate of 40 percent from March 1 to March 31.
20. See IPEA 1991.

Table 5.2 Percentage Quarterly Growth Rates in Brazil: 1988–1996

Year/Quarter	Gross Domestic Product	Agriculture*	Industry*	Services*
1988				
First	1.6	—	—	—
Second	−1.2	−2.3	−2.7	0.8
Third	−0.5	−0.8	−1.9	0.0
Fourth	−1.9	1.6	−2.8	−0.8
1989				
First	1.2	3.9	0.0	1.6
Second	4.5	−0.8	7.6	3.1
Third	1.1	−3.8	1.8	0.7
Fourth	0.0	2.3	−0.9	0.7
1990				
First	−2.5	−6.9	−2.7	−0.8
Second	−8.2	4.1	−15.4	−3.8
Third	7.4	1.6	12.8	2.3
Fourth	−1.9	1.6	−4.8	0.0
1991				
First	−4.8	−3.1	−6.0	−1.6
Second	6.6	0.2	12.8	3.8
Third	2.0	5.4	1.2	1.0
Fourth	−2.8	0.6	−5.3	−1.0
1992				
First	−0.8	1.7	−2.4	−0.5
Second	−0.3	−0.3	−1.5	0.3
Third	−0.3	0.8	0.2	−0.5
Fourth	0.8	0.4	1.7	0.4
1993				
First	2.2	−1.9	3.6	1.8
Second	2.3	1.0	3.2	2.2
Third	−0.6	−2.2	−0.8	−0.4
Fourth	0.5	2.6	0.3	0.5
1994				
First	2.2	6.6	1.7	1.2
Second	0.7	1.1	1.3	−0.1
Third	3.1	0.7	4.2	3.0
Fourth	3.4	1.5	5.0	2.9
1995				
First	2.4	3.0	2.6	1.7
Second	−3.2	−1.7	−6.6	−0.6
Third	−1.2	0.2	−3.5	0.3
Fourth	2.0	4.3	1.5	2.2

continued

Table 5.2 (continued)   Percentage Quarterly Growth Rates in Brazil: 1988–1996

Year/Quarter	Gross Domestic Product	Agriculture*	Industry*	Services*
1996				
First	0.1	−3.0	1.5	−0.7
Second	1.5	0.1	1.7	1.8
Third	3.0	6.0	3.7	1.7
Fourth	1.6	5.6	0.2	2.2
1997				
First	−0.5	−4.0	0.9	−1.3
Second	−0.8	0.9	−2.5	−0.3

Source: Data from IPEA. Various issues of *Boletim Conjuntural.*

* Seasonally adjusted.

the elimination of the export incentive program, caused an 8.7 percent decline in exports in 1990. Imports rose by 11.5 percent, due not only to the overvaluation but also to an increase in petroleum prices that resulted from the Iraqi crisis. With the liberalization process, they might have increased even more had there not been an economic recession.

Collor II

After an initial drop following the announcement of Collor I, inflation started to rise again in July as a result of the relaxation of price and wage controls and the erratic remonetization process. As inflation continued to accelerate at the beginning of 1991, and the placement of government papers encountered increasing difficulties, Collor's economic staff, headed by Zélia Cardoso de Melo, implemented a new economic package on 1 February. This time, the strategy concentrated on a limited financial reform consisting of the elimination of the "overnight" and an attack on inertial inflation through a price and wage freeze and the elimination of various forms of indexation.

The overnight was replaced by financial application funds, whose composition was regulated by the government. A minimum of 43 percent had to be in federal government papers or state papers that had the backing of the Central Bank, a regulation intended to guarantee a minimal demand for them. Thirteen percent had to be in economic development bonds and social development bonds, which were created to finance new investment programs in the industrial and social areas. Forty-two percent of the funds were left to be invested at the discretion of financial institutions in either private papers or state papers without the backing of the Central Bank, while the remaining 2 percent were to be maintained as reserves in the form of demand deposits.[21]

The yields of this fund were to be based on a *"Taxa Referêncial"* (TR, reference rate), which was calculated on the basis of expected future rates of private (CDS) and federal papers. The government's objective in establishing this system to replace the old indexation schemes was to eliminate the "inflationary memory," making it possible for expectations of falling inflation rates to be incorporated into current price formation. The same objective of having future expectations rapidly incorporated into current adjustments was behind the change in wage policy, which consisted of a unification of the dates for wage renegotiations (*dissídios saláriais*).

Under Collor II, the perennial quest for fiscal austerity consisted of attempts at better management of cash flows and a tightened grip on the expenditures of state enterprises. Among the main initiatives was the blocking of 100 percent of the budget of the Ministries of Education, Health, Labor, and Social Development, as well as 95 percent of the funds originally destined for investments. The release of funds to these ministries was made dependent on the approval of the Ministry of Economics and the availability of resources. In addition, a committee under the direction of the Ministry of Economics was created to control state enterprises, which were required to reduce their real expenditures by 10 percent by the end of 1991. These measures complemented the increase in public tariffs that had taken place prior to the price freeze. Finally, the government reduced the transfer of funds to states and municipalities while still observing the minimum level imposed by the constitution.

Although the Collor II measures had a short-term impact on prices (whose monthly rise fell from 21 percent in February to 6 percent in May), the economic team responsible for it was replaced in May 1991, before the long-term impact of all Collor II policies could be felt. The principal reason for the change in the Ministry of Economics can be found in the increasing weakness of political support for Zélia Cardoso's economic team, which was seen as excessively centralizing and author- itarian. The strong interventionism of the Collor I Plan (especially the freezing of financial assets) and its eventual failure, the imposition of another price freeze, and a new form of indexation had a strong negative impact on the private sector and the media. The new minister, Marcílio

21. See E. C. L. Rego 1991: 162, and *Conjuntura Econômica*, February 1992: 13.

Marques Moreira, took over and declared himself against any type of shock treatment. This statement, and his background as a former ambassador to Washington and banker, made him very popular with the private sector.

The new economic team's short-run concerns concentrated on controlling the cash flow and the money supply, as well as unfreezing prices and preparing for the release of the remaining blocked assets (which amounted to 6 percent of the GDP). It also guaranteed the continuity of the privatization process and the opening of the economy (see Table 5.3, showing the decline of average import tariffs). In fact, actual privatizations began in October 1991, and by the end of the year five state enterprises had been sold, bringing in total revenues equaling 0.5 percent of GDP (Baer and Villela 1994).

Table 5.3   Percentage Average Import Tariffs in Brazil

Year	Average Tariff	Standard Deviation
1987	51	26
1988	41	17
1989	35	20
1990	32.2	19.6
1991	25.3	17.4
1992	21.2	14.2
1993*	17.1	10.7
1994*	14.2	7.9

Source: IPEA 1991b: 67, 76.

*Projected.

With respect to cash-flow controls, satisfactory results were achieved primarily by having public servants' wage increases fall behind the rate of inflation. Real-wage expenditures thus declined by 13 percent.[22] Public investments also declined and stood at only 30 percent of what had been programmed for the year. Service expenditures on the domestic public debt declined by 80 percent, which was mainly a result of the reduction of domestic debt by 1.5 percent of GDP through the process of under-indexation in Collor II.

22. General wages were also affected in September 1991, when Congress passed a law establishing that the minimum wage and a portion of all salaries up to a maximum of three minimum wages would be adjusted every four months by 100 percent of the accumulated inflation during the period. Also, an interim wage adjustment in the middle of the four-month period was granted equal to 50 percent of the accumulated inflation over the previous two months.

Despite the significant decline in expenditures, which fell by 63.8 percent in real terms, the primary surplus was only 1 percent of GDP and the operational deficit for 1991 as a whole was 1.75 percent of GDP. This was because government real income had declined by 65 percent, due to the de-indexation of taxes,[23] various disputes over the payment of other taxes, and a decline in the tax liabilities of enterprises to compensate for overpayments under Collor I.

These fiscal efforts were more than counterbalanced by monetary expansion. In August and September, there was an excess of liquidity due to the beginning of the release of blocked assets, which resulted in negative interest rates. Table 5.4 shows that the average quarterly growth of the money supply was 8.5 percent in the second quarter and rose to 13.5 percent in the third quarter, while M2 rose from 8.7 to 15.7 percent. This increase and the lack of any strong anti-inflationary measures by the government resulted in an explosion of inflationary expectations. The monthly inflation rate rose from 16 to 26 percent in October, and a crisis broke out in the foreign exchange market, where there was strong speculation against the cruzeiro. The government responded by sharply increasing interest rates, which reached 6 percent a month in real terms after September, and devaluing the cruzeiro by 14 percent in real terms. These measures succeeded in controlling the October crisis. However, the high interest rates caused a substantial inflow of capital, which contributed greatly to new increases in the money supply—the monthly growth rate of M1 in the last quarter rose to 21.1 percent and of M2 to 32.7 percent.[24]

Real GDP increased by approximately 1.1 percent in 1991, with most of this growth concentrated in the second quarter and linked to the price freeze. The high real interest rates prevailing in the second half of the year and the reduction in government expenditures led to a substantial decline in growth in the third quarter, and to a negative real growth rate in the final quarter of that year.

Toward the end of 1991, the Marques Moreira team introduced yet another new antiinflation program for 1992–93. This was based on very tight credit,[25] a gradual strengthening of public finances, and an exchange

23. The reason for this was that the judiciary declared the TR illegal as an indexing tool for taxes.

24. See *Conjuntura Econômica*, February 1992.

25. High interest rates were also required to deal with the remaining blocked assets, which at the end of 1991 amounted to about 3 percent of GDP. The release of blocked assets was completed in August 1992.

Table 5.4 Prices and Money Supply in Brazil (average monthly growth rates)

Year/Quarter	Prices	M1	M2	M3	M4
1988					
First	18.3	4.7	11.8	15.7	15.9
Second	20.2	16.4	26.7	23.0	22.3
Third	23.4	15.7	22.7	23.0	23.0
Fourth	28.2	34.6	30.4	28.9	28.4
1989					
First	17.5	12.2	20.4	21.5	19.0
Second	14.9	19.7	14.4	12.9	14.4
Third	37.8	21.1	33.1	30.4	30.1
Fourth	44.5	56.2	50.6	45.0	46.7
1990					
First	75.0	91.7	24.4	28.4	27.4
Second	9.8	24.7	32.4	27.9	33.2
Third	12.5	8.0	9.2	11.5	13.5
Fourth	16.0	19.3	15.7	15.9	15.6
1991					
First	16.1	14.8	16.0	16.4	15.1
Second	8.4	8.5	8.7	9.1	11.2
Third	14.8	13.5	16.3	15.1	16.2
Fourth	24.6	21.1	32.7	32.5	29.5
1992					
First	24.1	9.3	32.2	30.4	32.3
Second	20.8	24.6	26.7	25.7	26.8
Third	24.9	21.8	23.9	23.9	24.6
Fourth	24.2	32.0	26.0	26.5	26.6
1993					
First	27.7	16.7	26.3	26.8	27.1
Second	30.4	28.4	26.9	28.1	28.9
Third	34.2	29.2	32.5	33.8	33.9
Fourth	36.1	47.2	33.9	41.0	40.1
1994					
First	43.1	26.4	41.2	41.9	41.8
Second	43.4	46.9	51.7	53.8	52.9
Third	9.8	13.9	1.7	3.0	1.9
Fourth	1.9	12.8	1.4	1.9	3.3
1995					
First	1.4	−4.6	−3.0	−1.8	2.4
Second	1.7	−0.6	2.8	4.0	2.0
Third	1.5	1.5	7.7	5.2	4.8
Fourth	1.8	11.9	5.4	4.4	3.0

continued

Table 5.4 (continued)   Prices and Money Supply in Brazil

Year/Quarter	Prices	M1	M2	M3	M4
1996					
First	0.9	−4.1	3.4	2.3	1.9
Second	1.2	0.7	4.2	2.7	1.8
Third	0.4	0.5	3.5	2.5	2.0
Fourth	0.5	6.5	3.9	3.9	2.7
1997					
First	1.1	8.7	2.8	2.9	1.5
Second	0.5	−0.1	1.2	1.2	1.4

Source: Calculated from various issues of *Conjuntura Econômica*.

Note: Average quarterly growth rates (percentages) are reported.

rate intended to maintain the real value of the cruzeiro. The government also sent a fiscal package to Congress for approval that included major changes in income taxes, reduction of the deductibility of payments of fringe benefits from the corporate income base, and a rise of tax rates for higher tax brackets. There were increases in some indirect taxes and elimination of many minor taxes. In addition, efforts were made to collect tax arrears and improve tax administration. Most of the measures in this fiscal package were not approved by Congress. In December 1991, Congress did pass some emergency measures that consisted of indexing all taxes and modifying income tax legislation.

For a number of reasons, however, the fiscal situation in 1992 weakened. In the first half of 1992, government revenues were lower than programmed because of continuing disputes over the payment obligations of social security taxes (the FINSOCIAL tax and its successor COFINS), larger-than-expected reductions in corporate tax payments in compensation for overpayments in 1990, and lower receipts from other taxes due to lower levels of economic activity. These revenue shortfalls were only partially compensated for by cuts in current and capital expenditures. Public finances weakened even more in the second half of 1992 due to increases in public-sector wages,[26] pension payments (a Supreme Court ruling ordered the government to provide increases retroactive to September 1991), and other current and investment expenditures. In addition, public utility prices were allowed to fall

26. Public wages increased due to adjustments that were to equalize wages among the three different branches of government (*isonomia salarial*) and payment of a thirteenth monthly wage in December.

sharply in an attempt to put a brake on inflation. Finally, due to tight credit policies in the first half of 1992, net government expenditures on servicing the debt rose from 0.6 percent of GDP in 1991, to 2.1 percent of GDP in 1992, even though interest payments on the external debt were declining. For 1992, the operational deficit amounted to 2.5 percent of GDP.

The tight monetary policy in the first half of 1992 resulted in yearly real interest rates in the *overnight* market of as high as 44 percent, as a result of the attempt to neutralize the large increase in international reserves (by US$14.3 billion from 1991 to 1992), the release of the remaining blocked assets, and the financial assistance that the Central Bank was forced to give to the Federal Savings Bank and a number of state banks that were facing severe liquidity problems. Because of the continued weakness of the economy, however, there was a relaxation of monetary policy in the second half of 1992, and real interest rates declined to 8 percent.

Inflation rates declined from 27 percent in January to 18 percent in April but then rose again to average 25 percent per month in the second half of the year. The return to these rates was attributed to the weak fiscal policy, as well as adverse expectations associated with the political crisis in the second half of 1992, which led to the impeachment of the president. In addition, the authorities were anxious to keep the real exchange rate from appreciating, and the stepped-up devaluations of the cruzeiro in connection with the inflation rate also fed renewed bouts of price increases.

Real GDP declined by about 1 percent in 1992. Most of the decline was in the industrial sector, especially consumer durables, for which production fell by 4 percent. This decline was due, in part, to low investments resulting from the high interest rates in the first half of the year and the political turmoil of the second half. The decline in real wages contributed to a decline in consumption expenditures. Agriculture made a positive contribution as a result of an excellent harvest and expanded by 6 percent.

The Itamar Franco Period: An Interregnum

By the time Itamar Franco took over as interim president in October 1992, it was clear that economic performance was not improving significantly. Inflation continued at a monthly rate of around 25 percent in last three months of the year, and in the first four months of 1993, it rose to a monthly rate of 28 percent, surpassing 30 percent per month by May. Although the GDP recovered slightly in the last quarter of 1992, it declined again in the first quarter of 1993. Workers continued to be laid off. There was opposition in certain quarters to privatization, and the process was temporarily stopped. There also was no consensus about how to implement a fiscal adjustment.

Itamar Franco's initial ineffectiveness in providing political and economic leadership did not improve once he graduated from being interim to full-time president. It took him more than four months to resume the privatization program, and it also took a considerable time to switch from a nationalistic stance vis-à-vis foreign capital to a more welcoming attitude. Also unhelpful was the instability of his economic team, as he changed finance ministers three times within a period of six months.

Until the middle of 1993, the successive economic-policy teams of Itamar Franco refrained from price freezes, seizing savings, new indexation, and breaking existing contractual agreements. As it became increasingly clear to the Itamar government that one of Brazil's major problems in coming to grips with inflation was the lack of a fiscal adjustment, a special temporary tax on financial movements (IPMF) was proposed and gradually passed by Congress. However, this tax was declared unconstitutional by the Supreme Court in September 1993. The government also made efforts to organize tax collection and counteract tax evasion more effectively, which had grown substantially over the previous years. By the middle of 1993, the privatization program was once again fully instituted and plans were broadened to include a number of infrastructure (such as electric utility and railroad) companies. The Itamar government also began to take a tough stance toward state and local governments.

In May 1993, President Franco appointed his fourth finance minister, Fernando Henrique Cardoso, who presented an austerity plan in June called the "Immediate Action Plan." Its centerpiece was a US$6 billion cut in government spending (amounting to 9 percent of federal spending and 2.5 percent of the spending at all levels of government—federal, state, and municipal). The plan also called for tightening up tax collection and resolving the financial relationships with state governments.

The state governments owed the federal government US$36 billion in 1993, and were about US$2 billion in arrears. Cardoso stated that the federal foreign loan guarantees would be withheld from states until these arrears were cleared and that state governments would be required to allocate 9 percent of their revenues to clear their debts with the federal government. Steps were also being taken to restrain state government-owned banks from creating money. In the 1980s and early 1990s, it had become the practice of many states to borrow from their banks. Such borrowing became so unrestrained that many state banks became illiquid and had to turn to the Central Bank to rescue them. This became an additional source of pressure on the Central Bank to emit more money. By August, most states agreed to begin repaying their taxes to the federal government in monthly installments over a 20-year period.

A campaign was begun in mid-1993 to fight tax evasion, which had grown dramatically over the previous decade. It was claimed that the government was losing between US$40 and US$60 billion a year as a result of evasion.[27]

The "Immediate Action Plan" was put into effect as economic activity was rising again. Gross domestic product increased by 4 percent in the first quarter of 1993, in relation to the first quarter of 1992, in part due to higher real wages and to increased agricultural income. Rising economic activity also manifested itself in increased imports, especially of raw materials and machinery. From May 1992 to May 1993, industrial production grew at a rate of 16.3 percent, led by chemicals, electrical machinery, cars, and metal products, which together accounted for 65 percent of industrial growth.

Inflation, however, continued unabated, reaching monthly rates of over 30 percent in the middle of 1993. This led labor leaders and politicians to introduce a wage law requiring monthly wage adjustments for all low-income workers equivalent to monthly price increases. Although this law was at first passed, it was vetoed by President Franco. The government then succeeded in having Congress pass a wage law that limited monthly wage adjustments to 10 percentage points below the monthly inflation rate.

A Statistical Review of the Years 1987–1993

This period was characterized by stagnation. In three of six years, real GDP declined and the average yearly GDP growth rate was a mere 0.5

---

27. The government proposed that the country's largest firms, that is, those with a yearly turnover of more than US$150,000, should be taxed directly. They had previously assessed their own taxes. Cardoso also planned to begin court cases against 300,000 individuals who had not paid any taxes and another 115,000 who had paid only a fraction of what they owed. He also asked Congress to amend the constitution in order to allow the finance minister to jail tax evaders. See *Latin America Economy and Business*, July 1993: 2.

percent. Per capita GDP declined in four of six years, and the average yearly growth rate was −1.2 percent. By 1992, real per capita GDP was about 8 percent lower than in 1980.

Manufacturing was the worst performing sector, experiencing only two years of positive growth, while the average yearly growth rate in the period was −2.5 percent. Construction had three positive growth years, averaging a yearly −1.1 percent, while agriculture had four years of positive growth, averaging a yearly 3.7 percent. The biggest decline occurred in the capital goods industry, which averaged −8.4 percent a year, and the second largest decline occurred in nondurable consumer goods (−5.1 percent), followed by durable consumer goods (−4.6 percent) and intermediate goods (−3.7 percent). These figures were a reflection of a substantial decline in investments and consumption, with the latter being related to declines in income per capita. Industrial capacity utilization declined notably after 1989 (see Table 5.5), falling to the lowest level since the early 1980s in 1992.

Table 5.5   Percentage Monthly Industrial Capacity Utilization in Brazil

Month	1990	1991	1992	1993	1994	1995	1996	1997
January	78.6	68.0	67.8	71.5	74.8	80.1	75.1	77.3
February	76.8	66.7	68.5	71.4	74.2	79.1	76.8	77.0
March	72.4	69.1	68.1	75.0	76.8	82.8	78.2	79.1
April	59.6	71.9	68.9	74.1	75.0	79.8	77.8	79.8
May	68.2	73.4	70.6	76.1	76.0	80.6	79.3	79.2
June	71.1	75.3	71.4	75.9	76.1	79.4	77.5	79.8
July	76.55	78.3	72.8	75.2	77.1	78.0	79.4	—
August	78.2	77.2	72.2	75.6	79.8	77.9	79.5	—
September	78.5	74.1	72.2	75.7	79.8	70.1	79.9	—
October	77.3	74.2	74.1	76.0	80.2	78.2	80.1	—
November	73.0	71.7	72.8	76.8	80.9	78.8	80.1	—
December	64.9	67.6	68.9	73.0	78.6	75.1	77.6	—

Source: Data from *Conjuntura Econômica.*

Gross fixed investment as a proportion of GDP in 1980 prices, which amounted to 25 percent in the mid-1970s and stood at 22.9 percent in 1980, declined throughout most of the 1980s and reached a low point of 14.4 percent in 1992.[28] Much of the decline was due to the curtailment of government investments, which were almost 50 percent smaller in 1992 than in 1986. Private investments fell by 12 percent in the same period.

28. The decline in current prices has been small due to the substantial increase in the relative price of capital goods during the 1980s (Carneiro and Werneck 1992).

Table 5.6   Income Distribution in Brazil

Year	Top Decile	Top Quintile	Bottom Quintile
1983	46.2	62.6	2.4
1985	47.7	64.1	2.8
1986	47.5	63.4	3.2
1989	52.4	68.1	2.2
1990	48.7	65.0	2.6

Source: Data from IBGE. Various issues of *Anuário Estatístico*. Rio de Janeiro: Instituto Brasileiro de Geografia e Estatística.

Note: Figures are expressed as percentage of aggregate household income.

Since in national accounts the latter includes state enterprise investments, it should be noted that such investment was estimated to have declined by 34 percent between 1988 and 1992.[29] This notable decline in public investment was quite prejudicial to the country's future growth and efficiency. It meant that the country's infrastructure was becoming increasingly inadequate for the efficient functioning of the economy (apparent in deteriorating roads, the increasing inadequacy of the telecommunication system, and the threat of future breakdowns in electric energy supply) and that many directly productive industrial activities were falling behind technologically.

Brazil's notoriously concentrated income distribution became even worse during these years. The top quintile's share rose from 63.4 percent in 1986, to 68.1 percent in 1989, falling slightly to 65 percent in 1990. The bottom quintile's share fell from 3.2 percent in 1986, to 2.2 percent in 1989, rising slightly to 2.6 percent in 1990 (see Table 5.6). Various types of wage measures also showed a decline in the welfare of the labor force. While the legal minimum wage in early 1992 was 15 percent lower than in 1986,[30] real wages in São Paulo rose from 1986 to 1989, falling in the following three years to levels below that of 1986 (see Table 5.7). Employment levels in São Paulo's industries were steady until 1990, and thereafter declined noticeably, while hours worked fell after 1989. Finally, Table 5.8 shows that although open unemployment continued to be relatively low in Brazil's metropolitan regions, there was a notable increase in workers without work permits in 1991, and a steady increase in self-employed workers after 1986, indicating substantial growth of the informal sector.

29. These numbers are based on information in the reports of the Banco Central do Brasil and IBGE, various years.

30. See IBGE, *Anuário Estatístico*.

Table 5.7   Real Wages and Employment in Brazil

Year	Real Salaries (1978 = 100)	Employment in São Paulo's Industries (1978 = 100)	Hours Worked in Industry (1978 = 100)
1980	117	107	108
1981	122	100	95
1982	125	95	89
1983	110	88	80
1984	113	87	84
1985	140	95	95
1986	176	104	106
1987	167	106	107
1988	177	104	102
1989	193	105	102
1990	166	103	95
1991	146	95	85
1992	158	89	80
1993	169	86	80
1994	183	84	80
1995	193	83	79
1996	186	75	71
1997	188*	73*	68*

Source: Data from *Conjuntura Econômica.*

* Average as of June 1997.

In addition, studies by economists in the Ministry of Planning pointed to a decline in the educational and health services available to lower income groups. With the declining financial capacity of the state, there has been a decline "in the quality of basic education due to low salaries and an increase in school evasion; a breakdown of hospital and other public health services and an increase in rural endemic illnesses."[31]

Table 5.9 shows the inexorable rise of inflation during the 1980s and early 1990s, from yearly two- and three-digit levels in the years 1980–87, to a four-digit level from 1988 to 1994 (with the brief exception of 1991). Table 5.10 shows the monthly inflation rates in the 1986–94 period. Except for brief monthly one-digit levels during the various heterodox shocks, monthly rates, by the years 1992 and 1993, were in the twenties and thirties, reaching the forties in 1994.

A more positive picture presents itself when the country's external accounts are examined. Exports grew at an average yearly rate of 7.6 percent during the 1987–93 period (rising from US$26 billion in 1987 to

31. IPEA, 1992: 34.

Table 5.8 Unemployment and Status of Employed Workers in Brazil's Metropolitan Regions

Year	Unemployed	Workers with Work Permit	Workers Without Work Permit	Self-Employed Workers
1982	3.80	57.70	14.20	17.70
1983	6.70	55.70	13.40	18.00
1984	7.12	54.30	14.20	19.00
1985	5.25	55.60	13.90	18.60
1986	3.59	56.50	13.50	18.20
1987	3.73	56.30	13.40	18.60
1988	3.85	55.80	13.50	19.50
1989	3.35	56.10	13.00	19.80
1990	4.28	55.10	13.30	21.10
1991	4.83	51.60	15.40	22.80
1992	5.97	—	—	—
1993	5.32	—	—	—
1994	5.06	—	—	—
1995	5.50	48.40	24.10	22.00
1996	5.50	47.70	24.30	22.50

Source: Data are from various issues of Fonçao Instituto Brasileiro de Geografia e Estatística, *Pesquisa Mençal de Empreso.*

Note: Figures are percentages of the labor force.

US$39 billion in 1993). This was due both to an exchange-rate policy that kept exports competitive[32] and to the recession that forced Brazilian firms to substitute foreign for domestic markets. Imports stagnated until 1988, rising substantially in the following three years.[33] This increase was in large part due to the liberalization policies begun in 1989 and emphasized by the Collor government, though its small size and the decline in 1992 were reflections of the country's continued stagnation. The average trade surplus in the period was much larger than in the earlier 1980s, averaging US$14 billion.

An examination of the capital account shows heavy profit remittances in the years 1988–90, which declined thereafter, and a decline in the outflow of interest payments over the period, which reflected both arrears in payments and a declining international interest rate. Direct foreign investments, which had been small throughout the 1980s, picked

32. Exports were quite sensitive to the real exchange rate. Thus, the stagnation of exports in 1990 and 1991 was associated with the real exchange-rate appreciation in those two years, while the recovery of exports in 1992 was associated with a real devaluation.

33. The notable jump in imports in 1989 was also due to the substantial rise in food and raw material imports resulting from the decline of stocks, which was related to the impact of that year's Summer Plan. See *Banco Central do Brasil* 1989: 92.

Table 5.9   Percentage Yearly Inflation Rates in Brazil

Year	Rate
1980	110
1981	95
1982	100
1983	211
1984	224
1985	235
1986	65
1987	416
1988	1,037
1989	1,783
1990	1,477
1991	480
1992	1,158
1993	2,709
1994	1,094
1995	15
1996	9
1997*	6

Source: Data from various issues of *Conjuntura Econômica.*

* Yearly rate in July.

up in the 1990s, while long-term loans also increased substantially in the late 1980s and early 1990s. This reflected both progress in the country's foreign debt renegotiations, some degree of optimism by foreign investors in the country's long-term future, despite the current crises, and a substantial boom in the country's stock markets in the early 1990s.

Brazil's Stagflation, 1987–1993: An Interpretation

Brazil's Unresolved Fight for Shares

The root of the resurgence of inflation from the mid-1970s on was a "fight for shares" among various socioeconomic sectors that governments, committed to political opening, were not able or willing to prevent (Baer 1991: 45–57). With the return of civilian governments after 1985, this situation worsened as politicians were mainly interested in using the government to fulfill their electoral ambitions rather than in following consistent economic policies.

Table 5.10 Percentage Monthly Inflation Rates in Brazil

Month	1986	1987	1988	1989	1990	1991	1992	1993	1994	1995	1996	1997
January	18.0	12	19	36	72	20	27	29	42	1.4	1.8	1.6
February	15.0	14	18	12	72	21	25	26	42	1.1	0.8	0.4
March	−0.1	15	18	4	81	7	21	28	45	1.8	0.2	1.16
April	−0.6	20	20	5	11	9	18	28	43	2.3	0.7	0.6
May	0.3	28	19	13	9	6	22	32	41	0.4	1.7	0.3
June	0.5	26	21	27	9	10	21	31	47	2.6	1.2	0.7
July	0.6	9	21	38	13	13	22	32	25	2.2	1.1	0.1
August	1.3	4	23	36	13	15	25	33	3	1.3	0.0	—
September	1.1	8	26	39	12	16	27	37	1.5	−1.1	0.1	—
October	1.4	11	28	40	14	26	25	35	2.6	0.2	0.2	—
November	2.5	14	28	44	17	26	24	37	2.5	1.3	0.3	—
December	7.6	16	29	49	16	22	24	38	0.6	0.3	0.9	—

Source: Data from various issues of *Conjuntura Econômica.*

The resurgence of inflation in the 1970s was linked to the gradual political reopening of the country and to the world oil shocks. With the availability of foreign resources through debt financing, however, Brazil was also able to grow. In the first half of the 1980s, the debt crisis resulting from the interest rate shock and the world recession brought the inflation rate to a three-digit level, as the fight for shares (reflected in formal and informal indexing arrangements) was now taking place within a context of low economic growth.

The period examined in this chapter was one in which the fight for shares became even more acute, as economic stagnation lingered on. Any external or internal shock within this indexed economy resulted in a scramble by economic agents (firms and wage earners) to adjust their own prices as rapidly as possible. With the repeated failures of hetero-dox shock programs, this scramble was intensified as price readjust-ments were increasingly influenced by expectations of future price freezes and the speed of price readjustments increased. Thus, as was mentioned earlier, all attempts at a "social pact" were usually of a very short duration.

The fight for shares was made more acute by the requirements of the 1988 constitution which, as mentioned above, substantially increased the share of the federal government's tax receipts redistributed to the states and municipal governments. Because there was no equivalent transfer of government obligations, a newly built structural weakness developed in the federal government's fiscal position. Thus, in the "absence of foreign savings, this implied that the public sector . . . had, besides the already existing taxes and other usual sources of revenue, to extract additional resources from the private sector either through a further growth in the debt or through an additional inflationary tax."[34]

Mario H. Simonsen, Brazil's former finance minister, has stated that "the explanation of inflation resulting from the distributive conflict is not convincing . . . [and that] . . . inflation must be attributed not to the distributional conflict, but to the manner in which the government regulates it" (Rezende et al. 1989: 552). This is correct and, as we have shown in the Brazilian case, the various governments of the 1980s and 1990s were either not willing or not capable of devising noninflationary ways of dealing with the distributive conflict. That is, not being able to maintain a budgetary equilibrium and thus the stability of the money supply, the government undermined the credibility of the domestic

34. See Rezende et al. 1989: 552.

currency, thereby setting the stage for distributive pressures to manifest themselves through price increases.

The Constant Absence of a Fiscal Adjustment

In the period analyzed, Brazil suffered from both inflation and stagnation. This contrasts with most advanced industrial economies, in which long periods of stagnation have usually been accompanied either by no price increases or by very small rates of inflation (note: stagflation was talked about in the United States but for shorter periods). Brazil's stagflation came as no surprise to the observer, since both inflation and *stagnation* can be interpreted as being different manifestations of the same disequilibrium.

Over the years, Brazil's public sector experienced chronic budget deficits that were financed by increases in the indexed domestic debt.[35] The problem in the 1980s was the gradual decline of the government's credibility with the public, that is, there was increasing doubt about the government's capacity to service the debt and eventually to repay the principal.[36] This gradual loss of credibility required the shortening of the terms of financing, to a point at which most of the debt was being financed through the overnight market and at increasingly higher real interest rates. The high interest rates, combined with the large stock of debt, substantially increased the financial expenditures of the government, whose share in total government expenditures grew rapidly. This created a vicious cycle of rising debt, leading to a rising deficit, leading to further increases in the debt.

Brazil found itself in a situation in which an enormous number of financial resources were invested in the overnight market. This was extremely liquid and could at any time be turned into money, with the possibility of a capital flight into real assets. In 1989, for instance, while the stock of M1 was 1.7 percent of GDP, M2 was equal to 12 percent of GDP. Thus, there existed the real threat of a loss of control over the money supply due to the possibility of a rapid withdrawal from the *overnight* market, the exhaustion of the government's ability to finance its deficits through the issue of new debt instruments, or both. The

35. The reason Brazil's public has been holding government securities in a highly inflationary milieu is that they have been indexed since the mid-1960s.

36. Government debt as a proportion of GDP in many advanced industrial countries, which was in some cases as high as that of Brazil, did not cause similar problems because the governments of those countries never lost credibility with the investing public.

consequence was a growing loss of confidence and the rejection of the national currency, making it easier for the distributive conflict to result in price increases.

It is within this context that one finds an explanation for such questions as the following: Why did Brazilian firms grant nominal wage increases with little impact on employment levels? Why did Brazilian consumers accept price increases without significantly diminishing their purchases? In other words, why did the market sanction these price increases, allowing distributive pressures to manifest themselves through inflation? The answer is that all firms know that they can pass on increases in the prices they pay for inputs to their customers, since the latter prefer to keep buying more expensive products than to hold on to currency whose value, they believe, will continue to decrease at an accelerating rate. Of course, the inflationary process does not resolve the distributive conflict and the generalized indexation scheme "institutionalizes" and worsens the phenomenon.

Based on this diagnosis, the inconsistency of the various stabilization strategies attempted during the period under analysis may be worth pointing out. On the one hand, the successive shocks and price/wage freezes were not accompanied by a necessary structural fiscal adjustment. Thus, they progressively lost their credibility, and each successive shock had a lesser impact on inflation. On the other hand, the policies aimed at fiscal and monetary austerity were insufficient to attain a reversal of expectations, which was crucial for an effective stabilization program. According to our interpretation of the inflation crisis, confidence in the domestic currency depends on a permanent structural adjustment of public finances. Simply controlling cash flows, postponing certain expenditures, and devising temporary measures to increase receipts will not achieve the desired confidence, as these measures do not guarantee an effective future control over the money supply. Even more serious, however, is the attempt to control M1 in the short run without a fiscal equilibrium, since this will require very high real interest rates. This situation makes future problems worse and causes growing doubts among the general public about the government's financial stability as it increases the debt and the cost of its servicing.[37]

Besides its impact on price instability, the crisis in government finances and its implications described above also forced policy makers to maintain very high real interest rates in order to be able to place new

37. Some of these ideas are derived from Sargent and Wallace 1981. See also Paiva 1992.

debt issues in the market and maintain resources in the *overnight* market. The high interest rates and the general uncertainty in which the economy was finding itself were responsible for the decline of investments and economic stagnation. Without a fiscal adjustment, the trap of high interest rates was feeding the recession and inflation simultaneously.

Plano Real

In December 1993, Fernando Henrique Cardoso, then Brazil's finance minister, proposed a new stabilization program that was supposed to avoid some of the weaknesses of the previous plans. Unlike the previous plans, the new program was at first presented as a "proposal," which was to be amply discussed in Congress and implemented gradually. The program had two basic thrusts: first, a fiscal adjustment, and second, a new indexing system that would gradually lead to a new currency.

The principal fiscal adjustment measures consisted of (1) implementing an across-the-board tax increase of 5 percent; (2) designating that 15 percent of all tax receipts would go to a newly created Social Emergency Fund (*Fundo Social de Emergência*); and (3) cutting spending on government investments, personnel, and state companies by approximately US$7 billion. As the fund was only a temporary measure, the government announced long-term plans for constitutional amendments that would transfer to state governments and municipalities responsibilities in the areas of health, education, social services, housing, basic sanitation, and irrigation, and which would decrease the automatic transfer of federal tax receipts to state and local governments as contained in the 1988 constitution.

The new indexing system was introduced at the end of February 1994, and consisted of an indexer called the Unit of Real Value (URV, *Unidade Real de Valor*) that was tied to the dollar on a one-to-one basis.[38] The URV's quotation in cruzeiros reais rose daily, accompanying the exchange rate according to the prevailing level of inflation. Official prices, contracts, and taxes were denominated in URV, and the government encouraged its use on a voluntary basis by private economic agents. Gradually, an increasing number of prices were stated in URVs, although transactions occurred in cruzeiros reais.

38. For details on the creation of the URV, see *Conjuntura Econômica*, April 1994: 5–7.

By the middle of 1994, as an increasing proportion of prices were quoted in URVs, the government decided to introduce a new currency whose unit was equal to the URV. This was done on 1 July with the introduction of the "real," equal to one URV or one U.S. dollar and equal to 2,750 old cruzeiros reais. At the time of the price conversion from the old currency into the real, there was a waive of price increases in many supermarkets and stores, as many businesses took advantage of the public's initial confusion about relative prices in the new currency. In addition, many businesspersons also expected the introduction of a price freeze, which had been customary in previous stabilization attempts. However, the government refrained from any freezes, using its public relations network to suggest to the public that it minimize its purchases of necessities in order to force a price retrenchment. As the public now was in possession of a currency that it believed would retain its purchasing power, consumers were in a position to "bargain," that is, to wait and not pay for goods at the recently increased prices. In fact, very soon some prices began to decline, and the first results were felt in a decline in the weekly inflation rates.

Along with the introduction of the new currency, the government adopted a restrictive monetary policy. It consisted of a short-term limit on loans to finance exports, a 100 percent reserve requirement on new deposits, and a limit on the expansion of the monetary base of R$9.5 billion until the end of March 1995.[39] For the quarter from July to September 1994, the expansion had been limited to R$7.5 billion. By August, however, the government was forced to revise that number and admit an increase of R$9 billion by September. This had some impact on inflationary expectations, although most of the overshooting of the planned expansion was attributable to an increase in the demand for money.

The monetary authorities also kept interest rates high in order to control a possible increase in consumption and to discourage speculative stockpiling. As a complementary measure to discourage large capital inflows, which high interest rates might attract, the authorities fixed the selling price of the real as equal to one U.S. dollar, while they allowed the buying price of the real to appreciate according to market forces. With the substantial capital inflows and continued trade surpluses, the real indeed appreciated, reaching 84 centavos to the dollar in November.

The initial results of the plan were positive. Inflation was brought down from a monthly rate of about 47 percent in June to 1.5 percent in

39. For details, see *Conjuntura Econômica*, August 1994: 172–73.

September and 0.57 percent in December. In 1995, its highest increase was 2.6 percent in June and its lowest level was an actual price decline of 1 percent in September. As Table 5.4 shows, the monthly price stability continued to prevail in 1996. In addition, from Table 5.2 we can see that the initial impact of the *Plano Real* on economic activity was quite pronounced, in that the growth rate rose from 0.7 percent in the second quarter of 1994, to 3.1 percent in the third quarter and 3.4 percent in the fourth quarter. These increases were in large part due to rising sales, and were in particular a reflection of the purchases of lower-income groups whose real incomes were boosted by the fact that their monthly losses from quasi hyperinflation had disappeared. Although price stability continued throughout 1995 and 1996, it was maintained at the cost of a decline in growth and a worsening of the situation in the trade balance and public finances.

The appreciation of the exchange rate resulting from a policy of high interest rates (which were deemed necessary to avoid capital outflows when the Real Plan was introduced and were later necessary to finance the government deficit) convinced some policy makers that an appreciated exchange rate would also be a useful additional instrument to control inflation (this was called an "exchange-rate anchor"). Given that there was still a considerable inflationary residual in the economy, the real appreciation of the exchange rate continued throughout 1995 and 1996. The degree of appreciation varied depending on what price indexes were used to compare Brazil's inflation with that of its principal trade partners. For instance, through a comparison of the cost-of-living indexes, the real appreciation was estimated to have been about 47 percent in the first two years of the Real Plan. Since these indexes contain a large proportion of nontradable goods, especially services, whose prices increase more than tradables, some analysts have claimed that the correct comparison would be wholesale prices, which more faithfully represent tradable goods. Estimates of real exchange-rate appreciation based on the latter show an appreciation of about 29 percent.[40] Whether the appreciation represented an overvaluation of the real was a matter of considerable controversy. Some have argued that at the time of the introduction of the Real Plan, the currency was undervalued and that an appreciation of 30 percent would expose the formerly protected and high-cost Brazilian economy to healthy competition and thus force many sectors to increase their efficiency. Others maintained that such an

40. See *Conjuntura Econômica*, August 1996: 5.

appreciation was too severe and could result in permanent damage to many sectors.

The exchange appreciation, combined with the country's trade liberalization, caused a substantial increase of imports (from US$33 billion in 1994 to US$50 billion in 1995). Exports grew more modestly (from US$43 billion to US$46 billion), and thus Brazil experienced a trade deficit for the first time in 13 years. This continued in 1996. Although this deficit helped to stabilize the economy in that the huge increase in imports resulted in price-stabilizing foreign competition, some sectors (especially automobile manufacturers) found this situation so threatening that they convinced the government to reimpose higher tariffs and direct import controls in 1995 and 1996. The government stated, however, that this return to protectionism was only temporary, and its purpose was to give more time to the affected sectors to readjust.

The trade deficit, however, was more than compensated for by large capital inflows, which rose on a net basis from US$14 billion in 1994 to US$30.7 billion in 1995. This influx continued in the first half of 1996. Although substantial amounts of this influx consisted of direct investment (about US$4.8 billion in 1995 and close to US$7 billion in 1996), most of the inflow consisted of investments in government securities and funds for the stock market. A combination of lower interest rates in Brazil and rising rates abroad could easily reverse this flow.

The most worrisome aspect of the implementation of the Real Plan, in 1995–96, was the delay in attaining a basic fiscal adjustment. As the temporary measures to attain such an adjustment ran out in the course of 1995, the government was finding it difficult to get the constitutional amendments through Congress that would make it possible to balance the budget. These amendments involved such measures as abolishing tenure for public servants, readjusting retirement age, changing the amount and method of fiscal transfers, and so on. The rate of privatization during the first two years of the Real Plan also proceeded at a very slow pace, thus keeping government revenues from that source relatively low. Government expenditures, however, kept rising as a result of the rise in both government employment and wages, the rise in interest payments, and the necessity to rescue failing private and state banks that could not cope with operating in a noninflationary environment. In 1995, government receipts grew by 7.6 percent, while expenditures grew at a rate of 18.5 percent (*Gazeta Mercantil*, 14 August 1996: A-5). The operational deficit of the government amounted to about 3 percent of GDP in 1995, and the estimates for 1996 were not more promising.

The government deficit was financed by borrowing from the public at high interest rates. Although this was not inflationary because the Central Bank was not involved, it resulted in a rapidly rising government debt. The debt rose from R$63.4 billion in January 1995 to R$151.3 in May 1996, and it was estimated that by the end of 1996, this debt would have grown to about 40 percent of GDP. The government's dilemma was clear. With no fiscal adjustment and growing deficits, it had to maintain relatively high interest rates in order to finance them in a noninflationary manner. But high interest rates themselves made government debt servicing expensive, thus increasing the difficulties in expenditure reduction and making it difficult to stimulate growth and consumption.

The ultimate success of the Real Plan basically depends on two factors, the most important of which is that the temporary fiscal adjustment obtained from the *Fundo Social de Emergência* be made permanent through a constitutional amendment. Aside from the immediate positive impact it would have on inflationary expectations, this is a necessary condition for long-term monetary control. Together with the constitutional amendment, fiscal/monetary discipline also requires that the authorities be able to resist pressures from various sectors to settle distributional conflicts in an inflationary manner.

The Politics of Brazil's Quest for Stabilization

The assertion that price stabilization in Brazil is a political issue has become quite popular. This idea, however, should not be accepted without some important qualifications. It is indisputable that the fiscal adjustment necessary for stabilization requires a complex political arrangement for its implementation. Throughout this chapter, we have suggested that the successive economic plans devoted an increasing degree of attention to budget balancing as an anti-inflationary instrument. As this occurred, though, the difficulties this kind of reform faces in the political sphere became more evident.

In approaching this issue, some experts defended the necessity of a wide sociopolitical movement to trigger the institutional reforms that would lead to fiscal discipline. It has also been maintained that there is a need for all levels of public administration to act responsibly in order to achieve a balanced budget.

One cannot disagree with the desirability of a participant society and responsible political and public sectors. The question here concerns the timing involved in the process: will a new sociopolitical attitude lead to institutional reforms, or will a new institutional order mold different social, political, and economic behaviors? That this should all happen simultaneously would be an easy but very unrealistic assumption. Desirable widespread fiscal responsibility should be imposed from above, through a reformed institutional order.

Only when the government is forbidden to finance new expenditures through money creation can a political process be developed to force the state to deny new expenditure demands, bargain for reducing other expenditures, or create appropriate new tax revenues. While it is possible to approve politically advantageous projects without specifying how they will be funded, it is naive to expect any commitment to austerity from the public administration and from politicians in general.

As an illustration of this point, it is worth mentioning the scandal that broke out in October 1993, involving several Brazilian members of congress, construction companies, and members of the public administration. A scheme was revealed in which members of congress received bribes to introduce and get approval for projects to be carried out by certain construction firms. Although these projects were mostly only of local interest, they were included as amendments to the federal budget. No source of funding was usually specified, and prices were overstated. Investigators found evidence that the scheme had been in place at least since 1985, and involved billions of dollars.

Society's reaction to the episode and the measures taken against the people involved were satisfactory and seem to have reassured Brazil's democracy. One aspect that might have been overlooked in the midst of the indignation over this type of corruption was the legal channel that made the whole scheme possible: members of congress have the power to increase the federal government's expenditures almost indiscriminately. In most cases these projects were approved through negotiation in the congressional budget committee, and were not required to be discussed or voted on in the House of Deputies. With respect to the federal budget, one other example of the lack of an adequate institutional structure to enforce austerity is that the 1994 federal budget was not approved until October 1994.

Among the reforms necessary for public-sector austerity and stabilization to be achieved is a constitutional reform that would transfer obligations from the central government to the states to accompany the significant transfers of revenues in the same directions that were promoted by the 1988 constitution. This would make the central government's task easier and force local governments to use their resources in a more efficient manner than they have in the past.

Additionally, if the Central Bank were made more independent, it would force the behavior pattern of local and state governments to change. For instance, in the 1980s, many states used their commercial and development banks to make economically dubious but politically advantageous loans. The result was that many of these banks often faced the type of liquidity crisis that could undermine confidence in the banking system. This forced the Central Bank to "rescue" them by issuing large quantities of money for which it had not planned, which contributed to the rising rate of inflation. If the Central Bank were independent and these state banks faced a higher risk of insolvency, they would tend to act more responsibly. A more drastic measure to achieve such a goal would be the privatization of the entire state-banking system.

Through new legal parameters, it may be possible to change the behavior pattern of politicians and economic agents who have traditionally avoided market forces through government favors. The fight for shares will have to be explicitly resolved, not accommodated through monetary expansion and inflation. If economic agents (politicians and all levels of public administration included) are subject to market forces and the scarcity of resources, they will ultimately be forced to act in ways that could simultaneously increase efficiency and promote stability in the Brazilian economy.

6

Macroeconomic Adjustment in Chile and the Politics of the Popular Sectors

Manuel Barrera

The central theme of this book is the long-term political and social impact of the economic reforms that have been implemented in Latin America since the 1980s. Without a doubt these reforms, based on free markets, the insertion of national economies into the globalization process, and the withdrawal of the state from productive activities, represent a new development model. As is natural, the change from the continent's traditional development model to this new strategy brings with it profound social and political consequences that are analyzed in this book in four countries in the region.

The relationship between economic reform and political regimes is complex, given that the new development model has been implemented under both authoritarian and democratic governments. In the case of Chile, the reforms began under the military regime of General Pinochet and have been strengthened under two governments of transition to democracy. As the Chilean case suggests, the political analyst must move

Translated by Siobhan Harty and Philip Oxhorn.

beyond the general categories of "authoritarianism" and "democracy" when characterizing the political regimes which have carried out liberalizing reforms of the economy. It is obvious that the military dictatorship in Chile, with its strong interest in the development of national capitalism, was different from the classic military dictatorships on the continent. It is also obvious that the current regime is a restricted democracy, given the survival from the military government of important political institutions that restrict the scope of democracy and the severe economic and social limits that configure a market economy that is exclusionary with respect to important sectors of the population.

This chapter attempts to illustrate the social and political impact of the economic reforms through an analysis of the changes in the status of the Chilean popular sectors that have accompanied the process of implementing a new development model. As is well known, structural adjustment and its associated economic reforms are intended to impose fiscal discipline, liberalize markets, privatize state enterprises, and promote free trade and economic liberalization. Because the labor market has been made more "flexible," in the initial phase of the adjustment workers pay high costs in the form of unemployment, a decline in real wages, and precarious employment conditions. This has produced an overall relative decrease in employment in the formal sector of the economy but a notable increase in employment in small enterprises. Tables 6.1 and 6.2 confirm this observation.

Table 6.1 Structure of Nonagricultural Employment in Latin America

	1980	1985	1990
Informal sector			
Self-employed	19.2	22.6	23.9
Domestic service	6.4	7.8	6.9
Total	25.6	30.4	30.8
Formal sector			
Public sector	15.7	16.6	15.5
Private sector			
Large companies	44.1	36.5	31.6
Small companies	14.6	16.6	22.1
Total	74.4	69.7	69.2

Source: Estimates from Programa Regional del Empleo pora América Latina de Naciones Unidas, 1992, based on household interviews and official sources.

Note: Figures are expressed as a percentage of the total economically active population outside agriculture.

Table 6.2 Urban Unemployment and Wage Structure in Latin America

Year	Urban Unemployment	Minimum Wage	Industrial Wage
1980	6.7	100.0	100.0
1981	6.6	96.9	102.4
1982	8.4	94.2	100.6
1983	9.8	91.8	95.0
1984	10.0	89.7	93.4
1985	10.1	86.4	91.0
1986	9.2	84.7	93.2
1987	8.3	85.2	97.1
1988	8.5	81.2	93.7
1989	7.9	74.1	89.0
1990	8.0	67.0	84.6
1991	7.8	65.0	82.5

Source: Based on household interviews and official statistics provided by Programa Regional del Empleo pora América Latina de Naciones Unidas, 1992.

Note: Figures are percentages of the total economically active population with 1980 used as a baseline (1980 = 100).

Within the above general framework, the Chilean situation has the following particularities:

1. The economic adjustment started after 1975, well before the adjustment in other countries of the region. This policy is presently consolidating itself as the new economic strategy for growth.
2. The costs of macroeconomic adjustment for the popular sectors in terms of unemployment (the rate and length of unemployment) and a reduction in real wages have been much higher in Chile compared with the averages for Latin America as a whole.
3. The restructuring process was initiated by a military government. The entire initial phase (1975–85) took place under a military regime. Since coming to office in March 1990, the democratic government has continued these neoliberal policies, with the result that a broad consensus has developed around the development strategy in this period. Presently, this consensus includes both the government (a center-left alliance) and the opposition (the right), management groups, labor unions, intellectuals, the media, and public opinion. One of the state's policy priorities, the fight against poverty, is even part of this consensus. Only the Communist Party is not included.
4. As of early 1996, GDP had been steadily rising for twelve years, national savings and investment rates had reached unprecedented

levels in the history of the country, inflation had continued its downward trend, the employment situation had ostensibly improved with the unemployment rate oscillating between 4 and 6 percent since 1992, real wages and even the minimum wage had shown a slight upward trend, and the perennial shortage of foreign exchange had given way to an oversupply of foreign currencies.

5. Free markets, an open economy, and deregulation were all achieved principally through orthodox measures that will ensure the continuation of market principles for the medium to long term. The Chilean adjustment program adhered to the structural adjustment and stabilization policies of the International Monetary Fund (IMF) and the World Bank. The Chilean experience is therefore representative of the results that can be expected in other developing countries that follow these same programs. This is particularly the case regarding the social costs and distributional effects of these programs.

6. The economic change that resulted from this new development strategy was sufficiently dramatic to warrant the observation that there was a "foundational dimension" to this policy, not only relative to economic restructuring but also to the creation of a new social order. This dimension is a given, because it has created a modernizing capitalist class that plays a leading role in economic growth and modernization (Garretón 1984). In this renovated social order, workers have a new status and social position, manifested in the following: in the insertion of workers and unions into the business enterprise and society; in the improved relationship between workers and their organizations, on the one hand, and the state and political parties, on the other; in the characteristics and functioning of the labor market; and in the organization of production remuneration, as well as in the professional qualifications of the workforce.

7. At the macrosocial level, it is obvious that the popular sectors have been profoundly affected by the economic restructuring. The consequences of this vary, depending upon the area of examination. The increasing flexibility of the labor market means that workers are inserted into this market in a variety of ways. Socially, the potential for organization and articulation on the part of the popular sectors has been reduced, notwithstanding the existence of microorganizations that carry out survival and solidarity activities. From a political perspective, it is obvious that the importance of the popular sectors in state decision making, in policy making at the level of political parties (especially the parliamentary left), and even

in civil society has been weakened. As a whole, civil society has experienced a process of atomization and disintegration during the seventeen-year authoritarian period. The reconstruction of a civil society, in which popular sector movements would play a dominant role, has not taken place during the four years of democratic transition.

I will attempt to analyze the relationship between economic restructuring and the status and position of the popular sectors in Chile.

Popular Sector Insertion in the Labor Market

Since they were first introduced in 1974, stabilization and adjustment policies have had a profound impact on the labor market, altering its traditional structure and breaking with historical tendencies in the areas of employment, salaries, and labor relations. Some of the main effects are outlined in this section.

Employment

For fourteen years, stabilization measures and economic restructuring policies have had dramatic consequences for employment. For a four-year period, figures for open unemployment exceeded 20 percent of the available workforce (see Table 6.3). But while there were 1.3 million unemployed and registered in emergency employment programs in 1982, by 1990, unemployment had been reduced to 300,000. This means that from 1982 to 1990, one million Chileans changed their occupational situation. This figure is extremely high if one remembers that in 1980 the Chilean workforce was 3.6 million and in 1990 4.8 million.

Confirming that the adjustment polices caused a change in the structure of the labor market, one economic study noted that, "In the period 1973–83, two significant structural changes have affected the Chilean productive structure and, as a consequence, the capacity of this structure to generate employment opportunities: these changes are the new role of the state and the commercial opening" (Meller 1984: 30). As a result of these changes, the industrial and public sectors have a smaller capacity, both in relative and absolute terms, to produce employment opportunities. This has been compensated for, in part, by the expansion

Table 6.3   National Unemployment Rates in Chile

Year	Unadjusted Rate	Adjusted Rate	Year	Unadjusted Rate	Adjusted Rate
1961	8.0	8.0	1978	14.1	18.3
1962	7.9	7.9	1979	13.6	17.5
1963	7.5	7.5	1980	10.4	15.7
1964	7.0	7.0	1981	11.2	16.1
1965	6.4	6.4	1982	19.4	26.4
1966	6.1	6.1	1983	15.0	28.5
1967	4.7	4.7	1984	15.5	24.6
1968	4.9	4.9	1985	12.2	21.0
1969	5.5	5.5	1986	8.8	13.9
1970	5.7	5.7	1987	7.9	10.8
1971	3.8	3.8	1988	6.3	7.0
1972	3.1	3.1	1989	5.3	5.3
1973	4.8	4.8	1990	5.7	5.7
1974	9.2	9.2	1991	5.3	5.3
1975	14.5	16.8	1992	4.4	4.4
1976	12.9	17.8	1993	4.5	4.5
1977	11.8	17.7	1994	5.9	5.9
			1995	5.4	5.4

Source: Data from various issues of *Encuesta Nacional de Empleo.* Instituto Nacional de Estadísticas, Santiago.

Note: Figures are expressed as a percentage of the total economically active population. The adjusted rate includes persons working in the emergency employment programs Programa de Empleo Mínimo and Programa Ocupacional para Jefes de Hogar (1975–88).

of both the trade and financial sectors, due to the removal of restrictions on imports and the capital account.

The economic study quoted above calculated that 15 to 25 percent of the increase in unemployment, for the period 1975–81, was due to the change in the role of the state. Ten percent of the job losses in the industrial sector, for the period 1974–81, were due to the commercial opening (Meller 1984). These changes in the economy produced large population movements between the different economic sectors. Whereas agriculture employed 22 percent of the active workforce in 1970, this figure had declined to 17.4 percent by 1985, the year in which the transitional phase of the adjustment process was completed (García 1991). The percentage of the active workforce employed in manufacturing decreased from 17.8 percent in 1970, to 15.1 percent in 1985. Meanwhile, employment in the commercial sector increased from 12.1 percent in 1970, to 20.4 percent in 1985, while in the service sector employment went from 30.8 to 34 percent in the same period. In those sectors in which workers were traditionally strongly organized and powerful (mining, the manufacturing industry, and construction), employment decreased by 6.4 percent in the period 1970–85. In the commercial and service sectors, the union movement is weak, with either no tradition (commerce) or little tradition (some services) of organizing.

Another significant development for the period 1973–83 was the declining importance of salaried workers relative to self-employed workers. This tendency strongly reversed itself, however, from 1985 onward, although there has been a significant expansion of small- and medium-sized businesses. The changes in the distribution of the work-force among different economic sectors and the changes in occupational categories have had repercussions for the size and character of the working class and, therefore, on its ability to organize.

There has also been an industrial restructuring in the period 1970–90. In particular, a strong increase is evident in agro-industry, wood and furniture, chemicals, ceramics, and glass. By contrast, there has been a relative decline in iron and steel, metalwork, textiles, garments, and footwear.

From the perspective of economic development, the new strategic sectors are very different from the previous ones insofar as union organization is concerned. These new strategic sectors are the financial sector, where the upper middle class is gaining ground; the fruiticulture industry, in which there has been a sharp influx of temporary workers; woodcutting, in which geography forces workers to be dispersed among different forest regions; commerce, in which there is a low rate of unionization; dock workers, who due to their privileged legal position prior to the military regime were barely integrated into the union move-ment and are now experiencing difficult hiring conditions; and copper mining, which is the only sector in which unions are powerful, both historically and at present, and the features of the traditional mining enclave are still in evidence. However, copper miners now have salaries that are much higher than the average for all workers.

Those groups that have had a history of traditional unionism, such as textiles, metalwork, construction, nitrate and coal mining, and teaching have experienced economic changes which have weakened them, whether due to new forms of hiring (construction) or the new model of organic insertion into the state apparatus (education).

The integration of the national economy into the international economy, precipitated by the structural adjustment, has debilitated union strength, as a result either of the nature of the new strategic sectors or the new ways in which the workforce is regulated. In an earlier work

(Barrera 1989), I discussed the five modes through which the Chilean working class has been introduced into the labor market since the articulation of a mature capitalist economy: informality, exclusion, precarious employment, the growth of the tertiary sector, and formal and traditional employment. Given that the most militant workers' organizations historically arise in the formal sector of the labor market and that today this sector is made up of only a fraction of the total number of workers, the importance of the informal sector, the process of exclusion, and employment insecurity all tend to weaken union strength.

Remuneration

The whole process of stabilization and economic restructuring has been accompanied by a fall in real wages. In the first instance, there was a sharp drop that corresponded with the beginning of the process but was attenuated as the structural adjustment policies took force. However, this tendency was interrupted by the recession of 1982–83, the consequences of which were another fall in real wages. This second drop, however, was not as great as that which occurred in the first years of the adjustment process, and it was only beginning in 1988 that a clear and persistent recuperation in wages was observable (see Table 6.4).

As should be obvious, an aggregate index of wage earnings for the entire workforce would not reflect the real situation of the various employment sectors. If one examines the path of the minimum wage index, it is clear that workers who received only the legal minimum wage have experienced such a dramatic drop in their wages that even in 1992, their real income was less than what they earned in 1974, the first year of the structural adjustment program. Table 6.5 shows how low-income workers have been living in debilitating circumstances, even during years of economic growth. The drop in the legal minimum wage has been greater than that of total wages. In other words, poor workers have become poorer than all other workers combined. The position of minimum wage earners is the most extreme of all wage earners. What percentage of total GDP is represented by wages, and what have been the changes in this proportion over the last 20 years? Figures for the period 1970–90 reveal that the contribution of wages to national spending has not risen substantially, as one would expect with the growth of GNP (see CEPAL 1989a, 1990).

The economic situation of the working class deteriorated during the years of the structural adjustment program, while the situation of the population in general revealed the profound inequalities that were

Table 6.4   Index of Real Wages in Chile

Year	Index	Annual Variation (%)
1970	100.0	—
1971	125.3	25.3
1972	126.6	1.0
1973	—	—
1974	64.1	—
1975	62.0	3.3
1976	65.4	5.5
1977	70.7	8.1
1978	75.1	6.2
1979	81.4	8.4
1980	88.5	8.7
1981	96.4	8.9
1982	96.1	−0.3
1983	85.8	−10.7
1984	85.9	0.1
1985	82.2	−4.3
1986	83.8	1.9
1987	83.6	−0.2
1988	89.1	6.5
1989	90.8	1.9
1990	92.4	1.8
1991	96.9	4.9
1992	101.3	4.5
1993*	99.9	—
1994	105.0	5.1
1995	108.7	3.5

Source: Data from various issues of *Encuesta Nacional de Empleo.* Instituto Nacional de Estadísticas, Santiago.

Note: The year 1970 was used as a baseline (1970 = 100). In 1970–72 and 1980–92, the figures were deflated using the official Consumer Price Index. In 1974–78, the figures were deflated using a Consumer Price Index adjusted by the Corporación de Investigaciones Económicas Para Latinoamerica.

* April through December average from the new hourly wage index, with April 1993 equal to 100. These data are not comparable with earlier data.

accentuated during this period. In effect, studies of poor and destitute households demonstrated that in the eighteen-year period from 1969 to 1987, the percentage of destitute households increased steadily, as did the percentage of households experiencing poverty. The total of both categories went from 28.5 percent of households in 1969 to 38 percent in 1987. In other words, in the first years of the implementation of the

Table 6.5 Real Legal Minimum Wage in Chile

Year	Nominal Value in Pesos	Real Minimum Wage (base 1981 = 100)	Annual Variation (%)
1981	6.222	100.0	—
1982	6.222	91.0	−9.0
1983	6.534	75.1	−17.5
1984	6.534	62.6	−16.6
1985	8.100	59.4	−5.2
1986	9.353	57.4	−3.4
1987	10.525	53.9	−6.1
1988	12.936	57.8	7.2
1989	16.836	64.2	11.2
1990	22.666	68.6	6.8
1991	30.083	74.8	9.0
1992	36.266	78.1	4.4
1993	42.916	82.0	5.0
1994	49.587	85.0	3.7
1995	56.087	92.0	8.3

Source: Data from various issues of *Encuesta Nacional de Empleo.* Instituto Nacional de Estadísticas, Santiago.

adjustment program, the percentage of households living in poor or destitute conditions surpassed 35 percent of all households. Tables 6.6 and 6.7 summarize the terrible social cost that these years have had for marginalized sectors in Chile.

Family budget surveys confirmed that extreme inequality increased during this period. The income share of the poorest sectors systematically decreased as it increased by 24 percent for the wealthiest sectors of the population, rising from 44.5 percent in 1969, to 55.4 percent in 1992. In 1992, only 13.8 percent of total income was received by the two bottom quintiles of the population.

Table 6.6 Percentage of Households Living in Poverty in Chile

	1969	1987	1990	1992	1994
Indigent households	8.4	13.5	11.6	7.2	6.6
Poor, nonindigent households	20.1	24.5	22.9	20.5	17.4
Total poor households	28.5	38.0	34.5	27.7	24.0
Nonpoor households	71.5	62.0	65.5	72.3	76.0
Total households	100.0	100.0	100.0	100.0	100.0
Total poor persons	ND	5,571,000	4,510,000	4,348,000	3,916,000

Sources: Data from various years of the *Encuesta CASEN* report, Ministerio de Planificación Nacional, Santiago, compiled by Pollack and Uthoff 1990: 1,969. ND, not determined.

Table 6.7 Percentage Income Distribution for All Households in Chile

Income Quintile	1968	1992	1994
First	7.6	5.0	4.6
Second	11.8	8.8	8.6
Third	15.6	12.4	12.4
Fourth	20.5	18.4	18.4
Fifth	44.5	55.4	56.1
Total	100.0	100.0	100.0

Sources: Data from the 1969 *Family Budget Surveys*, Instituto Nacional de Estadísticas, and from the 1992 and 1994 *Encuesta CASEN* reports, Ministerio de Planificación Nacional, Santiago.

Calculations of the Gini coefficient demonstrated the deterioration in income distribution. This trend reached its highest degree of concentration during the period of recession from 1982 to 1984, which produced a Gini coefficient of 0.54 (Meller 1992: 21). The pattern of income distribution was the same in 1991 as it had been 1980 (MIDEPLAN 1992). A more concentrated income distribution, a sharp deterioration in real wages, and an increase in poverty levels all indicate that the economic sacrifices associated with the structural adjustment were largely borne by the working class. This situation was accompanied by a deterioration in labor relations, at the expense of unions and workers.

Labor Relations During the Adjustment Period

The macrosocial framework within which labor relations were conducted during the military regime was characterized by authoritarianism and structural adjustment. The concurrence of these economic and political circumstances is what set the Chilean experience apart. Neoliberalism could never have been the main pillar of a new social and economic model without authoritarianism, since it is unlikely that an unrepressed society would have willingly borne the costs that adjustment passed on to it, as the experience of other Latin American countries has demonstrated.

As far as labor relations were concerned, the authoritarian period ushered in systematic police, legal, and administrative repression, especially during the years 1973–79. By this means, the regime attempted to eliminate the union leadership that had supported the Popular Unity government and, by extension, the majority segment of the movement that was most experienced in terms of defending the rights of workers.

Together with the physical repression, the government decreed certain ordinances aimed at suspending the process of collective bargaining and making it difficult for unions to assemble. Armed with these antiunion measures, de facto repressive and normative in nature, the regime ensured that union activity would be rendered very difficult. The result was that union organizations at the level of the firm existed in name only. Nevertheless, these unions did not lose their legal status, although they lost most of their usual functions. This whole process, which extended from the moment when the military assumed power in 1973, until it enacted a new labor law in 1979 (the *Plan Laboral*), has been analyzed in detail elsewhere (Barrera 1980; Ruiz-Tagle 1986).

The *Plan Laboral* reinstated workers' rights that had been suspended in 1973. However, not all rights were reintroduced, for example, the right to elect union leaders and to bargain collectively. In analyzing the laws that comprise the *Plan Laboral* and their application, the attempt to make labor relations (contracting, collective bargaining, union organizations, labor-employer relations) compatible with the operation of the new economic processes stands out. The principal emphasis was on making the labor market more flexible, which was accomplished through legislative mechanisms that endeavored to remove any rigidities that might distort the mobility of the labor factor. Through legal, administrative, and economic measures in the areas of hiring and firing; incorporation of technology into the workplace; and organization of a system of workforce training (for which firms would not incur any costs), it would be easier to reduce, recruit, disqualify, or qualify workers.

In order to ensure that labor conflicts did not go beyond the level of the firm, the legislation established a system whereby agreements concerning wages and working conditions were arrived at without the intervention of external agents, that is, without any mediation on the part of the state or political and social actors. The state had the appearance of being neutral and unaffected either economically or politically by labor conflict. In reality, it was insulated by legal norms. The risks associated with strikes, for example, were directly assumed by the parties involved. The labor legislation, as well as the institutionalization of a new political model, attempted to prevent unions from moving beyond economic/wage claims. The capacity for trade union action, especially in terms of collective bargaining, was reduced to the level of the firm. The formal neutrality of the state in workers' relations was situated within a restricted legal framework regarding union activity, and within an economic setting characterized by a high level of unemployment and an ostensible drop in real wages. The economic adjustment produced a concentration of capital that, together with the legal nonexistence of political parties and

Parliament, made for an incapacitated union structure at the level of the firm that had to face, alone, an organized capital class.

Table 6.8 demonstrates the low level of unionization in the years immediately following the implementation of the *Plan Laboral*, a phenomenon that coincided with both the final years of the first phase of the adjustment and the military government in general. It is also interesting to note the increase in the number of unions that, on average, had small memberships. The last two columns of the table, calculated using official data, show that unionization was relatively weak and dispersed and that the unionized population was small relative to the workforce in general. However, these figures do show there was an increase in union affiliation under the democratic government.

Table 6.8   Union Membership in Chile

Year	Workforce	Total Unions	Total Membership	Members per Union	Unionization Rate
1981	3,369,400	3.977	395.951	99.6	11.7
1982	3,069,100	4.048	347.470	85.8	11.3
1983	3,149,500	4.401	320.903	72.9	10.2
1984	3,268,100	4.714	343.329	72.8	10.5
1985	3,537,400	4.994	360.963	72.3	10.2
1986	3,895,700	5.391	386.987	71.8	9.9
1987	4,010,800	5.883	422.302	71.8	10.5
1988	4,265,800	6.446	446.194	69.2	10.5
1989	4,424,800	7.118	507.616	71.3	11.5
1990	4,459,600	8.861	606.812	68.5	13.6
1991	4,472,700	9.858	701.355	71.1	15.7
1992	4,472,700	10.725	723.100	67.4	15.1
1993	4,985,700	11.369	682.704	60.0	15.1
1994	4,988,300	12.109	661.966	54.6	13.3

Source: Data from various issues of *Anuário de Estadísticas.* Dirección del Trabajo, Ministerio del Trabajo y Previsión Social.

Labor relations within the firm carried the stamp of authoritarianism. Legislation allowed for the complete subordination of workers to management, which was further aggravated by the regulation of labor. It became easier to dismiss workers, while the process of hiring workers became more flexible so that precarious employment conditions extended into the formal sector, including its most modern sectors. The precariousness of employment (contracts for a fixed period only and so on) dealt a hard blow to unions since workers employed under unstable conditions cannot easily become unionized. Extensive subcontracting tended to atomize the trade union within the traditional method of organizing the workforce in Chile or simply made unionization impossible.

Authoritarianism in labor relations within the firm at times included open repression, arbitrary dismissals, and antiunion policies on the part of management. In addition, the labor "climate" within the firm was unpleasant for workers, and working conditions generally deteriorated during the adjustment period. Management was just as authoritarian and repressive as the military government. In reality, labor organizations were one of the permanent sites of repression during the military regime. At times, this happened with the complacency of management, which placed workers in a weakened position as in, for example, the case of the textile sector (Henríquez 1991).

The above discussion supports the conclusion that labor relations during the entire military regime and, therefore, during the whole first phase of the structural adjustment program were traumatic for workers. Power relations were asymmetric, and the subordination of workers was assured by the repressive legal, economic, and administrative controls in place.

A study (PREALC 1992) conducted of the social and economic consequences of the adjustment process for the popular sectors in all of Latin America concluded that the social costs of structural adjustment were inevitable, since in every country that implemented these programs these costs were encountered. Nevertheless, it was clear that there were alternatives available to reduce or redistribute these costs. Another conclusion reached by the study was that the costs of *not* implementing these adjustments during the critical period of the 1980s were higher for the popular sectors in social and economic terms than those associated with restructuring (the cases of Argentina, Brazil, and Peru can be compared with those of Bolivia, Costa Rica, Chile, Jamaica, Mexico, Uruguay, and Venezuela).

In the Chilean case, it is possible to confirm that, although the social cost was very high, since the initial stage this tendency has reversed itself. Therefore, what needs to be examined are the characteristics assumed by the labor market and the insertion of the popular sectors into this market at the time when the consolidation of the new social and economic order was taking place. In effect, Chile is now experiencing a transition from a pattern of accumulation and regulation that first emerged after World War II and which initiated a mode of production and regulation, as well as a certain form of labor relations, defined in normative terms. The country is moving toward a new pattern of capitalist accumulation and regulation in terms of both economics and labor, according to which, compared with the previous one, workers have a more precarious status and are essentially defenseless. In fact, one of the more relevant characteristics of the new economic and labor order is that it appears to confirm that a high percentage of the workforce will experience marginalization and informality, as Table 6.9 demonstrates.

Table 6.9   Nonagricultural Employment Structure in Latin America and Chile

	1980	1985	1990
Latin America			
Informal sector			
Independent workers	19.2	22.6	23.9
Domestic service	6.4	7.8	6.9
Total	25.6	30.4	30.8
Formal sector			
Public sector	15.7	16.6	15.5
Private-large firms	44.1	36.5	31.6
Private-small firms	14.6	16.6	22.1
Total	74.4	69.7	69.2
Chile			
Informal sector			
Independent workers	27.8	24.4	23.6
Domestic service	8.3	9.8	8.1
Total	36.1	34.2	31.7
Formal sector			
Public sector	11.9	9.9	7.0
Private-large firms	37.7	36.8	43.0
Private-small firms	14.3	19.1	18.3
Total	63.9	65.8	68.3

Source: Estimates from Programa Regional del Empleo pora América Latina de Naciones Unidas, 1992, based on household surveys.

Accordingly, for Latin America as a whole, employment in the urban informal sector increased between 1989 and 1990, while in the formal sector employment increased in small firms. In Chile during the same period, employment in the urban informal sector decreased, but it continued to represent an important percentage of the working population. Public-sector employment decreased significantly, and there was an increase in employment in small firms. The Chilean situation corresponds to a pattern of dismantling the state's productive functions and rationalizing the modern industrial sector, which has favored the expansion of subcontracting and the development of small firms in which there are opportunities for good quality jobs. Some of these jobs are in the informal sector. It is possible to assert that a process of articulation has been established between the modern capitalist sector of the economy (or that sector in the process of productive modernization) and a segment of the informal, noncapitalist economy (Díaz 1993). This articulation obviously changes the traditional scenario of two parallel economies that never touch each other. As a result, the informal economy has become more complicated, and it remains uncertain whether, through a process of technology transfer, opening of commercial channels, and creating subcontracting relations, jobs in the informal sector—or at least a portion of these—will be able to generate adequate incomes. Training and the extension of credit are preconditions that must be satisfied for this to take place.

However, it is obvious that for most of the informal sector, the precapitalist characteristics that this economy exhibited in the previous pattern of accumulation continue to dominate. This section of the informal sector exists apart from the processes of modernization, rationalization, and internationalization. As well, the informal sector does not possess the traditional capacity for organizing and mobilizing that we have seen in trade union movements. This logic behind organizing is unclear to the informal sector. Analysis of the organization and mobilization of the economically marginalized popular sectors takes us out of a labor market scenario and places us in the environment of the city and its *poblaciones*. Various authors have maintained that the identity of "*lo popular*" that is created within this environment is stronger and more authentic than that found in the more traditional social movements (Oxhorn 1995b).

The Social and Political Inclusion
of the Popular Sectors

Economic reform has had a profound impact on the social and political status of the popular sectors. Throughout Latin America, these sectors have experienced a considerable decrease in their standard of living, and as noted, the employment situation and the forms of contracting workers have become unstable. Labor legislation has become less rigid and the state has abandoned the concept of protecting the most vulnerable section of the workforce. A large portion of the workforce cannot be organized, and for the workforce as a whole, the general tendency in Latin America has been to weaken the power of the union movement, a trend that is as much a result of legislation as it is a result of real economic processes.

The new social consensus has assigned employers a fundamental role in the new development strategy. The protagonist class in the historical advancement of humanity, at least in the socialist utopia, was the working class. This has been the guiding principle for action for the Latin American labor movement, even its non-Marxist elements. The new social consensus has eliminated this utopia and instead has assigned to the adversarial class the role of protagonist. The processes of change that are occurring at the microsocial level in firms, the tendency toward the destructuring of certain industrial branches and regions, the disarticulation of production chains, and the expansion of the tertiary sector within the economy and the workforce have all been decisive developments in the reduction of union strength.

The popular sectors in Latin America have not been without a response to these developments, but this response has sometimes taken the form of violent reactions on the part of the masses. The response has been poorly structured and has not offered an alternative program for adjustment and reform, which has been evident in Chile, Bolivia, and Venezuela and recently in Argentina and Mexico. These protests have at times been relatively spontaneous, without any political or union direction of a national or international nature. Some of the protests, for instance in Chile, have had as their explicit objective the overthrow of the military government, whereas others clearly have been popular uprisings against economic-adjustment measures, such as those that occurred in December 1993, in a province of Argentina. In Venezuela, the violent uprisings of the populace have had a dual purpose: first, they have been directed against the former president, Andrés Pérez, and, second, they have served as a protest against an intolerable economic situation.

These violent reactions have obviously achieved greater visibility, the results of which have been diverse, from the fall of a president (Pérez in Venezuela) to the opening up of the political system (as in Chile), which resulted in moderation of the drastic nature of the measures.

At the level of the popular sectors—unemployed or working in the informal sector—these adjustment measures have produced certain economic and solidarity practices of profound social, political, and moral significance. These practices have been oriented to what Razeto has termed "the popular economy of solidarity and labor," which is a veritable survival strategy. The informal worker, traveling salesman, and community market, the small firm self-managed by its workers and a large variety of microfirms run by families, individuals, or groups, are all part of this popular economy, which involves production, distribution, and consumption activities conducted by an abundant workforce. Their material, financial, and technological resources are of diverse origins and quality, and the economy has received support in the first instance from nongovernmental organizations and later through the state's social policies. This popular economy of solidarity and labor emerged under the military regime and continued into the democratic transition phase in the urban informal sector that, we have already noted, grew throughout Latin America and in Chile has remained at around 30 percent of the urban workforce.

As it has evolved, this economy has transformed itself into a veritable social safety net, in that the permanence of this particular type of economy translates into many opportunities, given that the international economic opening and free market have generated a process of rationalization and productive modernization in only one sector of the economy, a relatively small sector from the perspective of the workforce. For this reason, it is possible for civil society within the popular sectors to develop along this path, which has a logic entirely contrary to that of neoliberalism. If this were the case, the popular sectors could consolidate those community actions they perform, such as forming communal kitchens, creating day care for children, constructing housing, and creating shopping centers (which in Chile are suggestively referred to as "shopping together"). According to several Chilean scholars, this popular economy could lead to a sociopolitical project of the popular sectors, supported by the democratization process. But perhaps such a project is an overblown and romantic conception of the political possibilities associated with grassroots organizations.

Another reaction on the part of the popular sectors to the economic adjustment has been the incorporation into the labor market of women, youth, and children from the poorest socioeconomic sectors. All of these people are working in jobs of the lowest quality. As more and more heads of households (men) lose their jobs, the "secondary" workforce (women and children) are incorporated into the labor market, with all of the negative consequences this poses for popular sector families.

The strategy of the union movement at the national level, promoted as it is by democratic governments and international organizations such as the International Labor Office, has been one of social "concertation," that is, the strategy has been to promote agreements between workers and employers of a national character and consensual nature. A consequence has been a realization that a conflict-driven strategy—long prevalent in the Latin American labor movement and especially in Chile—is not the most appropriate one to deal with the problems workers face in the economic model of free markets and an open economy. Behind the union's strategy is the theory that competitive advantage requires an agreement between employers and workers on issues such as wages, unemployment, and working conditions. From the perspective of employers, the most essential thing to preserve is a flexible labor market, since this is considered indispensable for a competitive economy at the international level. From the perspective of workers, a flexible labor market must come with certain guarantees against layoffs. In general, social concertation has not given workers a larger role in matters dealing with technological change, restructuring of firms at the sectoral level, or even the training and retraining of the workforce. However, at the level of national policies, such as setting the minimum wage and economic strategy, unions have been considered an important social actor in Chile, one with whom the transition government has had an easy-going relationship.

The "flexibilization" of the labor market has also meant the abandonment of the principle of tripartite labor relations, that is, the intervention of the state, management, and unions, with the state acting as protector of the weakest actor. Implicit in social concertation is the principle of bipartite relations with the abstention of the state, which appears as a neutral actor and assumes the role of facilitator. Since the adjustment process has weakened the position of labor while strengthening that of the capital class, labor relations have become increasingly asymmetric. This is especially serious for workers, since the firm has become the arena where salaries and working conditions most frequently are negotiated. Collective bargaining at the level of the firm has become the only mechanism through which workers can make claims and realize gains.

In the preauthoritarian period, Chilean workers made use of the strike as a weapon during labor conflicts, when it was used not only against management in the private sector but also against the state by groups such as teachers and nonprivatized health care practitioners. Both of these sectors were reformed under the military government, which resulted in a deterioration of their wages from which they have yet to recover. These strikes represented a difficult confrontation for democratic governments and revitalized the general struggle of workers in the country. In the 1990s, labor conflict is the only expression of conflict that is permanent and does not threaten a rupture of the social and political order. The objectives of strikes have been economic.

The dominance of the particular kind of bipartite labor relations discussed above (associated, moreover, with the discrediting of Marxism, which in various countries of the region had and continues to have an influence on unions) has forced the union movement to move in a direction that reconceptualizes its role in the economy and society of Latin America. Within this new conceptualization, the themes introduced by the macroeconomic reform that liberalized the market will have to be clearly set out. It is evident that since the reform, the classic strategy used by unions is obsolete. Microcorporate organizations will be more important than partisan links. Proposals with regard to economic strategy will get a better audience among workers than anticapitalist and anti-imperialist statements.

In this new context, unions can represent either the whole of the subordinated sectors—which has been its ambition since the nineteenth century—or only the unionized sector of the workforce, as the logic of that particular combination of free market and economic liberalization with democratization would appear to dictate. Faced with a union movement that represents only itself, the rest of the popular sectors will not have any social representation along this route. Moreover, given that the political parties on the left presently are attempting to sell themselves as representatives of the "common interest" and not of the class interests of the lower strata, the popular sectors will have no choice but to represent themselves. It is not clear that this will happen in the short term.

Conclusion

I have argued in this chapter that in the Chilean case, the coordinates that delimit the situation of the popular sectors are first, the process of democratization and second, the policies of adjustment and macro-economic reform. These are the signature of the 1990s, just as the debt crisis was for the 1980s. Within this framework, popular sector politics can be characterized in the following way:

1. The recomposition of civil society following its disarticulation by the authoritarian regime has not occurred as quickly as was originally anticipated. In fact, social movements have been weakened and

some—such as those in the *poblaciones*—that were of decisive importance during the fight against the dictatorship have disappeared from the social scene. Even movements as traditional to Chilean politics as the student movement have met a similar fate. At the same time, the so-called new social movements (feminist, ecological) have not succeeded in establishing themselves, despite the enthusiasm of various intellectuals.

2. The most important popular social movement is without doubt the union movement. However, its status has been diminished greatly in society. Within the framework of a "level" society in terms of popular sector organization and mobilization, the unions could have established themselves as the defenders of the interests of the marginalized sectors. However, this was not to be the case. The union movement has focused on the corporate interests of its members.

3. The transition to democracy has been characterized by a gap between political elites and the people. Political life has been closely tied to the institutional environment, and in society there has been an absence of participation on the part of various social sectors. In some sectors (youth), there is apathy and disinterest with regard to all that centers around politics.

4. In light of what has been said, it is worth considering whether the weakening of civil society is the result of the nature of the new pattern of accumulation and regulation. Put differently, is it not the macroeconomic reform that necessitates a more individualized lifestyle centered primarily around income and subsistence, as opposed to solidarity and social participation?

5. If this is the case, the reconstitution of civil society following the pattern associated with the period of inward-oriented development is no longer possible. Civil society, and the social movements associated with it, would have a new character. Perhaps the impulse that now motivates groups is of a more economic than political nature. Among the unemployed and underemployed, subsistence will have priority over citizenship. Among the fully employed, work and income will have preeminence over political or social participation. The fundamental demand for some will be the right to consume, and for others it will be the pleasures associated with consumerism. The social or political utopia has disappeared.

6. The adjustment process had a severe impact on the popular sectors in terms of unemployment, cuts in wages, and unstable hiring practices. Once the principal reforms were consolidated, the situation began to

reverse itself. However, within the so-called urban informal sector (to which should be added a rural informal contingent), there is a mass of poor and extremely poor whose ultimate destiny is unknown. Although there is evidence that good quality jobs have appeared within this sector, the future course of this development is not clearly discernible. One hypothesis is that a definitive social and economic exclusion of marginalized sectors has occurred. A second hypothesis is that the development process will eventually include this population. It is difficult to accept these two extreme positions. What might happen is that the state's social policies, together with private-sector demand for workers, will finally incorporate a large proportion of this "excluded population."

7.   One of the most interesting observable phenomena in the economic strategy of the popular sectors is the creation of self-employment opportunities through the formation of microenterprises. It is the popular segment of the private sector that is experiencing strong growth as it vigorously attempts to be incorporated into a labor market situated in the gaps or voids that result from the globalization of goods and services. The logic of this popular segment is not a capitalist logic but rather one that emerges from a primary form of association. Family or friendship ties bind those participating in micro-entrepreneurial activities, and these ties are motivated by questions of subsistence, the self-creation of one's own means of earning a living, and labor independence. The movement toward creating microenterprises is one of the few signs of vitality within popular civil society. In the future it can perhaps become a vehicle of inclusive participation in the march toward an integrated society.

8.   The return of democracy has meant notable changes for unions and workers. First, political freedom makes it possible to realize union activities and assert rights according to the rule of law, without danger of repression. Second, the labor movement has come to occupy a preeminent place in the public arena, favored perhaps by the inactivity of the other social movements that were active during the years of the dictatorship. In this way, the labor movement has, as has happened in many other moments of the country's social history, become the representative of all of the subordinate sectors as a whole. In recent years, it has begun to share this distinguished position in the public arena with organizations of professionals, particularly teachers (who are members of the *Central Unitaria de Trabajadores*, CUT) and doctors, whose primary organizations are

the *Colegio de Profesores* and the *Colegio Medico*. It should be noted that the program of the democratic government and the party alliance that sustains it intended to devolve to the labor movement an important role in the relationship between the state and civil society. In this way, the policy of social concertation was put into practice even before President Aylwin assumed office. A basic consensus on the program for democratization and development of the country was sought through discussions between the government and representatives of business groups and the CUT.

In recent years, the democratic government has been able to achieve improvements in labor legislation, regulation of work, and communication with unions. These actions have at times caused confrontations with the political opposition and business groups, but in reality important changes in these spheres have been realized. These can be considered to be more or less profound according to one's expectations regarding the possibility for the immediate repair of democratic institutions.

The government continues to persist in its efforts to improve labor legislation, particularly laws related to expanding the scope of collective bargaining. It is making efforts to amplify and improve its ability to enforce compliance with labor laws by firms, and continues to grant the CUT—organized labor's national leadership—a status as a premier national actor.

In terms of development policy, the struggles against poverty and for development with equity have been declared a priority during the six-year term of President Frei. Employment and wage indicators have improved demonstrably since 1990. However, there remains a long union and political road to travel in order to achieve an equitable distribution of wealth and social power between business and workers.

7

Trade Unions and the Corporatist System in Mexico

Francisco Zapata

Labor forms a constitutive part of the Mexican political system, making it very important to evaluate its role in the process of restructuring the country's political and economic systems. One cannot ignore that the insertion of the labor movement into the corporatist system is a determining factor in the process of transformation that has been taking place in Mexico since the beginning of the 1980s. By defining itself as part of that structure, the Mexican labor movement cannot disassociate itself from the state as an autonomous actor capable of defining alternatives or projects that are situated outside the general framework of the state of which it forms a part. This dependence has been the central characteristic of the labor movement within the structure of the Mexican state.

It would thus be a mistake to analyze union activity in Mexico as though it were part of an autonomous strategy expressing a project external to state structures and based on corporatism. This restriction permeates any consideration of the relationship between unions and economic restructuring

Translated by Philip Oxhorn with the assistance of Carmen Sorger.

in Mexico. It is particularly true if we ask ourselves if labor has or does not have a project that could challenge the measures that the state has taken to restructure the productive structure of the country.

On the basis of this caution, some reflections are presented here on the impact that economic restructuring has had on the Mexican labor movement. First, I discuss the issue of the continuation or rupture of corporatism. In spite of an apparent consensus in favor of the second alternative (rupture), the issue is not, in my opinion, resolved. Second, on the basis of the previous argument, I focus on the actual implementation of the Pact for Stability and Economic Growth (PECE), which is a good example of the way in which Mexican corporatism has operated since 1987. How the different components of the Mexican labor movement reacted to the implementation of the PECE and how they have evolved in the recent period of restructuring, privatization, and macroeconomic crisis are examined in detail. I conclude by arguing that Mexican corporatism is a multifaceted phenomenon that has been able to operate under very different historical circumstances.

The issues posed in this chapter are directly related to the more general question of the transition between development models that has been going on in several Latin American countries since the oil crisis of 1973, and the debt crisis of 1982. As a result of both events, the old development model based on closed economies, with a strong state economic sector and implementation of populist social policies, has been gradually replaced by open economies, privatization of state-owned companies and substitution of public welfare policies by privately owned social services. This transition poses a series of questions related to the specific form that the transition takes in different historical situations, because these condition the process in each country. In this respect, my focus on Mexico emphasizes the central role that corporatism plays in this specific transition, thus making it hard to subsume what happens in this country into more generic arguments about the rise of the neoliberal development model in countries such as Chile, where a military dictatorship took it upon itself to make this transition by erasing the old political and economic system.

Continuation or Rupture of Corporatism?

In order to correctly evaluate the relationship between the labor movement and the corporatist system, I offer the hypothesis that unions, employers, and the state continue interacting through the structure that was established in the 1930s, in particular by the government of Lázaro Cárdenas (1934–40). This structure was based on the ideological principles laid out during the previous decade by Vicente Lombardo Toledano, a key intellectual in the design of that system (Zapata 1990a, 1995a). I therefore assume that the PECE,[1] whose first version was signed in December 1987, did not fundamentally change the character of the relationship that these actors have had among themselves and especially with the state. Unions and the business chambers recognize their subordination to the state and at the same time contribute to the achievement of the state's objectives. From this perspective, the PECE did not pave the way for important changes in the structures of interaction among these actors. Perhaps the institutions in which these three participants acted together, such as the National Commission on Minimum Wages, the Institute for the Promotion of Housing for Workers, the Mexican Social Security Institute (IMSS, *Instituto Mexicano del Seguro Social*), and the Evaluation Commission of the PECE, further developed the nature of those static relations and the rhetorical nature of many of their public expressions.

A good example of this situation can be found in the negotiations dealing with the reform of the Federal Work Law (LFT) that took place in 1989–92. Although social and political actors formulated proposals that would radically change regulation of labor relations,[2] these negotiations did not achieve any tangible results. This was essentially because of the opposition openly manifested by the Confederation of Mexican Workers (CTM) to the reform of this law.[3] Despite this opposition, some leaders, such as Francisco Hernández Juarez, secretary general of the Telephone

1. The text of the first PECE appeared in Banco Nacional de México, January 1988. It was analyzed in "Ni pacto, ni solidaridad," *El Cotidiano*, no. 21, January–February 1988. Its implications for the relationship between the labor movement and corporatism were reviewed by Enrique De La Garza (1989).

2. In 1989, the National Business Chamber (*Confederación Patronal de la República Mexicana*) made a formal presentation regarding all the specific aspects of the Labor Law that it considered had to be changed. See "Propuestas preliminares que la Confederación Patronal de la República Mexicana presenta para la discusión del anteproyecto de una nueva Ley Federal del Trabajo (LFT): marco conceptual," June 1989.

3. See statements by Fidel Velásquez quoted in various newspapers on 26 December 1991, and 6 January 1992. For example, *La Jornada*, 6 January 1992, "They will not change Article 123, neither will they change LFT: Fidel Velásquez." Among other things, the leader said, "We have said very energetically that we do not accept in any way a change to the federal law because this would mean the loss of social peace. . . . There will be no changes as there were to [Articles] 130 and 27. Because this is not convenient for the time being. The law does not inhibit

Workers Union, did express favorable opinions about the reform based on a new vision of union-state relations. In any case, the resolution of this impasse was more a function of the general response to the restructuring of corporatism, in which the LFT plays a key role, than of any specific changes in the rules governing industrial relations in the country.

At the same time, the state was very successful in confirming its political support for the social security institutional apparatus, such as the State Employees Social Security Institute (*Instituto de Seguridad y Servicios Sociales de los Trabajadores al Servicio del Estado*) and the IMSS, although there has been a gradual process of stagnation in the membership of these institutions, especially since 1988. According to statistics on the number of people registered by the IMSS by area of economic activity,[4] membership is increasing only in the commercial sector. This means that while there is job growth in the informal sector and in microenterprises, and as more women are incorporated into the labor market, these workers are not registered with the social security system and are left without any coverage for health care or retirement. This suggests that the capacity of Mexican unions to put pressure on the distribution of social benefits (such as health care and social security) is now being questioned by politicians and the technocrats in charge of the government.

In sum, the current problem with the political structure of Mexico can be identified with the creation of conditions for a new consensus in which the trade-off for the 1940–70 period is reformulated in such a way that the elimination of certain benefits that are inconsistent with the new economic strategy will not contradict the political logic that makes economic change possible. This suggests, for example, that state intervention in industrial relations is being restructured in order to make it compatible with the global strategy of modernization that is taking place in the country. One can see that unions and businesses have accepted renovation of their traditional forms of interaction without proceeding to destabilize the system through the exercise of force. Therefore, they have been capable of maintaining a functional corporatist structure within their own structural limits.

It is clear that something is happening in the country, that corporatism in Mexico has been transformed and today operates clothed in the rhetoric of concertation. This raises several questions that are related to

---

enterprises from investing, or for others to do so because the federal labor law and Article 123 promote investments."

4. See the National Institute of Statistics, Geography, and Information (INEGI), *Cuadernos de Información Oportuna*, June 1992.

the implications of this transformation: Does it imply that there are fundamental changes in the central logic of corporatism, or only that corporatism is operating under temporary pressures derived from the difficulties of maintaining the old trade-off? Do present tensions derive from the successive crises that took place in 1982, 1987, and 1995, and the restrictions they imposed on the Mexican economy, or do they reflect more structural factors identified with a serious rupture within the corporatist system?

These questions emerged from the electoral results of the presidential elections of 1988 and 1994, and from the congressional elections of 1991 and 1997. In 1988, the Institutional Revolutionary Party (PRI, *Partido Revolucionario Institucional*) lost ground, and the president was elected with a very shaky majority, but the party succeeded in coming back both in 1991 and 1994, when it retained absolute control of the Chamber of Deputies and of the presidency. In 1997, however, the PRI lost control of the Chamber of Deputies, receiving 39.11 percent of the vote and electing 239 deputies, 48 percent of the total seats. From now on, the Mexican political system will be in unknown territory. It will have to learn how to engage democratic procedures and adapt to the considerable reduction of power on the part of the executive. These events also were the result of the appearance of a much more vigorous opposition to the PRI centered around the charismatic figure of Cuautémoc Cárdenas (Garrido 1993), who was elected mayor of Mexico City on 6 July 1997. In addition, the crisis of the labor movement and the weakness of its reaction to the decline in real salary levels and fringe benefits generated particularly critical situations from the point of view of the legitimacy of the system. If one adds the sudden appearance of a guerrilla movement in the state of Chiapas on 1 January 1994, political assassinations (of the PRI presidential candidate and of the PRI president in March and September 1994, respectively), and the consequent 1994–95 economic crisis, it is clear the stage was being set for an explanation of the deep tensions running through Mexican society. Last but not least, the death of Fidel Velásquez, in June 1997, created new challenges for the labor movement. Indeed, immediately following his death, tensions arose within the new organizations that have emerged to represent workers such as the *Foro El Sindicalismo ante la Nación* and the *Coordinadora Intersindical Primero de Mayo (Coordinadora)*.

The form that concertation took in 1987–94, therefore, does not necessarily imply that the corporatist structure changed its contents but that there were changes in its forms of operation. Conversely, the labor movement, business organizations, and governmental representatives interacted with one another more efficiently than ever before because now the challenges were immediate, putting pressure on them to resolve the country's problems. Caps on real salaries and the control of interest rates and prices were negotiated jointly, and over the period 1987–96 reflected a basic agreement among these actors.

In general terms, Mexican concertation showed that a structure exists in which the central actors of a corporatist system can interact on the basis of a nonideologically motivated consensus.[5] Thus, the viability of the existing concertation mechanism is much higher than when these elements are not present, such as is the case in Argentina or Brazil, where concertation policies have been much harder to implement. Furthermore, the concertation that took place in this context was not something new. These "actors" have performed in other "plays" in other circumstances, perhaps more positive than the existing ones, and are for now in a position to face the present challenges with much more maturity than if they did not have this shared history. Their capacity to find solutions acceptable to each one of them is strengthened by the presence of the corporatist framework.

It is thus evident that the current concertation is only a new name for the corporatism that has been functioning in Mexico since 1936. Yet, it is also evident that the existence of the corporatist model facilitates the construction of the model of concertation put into place since 1987. In effect, one can only explain the absence of massive resistance to techno-logical modernization, layoffs, revision of collective contracts, and re-structuring of businesses if the existing power of the corporatist control exerted by the labor leadership is considered.

For example, in cases such as the automotive sector, the Ford Motor Company was able to force workers into accepting salary reductions and reductions in social security in order to maintain the company's compe-titive edge in the future because it had the support of the CTM leadership throughout the confrontation with the workers.[6] The same thing happened in the privatized steel sector, where layoffs affected more than

5. That is, when this interaction does not correspond to the opposition of capital and workers that guides the behavior of social actors in other national contexts, as is the case in Bolivia, Chile, and Peru.

6. This was the case in the installation of the Ford Motor Company plant of Hermosillo (Sonora), where workers signed a collective agreement that was very different from that which predominated in the other plants of that company. See Shaiken and Herzenberg 1987 and Shaiken 1990.

30 percent of the workforce between 1990 and 1991. This was also the case in mining, textiles, food and beverages, oil extraction, and so on.[7]

It can be assumed that continued union control over various aspects of the life of workers is at a crossroads. In effect, the deterioration of this control that I have described is not reflected only in the inability of organized labor to confront decreases in real wages or the losses that collective work contracts have experienced. It is also reflected in the weakening of what once was organized labor's essential strength: direct access to state decision-making bodies and its capacity to regulate life on the shop floor of factories through its control over the internal and external labor markets. Today, the increase in layoffs, the introduction of new modes of subcontracting work, the flexibilization of working conditions, the imposition of salary levels based on increased productivity, the indiscriminate use of overtime, the wearing down of workers through accidents and occupational illnesses that induce increased turnover, and finally the open intervention of the labor authorities in favor of the economic restructuring project and the defenseless position in which workers find themselves given the subordination of their organizations to this project all reveal the true meaning of economic restructuring for the labor movement in Mexico (Zapata 1990a).

Furthermore, it is important to recognize that there have not been initiatives that would favor the creation of a direct relationship between businessmen and workers through collective bargaining. This could result in a higher negotiating capacity for unions that do not tow the official line, as well as for union representatives at the shop floor level in each plant. This absence reinforces our argument that despite formal changes in the operation of corporatism, substantial change does not exist in terms of the emergence of an autonomous union actor, either at the level of the industrial establishment[8] or the national movement.

This implies that concertation among the actors involved in production in Mexico does not have the same meaning as it does in other countries in the hemisphere. Elsewhere, concertation is associated with policies to increase the productivity of the workforce by involving workers in the

---

7. For a detailed discussion of this process, see Zapata 1995b.

8. Perhaps the only examples the union movements are assuming this form may be found is in certain enterprises in the automotive sector, such as Volkswagen of Mexico or Nissan Mexicana. There, for reasons that are unique to the workers in those plants, they have maintained organizations that defend an autonomous project and which are not linked either to the official union movement or such degraded forms of unionism as the "unionism with no workers" of the maquila and the "white unionism" of Monterrey (Montiel 1991).

future of the economy or in projects of technical innovation in which the participation of the workers is crucial. In Mexico, concertation preserves its political character without entering into the aforementioned areas. For this reason, it is difficult to imagine how Mexico will be able to resolve the current backwardness of its production methods in some branches of the economy through the existing institutions responsible for concertation.

One continues to see evidence of the top-down nature of corporatism, evident, for example, in the inability of committees like those of the PECE to make decisions responsive to the challenges that businesses face as a result of the implementation of the policies of economic restructuring. The difficulties that organizations such as the Federation of Workers in Goods and Services (FESEBES, *Federación de Trabajadores de Bienes y Servicios*) or the Confederation of Revolutionary Workers (COR, *Confederación de Obreros Revolucionarios*) have had in confronting the passivity with which official unionism met government initiatives are a clear example of this (Garabito 1991). In spite of having the support, at least rhetorically, of high state authorities, FESEBES obtained legal status only after its leader became directly involved in the resolution of the 1992 Volkswagen strike, and thus won the government's gratitude.[9] More or less the same thing happened when COR had to back down in a conflict that took place in the Cuautitlán plant of the Ford Motor Company. Here, after a prolonged confrontation with the CTM for the control of the rank and file, COR had to "retreat."[10] This situation repeated what had happened during the first years of the de la Madrid presidency, when the state also tried to find a new base of support for official unionism that was not centered in the CTM but in the Revolutionary Confederation of Workers and Peasants (*Confederación Revolucionaria de Obreros y Campesino*).

9. This was just barely achieved by September 1992, after the successful intervention of its general secretary, Hernández Juárez, in the resolution of the conflict that occurred in Volkswagen of Mexico's Puebla plant in July through August of the same year.

10. Rosa Albina Garabito stated that, "Under other circumstances, the project of the COR would have easily been assimilated by the government as an alternative for the internal recomposition of the Labor Congress. To the misfortune of the COR, its de facto location within the hegemony of the CTM, with its consequent implications for the political equilibrium within the state party, the proximity of the XIV Assembly of the Institutional Revolutionary Party (PRI), and the strengthening—or at least the stalemate—of Fidel Velásquez's project for sectoral organization vis-à-vis the citizens project of Luis Colosio (embraced by Mérida) provided a fertile social ground for initiatives such as that of the FSU, for the accumulation of contradictions in the heart of the Worker's Congress and, worse still, for the opposition of José Jesús Pérez to initiatives such as the re-privatization of banks, which together resulted in the failure of this project for union restructuring" (1991: n. 12).

Since concertation remains concentrated at the highest level, it is dependent on the presence of the state actor, and the state is not disposed to abandoning this position. Although government rhetoric tends to refer to the need to have concertation be decentralized or implemented at sectoral levels and to the need to renovate the historical pact between the state and workers, it is obvious that any such efforts have not reached business or labor organizations situated outside of the direct sphere of control of the Ministry of Labor and Social Security (*Secretaría del Trabajo y Previsión Social*).

Conversely, in some cases (such as the maquiladora industry located along the border of northern Mexico), workers are totally marginalized from any type of concertation. For example, the unions controlled by the Regional Confederation of Mexican Workers (CROM, *Confederación Regional Obrera Mexicana*), in the ease of the maquiladoras of the city of Tijuana, have established a policy of accepting the conditions established by business and the government in exchange for protecting the prerogatives of the union apparatus.[11] This was accomplished in such a way that workers are not aware of the conditions under which they are hired or of the existence of a union in the business in which they work. The absolute absence of workers in union activities, as mentioned, leads to the absurd situation in which "unionism without workers" appears to be the specific model that "maquila" managers, together with CROM labor leaders, want to implement. Nonetheless, it is clear that were this model generally applied to the other sectors of production, it would imply a definitive break with the corporatist pact, and such a move does not appear to be on the minds of the political leaders in the PRI.

Another example that shares some of the above characteristics is "white unionism," which is identified with the type of labor relations found in cities such as Monterrey, as well as other industrialized cities in Mexico such as Guadalajara. Here for the past few decades the institutions for representing workers have been closely tied to the labor relations departments of the enterprises (Vellinga 1979) or to confessional (nonunion) union organizations. This is the case of companies such as Hojalata y Lámina (HYLSA), in which the extent and depth of the relationship between the union and the enterprise make it impossible to speak about the autonomous representation of workers.

---

11. See the works by C. Quintero Ramírez (1990, 1991), who has examined the labor movement in the cities of Tijuana and Matamoros, and extensively documented the practices of CROM and the CTM.

Nonetheless, this type of "white unionism" is tied to structures of co-optation that are much more refined than those of the other type. This co-optation develops through mechanisms connecting the personal lives of the workers to the life of the business, for example, prizes and promotions that are tied to perceptions of differential loyalties, collaboration, and commitment to the internal norms of these establishments. Similarly, we see the development of an identity between worker and business that does not require a definition of unionism as independent of the authority of business but rather involves the latter assuming control over the workers' organization as its own responsibility.

Finally, "bureaucratic unionism," which is centered around the Federation of Unions of State Workers (FSTSE), has not played an active role in protesting against government policies that adversely affect its members (Zapata 1987, 1990c). Although the crisis did not affect public-service employment with the same force as it did jobs in the private sector (and this was precisely the reason why state workers were able to tolerate it more easily), public-sector salary levels were reduced to the same level or worse. For this reason, there could have been negative reactions to this situation. However, social peace has ruled, as it has in the rest of the unionized sectors of the country. Furthermore, this sector was the only one to experience an increase in its membership, which went from one to two million unionized members between 1975 and 1990. This increase can be explained fundamentally by the number of teachers who belong to the National Union of Educational Workers (SNTE, *Sindicato Nacional de Trabajadores de la Educación*), which represents more than 40 percent of the affiliates of the FSTSE. It is worth pointing out that, even though the National Coordination of Educational Workers (*Coordinación Nacional de Trabajadores de la Educación*)—a dissident faction that has been co-opted into the National Executive Committee of the SNTE—encouraged a series of labor conflicts during the period 1985–91, its central dynamic was related more to internal political tensions than to the internal opposition of some sectors, such as those in the states of Mexico, Oaxaca, and Chiapas, or to economic and social demands. Cook (1996) has clearly demonstrated that the internal dynamic of the SNTE is more closely tied to its political character than to the social project of this organization.

At the same time, employment in para-state enterprises experienced an increase of almost 50 percent between 1977 and 1987, which must have had an impact on the membership in national industrial unions. Notwithstanding this earlier evolution of public-sector employment, one should think that in recent years this tendency has tended to reverse itself as a result of policies encouraging privatization of state enterprises and rationalization measures in the public sector that intensified after President Salinas took power in 1988.

Concertation and Political Reform

The previous argument, however, oversimplifies the situation somewhat. We should keep in mind that the politics of social concertation was conceived of as the form that the corporatist pact would assume in the current period, and in which official unionism has played the role of guarantor. Concertation has been successful in curbing inflation, stabilizing the prices of public services, maintaining control over the exchange rate, and creating favorable expectations for the country's economic future. The uncertainty that dominated the economy at the end of 1987, and the impact on the political legitimacy of the 1988 presidential elections and the 1994–95 crisis have been replaced by a climate of relative certainty in economic matters and by the restoration of the PRI's predominance in electoral matters, as the 1994 presidential election clearly demonstrated.

In the Latin American context, the importance of the PECE mechanism as an instrument for social harmony and its apparent success have made Mexico the only case in which economic stabilization has followed attempts to harmonize relations among the principal corporatist actors. A comparative evaluation of these pacts for the cases of Argentina, Brazil, and Mexico demonstrates that the success in the latter has been directly related to the existence of the corporatist structure that predated the pact's implementation. In the other two countries from 1986 to 1991, various pacts were put into place, all of which have failed due to the absence of a substantive agreement between the interests of the state, businesses, and unionized workers.

Furthermore, it must be emphasized that the stability of the political system in Mexico does not rest only on the signing of pacts or agreements among the members of the corporatist structure. There also exists the constant efforts by the state and the workers movement to reiterate, frequently and rhetorically, the central role of unionized workers in the political alliance that sustains the system, and the movement's weight in determining the limits within which demands can be made in Mexico. Moreover, this stability is founded on the existence of institutions in the areas of social security, health care, and education that provide compensation for losses in buying power through collective mechanisms while the salary levels of the population shrink. Economic recuperation, which occurred from 1988 through December 1994, and is apparently advancing at a fast pace in 1997, as well as the support of workers for the political system, can be best explained by the renovated role these institutions assumed in the corporatist pact, rather than by strict analysis of the operation or functioning of labor unions.

A good indicator of the state's capacity to consolidate this alliance has been the inability of the opposition to recruit support among unionized workers. They have not substantially changed workers' pattern of political alliances.[12] The PRI continues to maintain a virtual monopoly over the ideological vision of workers, more because of the absence of a visible and viable alternative than as a result of their allegiance to the official project. After 1988, when public opinion could have foreshadowed an increase in the political strength of the opposition, the precise opposite occurred in that the PRI was able to regain its position in the electoral sphere in the 1991 congressional elections and in the 1994 presidential elections. In any case, the 1997 electoral results show, as I argued in the beginning of this chapter, that the strength of the political opposition should not be underestimated. The National Action Party (PAN), Democratic Revolutionary Party (PRD), Party of Work (PT, *Partido del Trabajo*), and Green Environmentalist Party of Mexico (PVEM, *Partido Verde Ecologista de México*) together received 52 percent of the national vote, and thus are in a position to form a "front" to challenge the PRI. This is exactly what happened in August 1997, when these parties succeeded in electing the president of the Chamber of Deputies (Porfirio Muñoz Ledo) who then could respond to Zedillo's State of the Nation Address on 1 September. Furthermore, the PECE's accomplishments were presented publicly as a success on the part of workers and not as the result of state policy. In this way, the workers' confederations seemed to be effective representatives of workers' interests. The state, in order to pay lip service to this political alliance, could easily pay the price of not taking credit for its implementation.

How can we summarize the results of the policy of concertation and reinforce our argument that it has not been a new way of making

---

12. This is despite the fact that in some areas where labor has protested in the state of México (Toluca), the city of Querétaro, and the mining and steel complex of Lázaro Cárdenas (Michoacan), among other places, the labor vote favored Cuautémoc Cárdenas in the 1988 presidential elections.

corporatism function? And how can we demonstrate that the form that unionism has taken in the process of concertation is a central aspect of the political reform underway in the country? It is clear that in economic terms, the PECE has revealed its central effectiveness. Inflation decreased to an average of 30 percent per year in the period 1990–93, from an average of close to 100 percent in the previous three years (1986–89). In 1993 and 1994, the long-awaited goal of a single-digit inflation rate was achieved. After the 1995–96 interlude, things are returning to normal, and inflation will not exceed 20 percent in 1997—quite an achievement for an economy that only twenty months earlier was facing inflation levels of more than 50 percent. For its part, the exchange rate stabilized at around 3.1 new pesos to the dollar, but in December 1994, as a result of a massive devaluation, it surged to 6 pesos to the dollar and later stabilized at around 7.5 pesos to the dollar in the period 1995–97. Interest rates tended to remain high all through the period, with a temporary decrease in 1992–94. Later in 1995, they increased to unheard of levels (in some months reaching 60 to 70 percent). This sequence had a precedent: indeed, in 1988–89 the average annual interest rates were equal to 50 percent and decreased to average rates of 20 percent per year in 1991 and 15 percent in 1993. Nevertheless, interest rates applied to credit provided by the financial system were the object of strong criticisms throughout the second half of 1992 and above all in 1993, as these were blamed for the recession that the country went through during this period. The inability to stop the speculative impetus that made stock market and financial investments the most profitable—much more so than those in productive activities—was a structural characteristic of the period from 1987 to 1995.

At the same time, social concertation has also made possible an ambitious program of economic restructuring oriented toward nontraditional exports, privatization of state enterprises (banks, telephones, and so on), and creation of conditions that are attractive to foreign capital. In this context, it can be observed that Mexico's entrance into the General Agreement on Tariffs and Trade in 1986, and the signing of the North American Free Trade Agreement (NAFTA) in 1993, were not as traumatic as many had expected. Apparently, Mexican industry found some export niches and reformed its modes of organizing production to make them competitive with those found in the rest of the world. Mexican-owned companies such as Cementos Mexicanos, Ingenieros Civiles Asociados, and VITRO were capable of penetrating foreign markets. They became authentic transnational corporations whose headquarters are located in

Mexico. This was also the case of transnational corporations in petro-chemical production (CELANESE) and the auto industry (Volkswagen, Nissan, Chrysler, Ford, General Motors), which benefited from the opening of the Mexican economy to free trade not only through NAFTA but also through the Mexico-Chile Free Trade Agreement and other agreements to which Mexico is a partner.[13]

It is difficult to predict what would have happened if some of the pre-requisites for the PECE had not been present. For example, if demands for salary increases had exceeded the capacity of the state to concede them or if there had been strong pressures in export sectors to improve the remuneration to their workers, inflationary pressures would have been inevitable. Concertation could have experienced difficulties if local actors in specific areas in the political and economic structure were unable to deliver the support of the people they claimed to represent, thus placing themselves in a vulnerable situation. The same might have occurred if the pressures derived from the breakdown of political legit-imacy had continued to widen the gap between civil society and the state.

That the results were favorable to the PRI, in 1991 and 1994, was not due only to an improvement in the opposition's negotiating position but rather to an aggressive campaign developed by the official party with the help of certain populist initiatives such as the National Solidarity Program (PRONASOL, *Programa Nacional de Solidaridad*). The PRI's electoral gain more likely reflected its own capacity to reassume its patrimonial role, which to a certain extent was associated more with the improve-ment of the macroeconomic situation than with anything related to ideology. In addition, in 1994, political assassinations and in particular the outbreak of a rebellion by indigenous groups in the state of Chiapas confronted the Mexican electorate with the dilemma either of deepening the political crisis by voting for the opposition or trying to stabilize the situation by renewing its support for the PRI. Salinas correctly calculated the PRI's electoral strategy and obtained support for the official presidential candidate, Ernesto Zedillo, who was elected with an absolute majority.

Nonetheless, to the extent that official election results differed from the actual vote count, as was certified by the representatives of political opposition parties that witnessed the counting, it is impossible to

13. The value of trade under the Mexico-Chile Free Trade Agreement reached US$750 million in 1995.

generate confidence and legitimacy in the citizenry with respect to the form in which power is generated. For this reason, even though concertation can provide economic stability, assure business expectations, and permit the electoral recuperation of the PRI, a great effort is still needed to realize the same objectives in the political sphere.

The presence of internal conflicts in the political apparatus of the PRI does not favor such an effort. In these internal conflicts, the renovators, supported by the president of the Republic and the party apparatus, confront the so-called dinosaurs, party members intent on maintaining the old order who are identified above all with the leadership of "official unionism."[14] These confrontations (which take place out of the public limelight) reveal the tensions that were caused by the strategy of political reform. It appears that this reform will not be as easy as the governing group, headed by the president, had believed. Only if the renovators are able to reach a durable pact on this reform with the opposition, especially with the PAN, and thus are able to find a consensus that would isolate both the "dinosaurs" and those who do not agree with political reform in the opposition's ranks, may there be a way out of the present dilemmas in which only a part of the modernization strategy (the one referring to the economy) has had the possibility of achieving concrete results.

In light of the above, the electoral system seems to be more important in the operation of corporatism and its reform than could have been imagined in abstract terms. Corporatism represents a form of citizenship development in which the political system is subordinated to the link between the state and the PRI.[15] In spite of the control that corporatism exercises over unions, the fundamental fact remains that there are workers and organizations at the base of this structure. If contradictions appear in the control that corporatist structures exercise over these organizations and their control over individuals, including their behavior in elections, it is possible that corporatism could begin to experience serious tensions threatening its survival. These tensions would translate

14. These conflicts have been expressed in the inability of the labor machine to elect deputies to Parliament in the same proportions as in the past. They are also expressed in the tensions between the national executive of the CTM and its state federations, which are closer to local and regional politics and force the national leaders to impose their views on them. For example, the candidates belonging to the CTM in the state of Tamaulipas were not elected in August 1991. In sum, the weight of "sectors" in the PRI has shrunk in favor of individuals who are aligned directly with the presidential project.

15. The best history of the PRI is by Garrido (1982). A recent analysis of the way in which the PRI is reacting to political pressures is by Díaz Amador (1996).

into a questioning of the policy of social concertation, because until now it has been limited to agreements among elites located within the corporatist structure. The corporatist structure's ties with the rank-and-file workers and peasants, as well as with bureaucrats, the middle classes, and businesspersons, are not as firm or institutionalized as the leadership of the corporatist apparatus would like, at least if we understand the electoral behavior of these groups to be a reflection of their position on corporatism. But at the same time, we must remember that in the absence of a concrete alternative to the control that the PRI exerts over the corporatist structure, this party can continue, by default, to maintain power in Mexico.

Conclusion

Despite Mexico's long experience in implementing strategies of social concertation, it still is not possible to draw unqualified conclusions. On the contrary, care must be taken not to interpret the current success of concertation as a projection of its continued viability. At the same time, we should be wary of excessive pessimism and attribute proper importance to the fact that the Mexican experience has by far been the most successful in the Latin American context, with the obvious exception of Chile where the military dictatorship headed by General Pinochet undertook the transition between models of development.

The labor movement has benefited from various tradeoffs, such as maintaining the social security apparatus, public education, and the policy of providing social services. Entrepreneurs have been sufficiently flexible so as to refrain from asking for price increases above those approved by government authorities. Workers have also benefited from a series of advantages given to the export sector. We can thus affirm that the operation of the pact has made it possible to maintain the essence of corporatism.

Where dark clouds appear, as we have just pointed out, is in the electoral arena. Internal tensions within the PRI apparatus, the result of the price the workers' sector must pay if these reforms are to be completed and exacerbated by the results of the July 1997 parliamentary elections, neutralize presidential initiatives to reform the political system. Given that the maintenance of the party apparatus represents a central aspect of the operation of corporatism as a whole, it would be difficult to expect abrupt changes. What is more likely is that there will be various initiatives intended to modify the party apparatus incrementally. To the extent that economic stability can be maintained for a sufficiently long period, it should be possible to patch together the renovation of the political system and in this way modernize it—if this is indeed the real aim of those who exercise political authority in Mexico.

The Mexican experience shows that when corporatism has been in force for a sufficiently long period, and when it has demonstrated its utility to the sectors that comprise it, the corporatist structures can be used in times of crisis to achieve objectives that are different from those for which it was originally created. Therefore, a prerequisite for the successful operation of social concertation in the current situation is the existence of a corporatist structure in which a long process of learning has facilitated the creation of mutual understanding among the political actors who constitute the system of domination in Mexico.

Nonetheless, all of these tensions and contradictions pose important questions: To what extent is this structure representative of what the citizens actually want? Given that corporatism appears to be attempting to systematically distort electoral results, how can democracy be created in this political context?

8

Interest Representation and the Party System in Mexico

Jean-François Prud'homme

Since the 1980s, Mexico, like other Latin American countries, has faced two parallel processes of transformation: first, the inward-oriented development model with strong state participation that had generated stable economic expansion was modified by structural adjustment and liberalization policies; and second, the system of interest representation that had been consolidated by the postrevolutionary regime experienced growing pressure to install pluralist channels of participation. These transformations may be summarized in two words: markets and democracy. As has been extensively discussed in the literature on transitions to democracy and the implementation of economic-adjustment policies, the coincidence of these two processes makes it difficult to establish a causal relationship between them.[1] The adoption of policies directed toward liberalizing market relations does not necessarily help the democratization of political relations. Nor does the existence of democratic political

Translated by Siobhan Harty and Philip Oxhorn.

1. An analysis of the Mexican case from that perspective can be found in Haggard and Kaufman 1995: chap. 8; Cook, Middlebrook, and Molinar 1994; and Centeno 1994.

processes constitute a guarantee for the successful implementation of market-oriented economic policies. The more successful Latin American experiences with adjustment policies appear to indicate that authoritarian contexts are more propitious for the implementation of such economic reforms.[2] In other words, as noted in the introduction to this book, the absence of "democratic obstacles" facilitates that process of implementation.

Even if this is the case, I am not convinced that the best way to conceptualize the relationship between the two processes is by defining it in terms of the conditions required for the successful realization of one project or the other. At least this is not the objective I am pursuing here. Rather, I explore the middle ground between *society-centered* and *state-centered* theories that have traditionally been used to address this problem. I aim to understand the complex set of interactions among social, political, and state actors set forth by the concomitant processes of reform in the economic and political realms. The Mexican experience shows that changes in one realm can sometimes produce somewhat contradictory effects in the other. For example, although it is certain that the application of economic liberalization measures contributes to the weakening of certain forms of political control, in many instances the conditions for the successful implementation of such measures imply an increase in political control, although through other means. This has been the fate of Mexican corporatist control over labor, whose traditional mechanisms have been weakened at the same time that it has been strengthened through the addition of apparently more modern ones, such as the repeated *pactos* reached by the state, unions, and business interests since the end of 1987.[3] Moreover, the political impact of adjustment policies tends to vary according to the nature of the activities in which the relevant actors are engaged. In particular, the impact of the same adjustment policy may lead some actors into actions promoting the democratization of the regime and others into actions directed toward supporting more exclusionary forms of political participation.

Rather than approaching the relationship between adjustment policies and democratization in a global way, or by viewing one as the precondition for the successful implantation of the other, I use an approach that stresses the existence of different realms, actors, resources, and strategies. In this approach, complex interactions are established between the

2. From the perspective of "governability," Ducatenzeiler and Oxhorn (1994) have argued convincingly to that effect. In the same way, Haggard and Kaufman (1995: 267–306) developed a more sophisticated argument for the case of what they call "dominant-party systems."

3. See Zapata, Chapter 7 of this volume, and Bizberg 1994.

economic and the political realms: both function as autonomous paths that provide actors with the possibility of using, in a somewhat interchangeable manner, resources associated with one path or the other.

In terms of strategies pursued by different actors, the effects of transformations in a given realm may acquire a different meaning in another arena depending on the strategic pattern of confrontation prevailing in the specific area. Resources can be drawn from one realm and used in a different fashion in another. For example, the successes of economic policies can be used by an authoritarian government to put a break on the process of political liberalization, while those same successes can be used by a center-right opposition party in order to demand a broader political opening. In the same vein, the failure of adjustment policies can be used by "hard-liners" within an authoritarian government to prevent any political liberalization, just as such a failure can be used by center-left forces to demand a greater political opening.[4] The possibilities of using resources positively depend on the pattern of strategic confrontation prevailing in the respective realms of action. There is no necessary correspondence in patterns of strategic confrontation between the political and economic realms.[5]

In a situation of political and economic stability, such as the one that prevailed in Mexico from 1946 until the beginning of the 1980s, the development model and the system of interest representation are self-reinforcing in a positive manner. In this scenario, an efficient and durable model of cooperation is consolidated between principal actors in both realms.[6] In and of itself, cooperation is compatible with any type of political system or development model. What changes, depending on the type of political system and development model, are the norms and procedures necessary for the functioning of cooperation. In moments of accelerated change within the development model and in the system of

---

4. Although the argument here is hypothetical, it stems from the Mexican political context. Center-right political forces may be read as the National Action Party (PAN, *Partido Acción Nacional*) and center-left as the Democratic Revolutionary Party (PRD, *Partido de la Revolución Democrática*), which are the two main opposition parties in Mexico.

5. I recognize that I do not take into account here the structural determinants of the economy, as emphasized by some authors, for example, Haggard and Kaufman (1995: 6). However, according to my argument, economic performance and the distribution of wealth can be interpreted in terms of fluctuations in the resources available to the political or economic actors.

6. I understand "model of cooperation" as the existence of formal and informal norms and procedures for conflict resolution that are known and accepted by the actors. See North 1990: chap. 2.

interest representation, the interaction between them produces debilitating effects that affect the level of cooperation.

In this chapter, I am interested in addressing one restricted aspect of the problem of cooperation in the context of economic restructuring and pressures for democratization in the Mexican political system. This aspect refers to the relations among the three principal political parties, the Institutional Revolutionary Party (PRI, *Partido Revolucionario Institucional*), PAN, and the PRD, and the negotiation of rules of the game acceptable to all of them. I begin by assuming that the difficult consolidation of a model of sustained cooperation in the economic realm has not been accompanied by a model of efficient and durable cooperation among the principal political actors. Whereas the pattern of consultation in economic policy making has been maintained since 1986, despite the financial collapse of December 1994, the road to cooperation in the establishment of rules for electoral competition has been more winding.[7]

The first part of this chapter demonstrates how the transformations in the Mexican development model are reflected in the party system and electoral competition. This task may appear enormous, but I think that it is possible to illustrate, in a broad way, some of the statements made above about the relationship between economics and politics. The second part explores in more detail the problem of cooperation among the principal political parties in negotiating rules of the game that are acceptable to all, with emphasis on the strategic dimension of their relationship.

The Development Model and Interest Representation

The model of cooperation that had guaranteed a stable form of development went through an accelerated process of transformation at the beginning of the 1980s, which resulted in conflicts over the definition of a new system of interest representation.

7. From December 1986 to October 1996, seventeen economic pacts establishing the main objectives of macroeconomic policy have been signed by the government, business associations, and trade unions, with the last one being the so-called Alliance for Growth (October 1996). See *Reforma*, October 1996: 17. It must noted that in spite of the financial disaster of December 1994, no real economic policy alternative has been put forward by any significant political or economic actor. During the same period, five electoral reforms were negotiated.

After the revolution, the lengthy process of consolidation of the new regime slowly led to the constitution of specific forms of economic and political organization in Mexico. The flexible nature of this process permitted adjustments at various junctures, while the existence of a broad consensus with regard to the regime's explicit and implicit rules of operation guaranteed its permanence. From an analytic perspective, we can speak of the existence of a development model and of a system of interest representation that is specific to postrevolutionary Mexico.[8] The models have complemented and reinforced each other: the proper functioning of the development model has permitted the production of those resources necessary for the maintenance of the system of interest representation, while the system's political stability has acted as a guarantee for economic growth.[9] The relationship between the political and the economic, on the one hand, and the political and the social, on the other, has maintained a level of expectation sufficient to ensure the reproduction of the rules of the system. Thus, an efficient and durable model of cooperation has been in place and has guided the actions of political and economic actors.[10]

In the economic sphere, once postrevolutionary state building was consolidated during the 1930s and World War II, the development model produced positive macroeconomic results and set the stage for a structural transformation of great magnitude. In the three decades following World War II, the economy grew at a rate that on average surpassed population growth by approximately three percentage points per year and, beginning in the mid-1950s, in a context of minor economic fluctuations, exchange-rate stability, and low inflation rates.[11]

8. Most analysts define the "classic period" as lasting from the beginning of the Aleman administration (1946) to the end of Díaz Ordaz administration (1968).

9. From a different perspective, Heredia (1991, 1994) has summarized well the workings of the interactions between the development model and the system of interest representation.

10. The use of the concept of "cooperation" may appear difficult to accept for those who believe that the longevity of the postrevolutionary regime was based only on coercion and co-optation. It is undeniable that coercion played a crucial role from time to time in the maintenance of the regime. However, during the regime's "golden years" the level of consensus surrounding the rules of the game was high and well internalized by vast sectors of Mexican society. Available studies on the Mexican political culture have shown how different sectors of the society used those rules to obtain goods from the political system. In fact, co-optation is not just a result of government action. In order to function, it has to be based on a certain level of acceptance of the rules of the game on the part of the "co-opted."

11. For a discussion of the development model, see the classic works of Hansen (1971) and Solis (1975).

In this development model, economic growth and macroeconomic stability reinforced each other in such a way that growth provided the increase in fiscal revenues required for increased public spending and generated the foreign exchange that this very growth demanded without having to devalue the peso. This meant that inflation could be kept under control. Together these factors created a climate in which opportunities for productive investment multiplied, leaving little room for financial speculation using potentially investible resources. This development model was complemented by a particular system of interest representation and provided the latter with the material base it needed to sustain itself over time. In turn, this system produced the "social peace" required for a climate of certainty that could maintain the investment process necessary for economic growth. The relationship of mutual consolidation between the development model and the system of interest representation was obviously the result of a process of institution building in a broad sense: that is, an incrementally produced agreement between the main political and economic actors on accepted norms and ways of presiding over political transactions.

The central axis of this virtuous circle running through growth to stability was the import-substituting industrialization (ISI) process, which over time paradoxically became the principal obstacle to the sustained expansion of the economy. Protectionism was the touchstone that kept the development model functioning. Although protectionism was ostensibly part of a development strategy that proceeded from the substitution of simple to complex goods, historically protection was instituted for those who demanded it, simply in exchange for demonstrating that they could produce an industrial good. This fact produced at least two problems that eventually led to the exhaustion of the model: (1) protection became a precondition not for only the appearance but also for the continued existence of protected industries; and (2) the agriculture-industry relationship did not succeed in maintaining the expansion of the former sector once public investment in agriculture lost its momentum. Two factors finally exposed the problems associated with this model of development and led the country into the debt crisis: first, the exhaustion of the dynamic momentum of ISI; and second, the consequences of the second oil shock and the changes in the international financial markets that led to the international crisis in the early 1980s. Adjustment to these new international conditions would mark, in a decisive way, the Mexican economy for the rest of the decade.[12]

12. For a detailed account of the causes of the crises, see Lustig 1992: chap. 1 and Kaufman 1988: chap. 2.

In the political sphere, the system of interest representation produced a relative stability that still was not without its periods of tension. These tensions were resolved by a mixture of selective repression and a process of inclusion and co-optation. The authoritarian nature of the system was undeniable, although it should be qualified as a moderate and pragmatic authoritarianism with a tendency to include certain social actors. Throughout its history, the regime developed a solid institutional network that implied the existence of formal and informal rules adapted to different political circumstances (Cornelius, Gentleman, and Smith 1989: 8).

In the postrevolutionary period, authoritarianism operated on the basis of an intense political exchange. The regime's much celebrated capacity for inclusion was based on a system of limited and hierarchical political exchange that took place in the highly regulated and codified spaces of corporatism, clientelism, and unequal party competition. The relations between individuals or groups and the political system were based on a complex set of mediations, some of which were more institutionalized than others. Each of the political spaces mentioned above had its specific formal and informal rules that were known and used by the participating actors.[13]

The regime's tutelary function, concentrated in the executive,[14] was expressed in the government's ability to exert an influence over (1) the recognition of those actors who could participate in the formal political system; and (2) the process of opening and closing that very system. The sphere of corporatist representation, principally articulated around the hegemonic party, was the pivot of the system of interest representation. There was also a second subordinated and truncated space for citizen representation that defined itself in relation to the hegemonic party system and semicompetitive elections. Within the historical particularities of Mexican authoritarianism, the ability of this space to sustain a democratic fiction stands out.[15] A system of cooperation among the principal

13. Earlier, I addressed the problem from a collective action perspective (Prud'homme 1994). Even though there have been many studies of corporatism in Mexico, very few of them have focused on an analysis of the rules of the game and the ways in which distinct actors used them to promote their interests. For an approximation of such an approach, see Durand, Prud'homme, and Márquez 1990. The same is true of the special type of party representation and unequal competition in Mexico. Many good analyses of clientelism have also used the same perspective, including the classic studies by Cornelius (1975) and Lomnitz (1977).

14. For a recent and relevant discussion on the role of the institution of the presidency in Mexico, see Casar 1993 and Weldon 1997.

15. Guerra (1985) emphasizes the paradoxical but functional relationship between democratic constitutional norms and authoritarian ways of exercising power during the Porfirio

political actors, regulated by well-defined codes and rules that were understood by all participants, was created by invoking this fiction. This system was the foundation for the period of *priista* peace.

In a manner similar to what happened with the development model, the same factors that maintained the stability of the system of interest representation were becoming obstacles for its continuance. Corporatism operated on the principle that only a limited number of actors would be incorporated into the formal system. Insofar as the social structure and the nature of political demands were diversifying, the rigidity of the system of interest representation impeded the incorporation of new actors and the processing of their demands. Moreover, it was not in the interests of the actors already represented in the system to increase the overall number of participants.[16] In order to maintain its tutelary function, the regime found itself faced with an obligation to manage increasingly complex and fragile cooperation models situated somewhere between state control and a blooming expression of pluralist interests. The *sexenio* of President de la Madrid may be characterized as a period of transformation and partial reintegration of the cooperation model. In the economic sphere, the *Pacto de Solidaridad Económica* was signed after a five-year period of negotiations. In the political sphere, the search for new rules of cooperation between political forces remained on the negotiating agenda.[17] The evident separation between the representation of economic and political interests, as if these were two completely distinct spheres, was a change that was attracting increasing attention. As long as the corporatist arena prevailed in the system of interest representation and part of it was also formally integrated into the hegemonic party, there was a close connection between economic and political representation. The signing of the *Pacto de Solidaridad Económica* in late 1987, as a separate sphere of bargaining between the main economic actors, made the weakness of the political parties in the process of aggregating economic interests more evident. The party system that had begun to consolidate itself was having a limited (if not nonexistent) impact on the intermediation of the interests of productive actors.

Díaz regime at the end of the nineteenth century in Mexico. Most of his conclusions would apply to the postrevolutionary regime.

16. This was one of the arguments for introducing the 1977 political reform that, among other things, allowed for the existence of a more diversified party system (see Middlebrook 1986).

17. For an overall balance of de la Madrid's *sexenio*, see Pérez and León 1987 and Bazdrech et al. 1992.

What was the specific impact of the transformations in the development model on the party system? As previously mentioned, it is important to emphasize the contradictory nature of the outcomes in the area of political representation that can result from measures of economic adjustment. The orientation of these outcomes depends on both the strategies pursued by different political and economic actors and the sphere from which these actors seek benefits.

The *sexenio* of President de la Madrid was fundamentally a period of rupture and attempts to reconstitute cooperative relations. It should be reevaluated in these terms. In the economic sphere, even though the objectives appeared clear, the strategies for implementing adjustment policies were based on a system of trial and error. In this sense, one can speak of "erratic" economic policies. As Jaime Ros has noted in various studies, three periods (1982–85, 1986–87, and 1987–88) were characterized by a similar number of distinct adjustment strategies.[18]

In the productive sphere, these periods were seen as separate moments in which different actors won or lost. But read from the political sphere, and more specifically from the party system, a unity between these separate periods is apparent that can help to explain changes in the relations among actors. There are at least four ways through which changes in the development model affected shifts in partisan rivalry.

First, at the beginning of the 1980s, the geography of electoral dissidence and opposition was principally northern and *panista*. This was the product of an encounter between a discontented private sector that exerted pressure on the government by threatening to support the center-right opposition and a renovated political party that had a more aggressive posture in canvassing for votes. On the one hand, we have an economic actor who, in order to have some influence on the design of the new economic model, ventured into the political arena. On the other hand, we have a political actor, the PAN, that wanted to take advantage of the effects of the economic crisis and errors in the adjustment policies in order to strengthen its political position and change the rules of the game in the party system. This coincidence of interests did not last a long time but was important in that it promoted the PAN's presence and the competitiveness of the party system in the northern region.[19]

18. See Ros 1992. For a review of the adjustment policies and their effects on the economy, see Casar 1993: chap. 1.
19. For studies on the relations between business interests and the PAN in northern Mexico, see Guadarrama 1987 and Mizrahi 1994.

Second, the official unions, which were most affected by the adjustment policies, adopted a strategy that had a double impact on the party system. In a positive way, they actively supported the adoption of a posture of political closure and steadfastness in the face of increasing competitiveness in the party system. After all, they had always been opposed to opening the system of interest representation in the electoral sphere, opposing the concept of "political democracy" in favor of one of "economic democracy." Moreover, in addition to their having been badly affected by the economic policies, there did not appear to be any way for official unions to use the party system in order to put pressure on the government. The increase in partisan competitiveness meant a still larger loss of political power for the unions. In a negative way, the inability of the official unions to ensure the functioning of the rules of exchange upon which corporatism rested made a populist option, such as the one supported by the coalition backing Cárdenas, appear all the more attractive. In a situation of economic crisis and steadily declining real wages, it was almost impossible for them to provide their rank and file with benefits.

In fact, it has been noted that in the 1988 election some unions, like the oil workers union (*Sindicato de los Trabajadores Petroleros de la República Méxicana*), backed the dissident presidential candidacy of Cuauhtémoc Cárdenas at the regional level. However, this should be seen more as an attempt at bargaining within the system that went beyond the usually accepted limits than as a sign of consistent support for the "*cardenista*" movement. As we know, the intent of pushing the game beyond the internal limits of the system ended with the well-publicized crackdown on the leadership of the oil workers union at the very beginning of the Salinas administration. In general, during the de la Madrid *sexenio* unions stood and acted against the opening of the party system.[20]

Third, as a result of the state's reduced capacity to deliver social assistance, there was an increase in the autonomy of certain social organizations. These ended up supporting the *cardenista* coalition in 1988.[21]

Fourth, disagreements with regard to the development model contributed to splitting the Democratic Current from the heart of the PRI.[22]

20. For more on union behavior during that era, see Bizberg 1990.

21. A good case study of the urban popular movement can be found in Farrera 1994. Tamayo (1992) has provided a brief history of how during the crisis of the 1980s many popular movements turned to representative democracy and party politics.

22. On the split within the PRI that led to Cárdenas's presidential candidacy, see Garrido 1993 and Bruhn 1997.

The last three developments are important for explaining the emergence of an electoral option that initially retrieved a popular and distributive economic project that has been labeled populist. Through the mere fact of competing electorally, this option had a strong impact on the cooperative relations of the party system.[23]

From the perspective of this chapter, the government of President de la Madrid represented a rupture in the existing model of cooperation. The hitherto self-reinforcing nature of the relationship between the development model and the system of interest representation started to produce negative effects, while the already-established cooperative relations in both spheres experienced strong tensions. Even though a model of cooperation between productive agents was successfully consolidated at the end of the *sexenio*, this was not the case for the party system.[24]

To a certain extent, one can speak of a process of "centrifugal diversification" of economic and political actors. This process implies the multiplication of autonomous actors and possible cooperative options. Those actors not only express different interests but also favor different ways of processing their differences. Resources available from the political and economic spheres are used in an interchangeable way by various actors in order to enhance their negotiation positions in each area and propose models of cooperation that are advantageous to them. In the party system, this centrifugal diversification did not translate into democratization, given that one of the actors, the PRI, has continued to control the rules of the game. Neither did it imply the creation of a model of cooperation, given that some of the actors could use a dominant strategy of confrontation. In fact, this is what happened throughout the Salinas administration within the Mexican party system: The existing basis for cooperation was not sufficient to guarantee the institutional processing of electoral contestation. At any moment, political parties could use strategies of confrontation with a reasonable expectation of winning at least something.

23. Other factors have obviously contributed to the increase in competitiveness in the party system, including the dynamism of the political reforms, the diversification of the social structure, and changes in the political culture, but they are beyond the scope of the present study (see Crespo 1992).

24. I obviously make a distinction between the consolidation of a new model of development and the performance of that model. The existence of a general agreement on rules and procedures among government, business, and trade unions is not an automatic guarantee of successful economic performance, as shown by the December 1994 financial collapse. However, contrary to what happened during the first half of the 1980s, the majority of organized economic actors still agree on the content of economic policy and the way it is formulated (tripartite negotiations). Moreover, there is no serious competing economic policy alternative.

As Mainwaring and Scully have argued, hegemonic party systems in transition mix processes of deinstitutionalization and reinstitutionalization: "In some respects, they are quite institutionalized but are becoming less so as electoral competition creates greater flux. In other respects, however, they are not very institutionalized but are becoming more so as political actors start to perceive parties and elections as legitimate" (Mainwaring and Scully 1995: 21).

Changes in a Hegemonic Party System

Traditionally, elections were of secondary importance in the Mexican system of interest representation, more a ritual than anything else. However, electoral legislation was organized in such a way as to permit the display of the tutelary function of the regime all the way through to the executive level. With the electoral law of 1946, the *Secretaría de Gobernación* assumed control of (1) granting legal political organizations the right to register in order to run for election, and (2) organizing and supervising the electoral process.[25]

In its classic version, the Mexican party system could be defined as the prototype of a hegemonic-pragmatic party system. Sartori defined this as a party system dominated by one party that does not allow real competition for power. Other existing political parties do not have any real possibility of forming a government. The obstacles to competition on an equal footing have more to do with the workings of the political system than with formal prohibitions (Sartori 1976: 230); the party in power exercises hegemony through noncompetitive elections.[26] The organization and supervision of elections are a part of the control mechanisms on which the regime's authoritarianism is based.

The political reform at the end of 1977 marked the beginning of a period of intensified change in the Mexican party system and in the electoral life of the country (Middlebrook 1986: 124–31). Gradually, the electoral sphere began to assume a fundamental place in the system of interest representation along the axis of political conflict.[27] How was this change reflected in the hegemonic party system?

25. See Molinar 1991.
26. See Hermet, Rouquié, and Linz 1982.
27. It must be noted that the political reform of 1977 created a party system in which opposition parties were highly dependent on the state, given that all of their revenues came

First, it is important to note that the unequal nature of competition in the system does not prevent secondary actors from gaining political ground. As unequal as it may be, political exchange is possible. In fact, this is what allowed the opposition parties to gain ground in the electoral arena throughout the 1980s and 1990s. But at the same time, this also explains the dismantling of the antisystem coalition of opposition parties in Mexico after the 1988 elections and the creation of a new configuration of relations within the party system. Behind the apparent convergence of forces against the regime and electoral fraud, there existed a constellation of distinct interests in which the survival and relative position of some organizations vis-à-vis other political forces were at stake.[28] From this perspective, the strategy of the opposition parties may be explained by their respective objective positions. The existence of a certain level of competition in the system permitted the PRI to reorganize its cooperative relations so that its "partners" achieved some successes, but not so much as to directly threaten the hegemony of the PRI. Nevertheless, the management of these cooperative relations became increasingly complicated and precarious. Concrete gains had to be provided for the junior partners, as the PRI's relationship with the PAN throughout the Salinas administration illustrates.[29]

Second, parties were able to monitor their actions. In other words, they could employ strategies designed to increase their political capital: some strategies were better than others, and some strategies were more compatible with each party's organizational characteristics. It was possible to choose between dominant strategies of cooperation and confrontation. However, the points of access to power in the hegemonic party system are difficult for opposition parties to reach. In the Mexican case,

---

from state subsidies—with the exception of PAN, which accepted those subsidies only in 1987—and their access to political representation was mainly through proportional representation. It is important to highlight this in order to understand how the nature of the party system limits the strategic behavior of opposition political parties. Under these circumstances, the costs of opting out are very high for an opposition political organization. To borrow an expression coined by Cavarozzi, Mexican political parties could be labeled "state-centric political parties" (see Cavarozzi 1994).

28. For an account of the transactions between the main political parties during the Salinas administration, see Prud'homme 1996.

29. Those gains were registered mostly at the state level when the PAN gained two governorships in the states of Baja California (1989) and Chihuahua (1992). In Guanajuato (1991), after an allegedly fraudulent election, a negotiation with the government resulted in the designation of a provisional *panista* governor. However, the PAN did not gain more ground in the 1991 national legislative elections.

the principal opposition parties tended to adapt their strategies for cooperation and confrontation at the national level to their organizational structure and geographical penetration. The "gradualism" of the PAN corresponded to its consolidated presence in certain regions of the country and to its high level of internal institutionalization. Paradoxically, the PAN's strong presence in certain regions prevented it from winning elections at the national level. The apparent "maximalism" of the PRD had much to do with its character as a charismatic party: despite its less-consolidated regional presence, it had greater possibilities of winning a national presidential election than did the PAN.[30]

Finally, change in the relationship between political parties took place incrementally within existing institutions and was the product of partial agreements between political parties. These agreements continue to be part of the institutional political game, and they respond to the dynamics of the party system. Their negotiation, therefore, must initially include all political actors who participate within the formal political system. In this case, legislative reform prevails over pact making as an instrument for the creation of agreements among actors. In recent years, the reform of the electoral legislation in Mexico has become an integral part of the process of measuring the relative strength of political parties. In fact, it is almost as important as the elections themselves. We need to regard both processes as two moments in the same cycle.

The dynamic of change in the hegemonic party system produced several effects that made it difficult to obtain general agreements with regard to the rules of the game. The first effect can be understood as one of the incompatibility between cooperation and the maximization of gains among actors.[31] In effect, the political parties did not yet appear disposed to distinguish between the acceptance of procedures and the acceptance of the results of those procedures. They were not willing to give up immediate benefits for future rewards, which translated into

30. The gradualist strategy PAN used was based mainly on limited cooperation, as was expressed by its endorsement of the three electoral reforms of the Salinas *sexenio*. However, its endorsement was conditioned upon the enforcement of the reforms and, obviously, the possibility for making real gains. It is possible to label PAN's strategy (documented in Córdova 1992 and Reynoso 1993) as one of limited cooperation guaranteed by a perpetual threat of noncooperation. On the other hand, PRD's strategy was clearly a strategy of noncooperation, as was made evident by its rejection of the first two electoral reforms of the Salinas *sexenio*. This strategy slowly evolved toward limited cooperation at the end of the period, as shown by its divided approval of the third electoral reform in May 1994 (see Prud'homme 1996).

31. This is a classic problem in the literature on transitions to democracy that is addressed well in Przeworski 1991: chap. 1.

confusion between strategies for negotiating the rules of the game and strategies for the accumulation of political power.

In this situation, the party system generated incentives that allowed the principal political formations to assume that they could win as much, if not more, without a consensual agreement with regard to the rules of the game than with such an agreement. In this way, the impossibility of arriving at a satisfactory agreement for all concerned parties became an element, among others, in the strategies used to attain power. Furthermore, for various reasons, the parties developed an interest in processing conflicts outside the agreed on rules. The resolution of state electoral conflicts in Mexico during the last *sexenios* illustrates this well. In San Luis Potosí, Guanajuato, Michocán, and Yucatán, electoral conflicts were resolved through negotiations between political forces in which each party's capacity for mobilization weighed very heavily in the denouement.[32]

The rules of the game that some actors agreed on resembled ephemeral guarantees that confirmed the state of political relations between those who subscribed to them more than they did norms that could maintain their efficient and formal institutionalization. In effect, they reflected fragile cooperative relations that were continually threatened by the prospects of noncooperation. Since 1986, each legislature has produced a substantial electoral reform, and the last legislature (1991–94) has succeeded in producing two. Already, after the announcement of the *Pacto de Los Pinos* (January 1995), it is known that one of the main items on this legislature's agenda will be approval of a "definitive" electoral reform. As may be seen, a cycle of reform-elections-reform has emerged that operates by trial and error and produces a recurring pattern of interaction between political forces in which cooperation alternates with confrontation over the rules of electoral competition. In fact, to accurately comprehend the power relations between political parties in Mexico, it is important to consider this cycle in its entirety.[33] By examining the amendments made to legislation since 1988, it is possible to identify the immediate interests of the parties which approved them.

32. This process came to be known ironically as "*concertacesión*," an expression invented from the fusion of the words *concertación*, which means "concerted agreement," and *cesión*, which can be translated as "surrender." It refers to a situation in which doubtfully elected PRI officials had to resign from their positions after a negotiation between the government and the affected and mobilized opposition party.

33. In 1986, at the end of President de la Madrid's administration, there was a constitutional reform in electoral matters that modified the assignation of seats in the Congress. As part of the same discussion, in February 1987, the *Código Federal Electoral* was also reformed. Those were the rules that governed the 1988 presidential election. In 1990, under the Salinas administration,

The pattern of change within the hegemonic party system that prevailed throughout most of the Salinas administration permitted relations of cooperation among the PRI, PAN, and smaller "satellite" parties. The PRD excluded itself from the results of the negotiation, preferring a strategy of confrontation. Obviously, even though its main demands were not fully incorporated into the reforms, it benefited from them as a participant in the party system. The situation evolved a few months before the 1994 presidential election toward what can be called relations of limited cooperation.

The difficulty in reaching an agreement regarding the rules of the game reflected a larger problem related to the creation of a political class in which the members of the various political clusters would recognize that beyond their obvious divergences of opinion, they shared common interests regarding procedures and the manner for engaging in political activity.[34] For the time being, the dynamic of change in the hegemonic party system, with all the particularities highlighted above, has not provided internal incentives to overcome the many differences.

This internal logic of party-system change provided only for the maintenance of the PRI's dominance and a slowing of the PAN advance. The relationship of cooperation between these two political forces was possible as long as the PRD was excluded from the agreements. The PAN

---

the electoral law was again substantially modified after a long negotiation with opposition parties. Known as the *Código Federal de Instituciones y Procesos Electorales* (COFIPE), the new law governed the 1991 national legislative election. In September 1993, a substantial modification of COFIPE was approved by all political parties with the exception of PRD, and these new norms were supposed to govern the 1994 presidential election. However, the Chiapas rebellion of January 1994 forced another major electoral reform that was approved by all political parties in May 1994. After the election of President Zedillo, one of the main items on the legislative agenda was the enactment of a "definitive" electoral reform. After 18 months of negotiations, parties approved constitutional amendments leading to substantial modifications of COFIPE. In November 1996, a new electoral law was approved with the sole majority vote of the PRI. However, most of its content was the result of a consensus agreement among the main political parties.

34. Traditionally in Mexico, the concept of a political class has referred to prominent members of the PRI. As long as political exchange took place mainly within the PRI, it was an appropriate use of the concept. All those *priista* politicians had a good knowledge of the formally and informally accepted rules of the game, shared common interests, abided by the rules of political recruitment, and were ready to face the sanctions associated with breaking those rules. The diversification of political options has created a problem in terms of the integration of a new political class. From this perspective, the consolidation of a model of cooperation within the party system must rest on the existence of accepted rules of the game, the consciousness of an overall common interest, and an accepted process of political recruitment. In other words, this model must rest on a new professionalization of politicians.

was using the possibility of an alliance with the PRD to strengthen its bargaining position, and the PRI was using the possibility of reaching legislative agreements with the PAN and other political parties to block the formation of an antisystem coalition and to isolate the PRD even more. And the PRD, as a "free-rider," was taking advantage of the limited progress in the electoral legislation without discarding the possibility of mobilizing against the inequity of the electoral system, which was where its real force rested. Given these circumstances, the party system was not offering incentives for reaching an inclusive agreement on the rules of the game. As I argued above, the dynamics of the party system during the Salinas administration promoted incentives encouraging political parties not to reach a consensual agreement on the rules of the game.

The only possibility for change from within the party system seemed to rest with the political collapse of one of the forces that was polarizing the negotiations, the PRI or PRD. This possibility seemed unlikely in the pre–1994 elections context. Only events external to the party system, such as the uprising in Chiapas, could push the parties toward a common ground in order to defend what they had in common: an interest in engaging in politics through institutional means. In fact, at the end of March 1994, this situation (external to the party system) led to interparty negotiations that produced an agreement on a new electoral reform supported by most deputies of the three major political forces in the country. The nature of the negotiations, which came to be known as the Barcelona Negotiations (*negociaciones de Barcelona*), implied a change per se in the party system. The small satellite parties, a folkloric artifact of the traditional Mexican party system, were virtually excluded from the negotiations and, with the exception of the newly created *Partido del Trabajo*, were wiped off the political map after the August elections. From the beginning of these last negotiations, it was clear that the installation of a model of limited cooperation in the party system meant the consolidation of a three-party system. Even so, the PRD's presidential candidate and an important group of deputies from its parliamentary wing declared themselves to be opposed to the reforms, which maintained the possibility for future strategies of confrontation.[35] The possibility of recurring dominant strategies of confrontation seemed more remote after the 1994 presidential election, which left little space for the organization of protests against electoral fraud, although most

35. Obviously, the possibility of using strategies of confrontation still remained. However, after January 1994 currents in favor of strategies of cooperation dominated the three main political parties.

observers agreed upon the need to go further in the reform of electoral institutions.

I have attempted here to demonstrate ways in which the problem of cooperation in the Mexican party system manifested itself during the Salinas administration. My argument is that although it has been possible to establish partial cooperative relations over the negotiation of the rules of the game between some political parties, its realization has depended on the possibility of confrontation and the exclusion of one of the main political actors, the PRD. For this reason, no efficient and stable model of cooperation emerged. The state of the system has encouraged the use of extrainstitutional resources for conflict resolution. Moreover, the nego-tiation strategies of the different parties for arriving at new rules of the game has continued to be associated with their respective strategies for attaining power. The prevailing dynamics in the party system alone were not able to provide the required incentives to promote an agreement between major political parties on the rules of the game. Only factors external to the party system that were threatening the system's very survival were able to compel the parties to move toward limited cooperation.

The 1994–1995 Economic Crisis

In December 1994, three weeks after President Zedillo took office, what initially appeared to be a slight devaluation of the Mexican peso resulted in creation of a financial crisis that had major repercussions for the economy.[36] The year 1995 was bad for the Mexican economy: Mexico was on the verge of defaulting on its financial obligations, the GDP decreased by 6 percent, inflation rose to 52 percent, and at one point interest rates reached 82 percent. The agreement on the goals of economic policy that had been reached at the end of 1987 broke down. Moreover, given the impossibility of reaching an accord on economic policy among the main economic actors, the government had to abandon the tripartite concertation formula and unilaterally imposed an economic package consisting of very strict adjustment measures.

The financial collapse translated into the political realm as a crisis of confidence in the government's capacity to control the situation. During most of 1995, relations between the government and the business sector

36. A good explanation of the crisis can be found in Sachs, Tornell, and Velasco 1996.

were tense. Beyond the folkloric aspects of the political struggle between the new president and his predecessor, former President Salinas, which lasted throughout 1995, a more fundamental struggle was taking place over the support of the business community. Official unions were also restless, threatening a general strike if their demands were not met. Finally, the existing rural movement of small indebted landowners, *El Barzón*, was impressively expanding its base to include the urban middle classes affected by the high interest rates. However, despite their discontent, neither of these groups was able to articulate a coherent alternative economic project.

As early as October 1995, the main economic actors returned to the model of tripartite concertation and approved the Agreement for Economic Recovery that outlined the general objectives of economic policy for 1996. A year later following the same pattern, they signed the Alliance for Growth. Both pacts represented a continuation of the economic policy that had been put in place in 1987. During 1996, the Mexican economy recovered at a steady pace, with an estimated growth rate of 4 percent of GDP and an inflation rate of 25 percent. This recovery has not yet been reflected in employment and wages.

In terms of my argument, although the financial crisis of December 1994 showed the fragility of the ongoing development model, it did not seriously jeopardize the cooperation among the main economic actors or the development model's direction. After a brief period in which neither the unions nor the business sector wanted to assume the cost of the crisis, they went back to the concertation formula. It must also be noted that the crisis did not favor the emergence of any sound economic-policy alternative. The actual policy is a continuation of the one that prevailed before the crisis, and there is no competing proposal.

The financial collapse also had effects on the political system, particularly on the party system. First of all, the crisis weakened the president's capacity to carry out his political projects. After the 1994 presidential election, one of the main items on the future legislative agenda was to achieve a "definitive" electoral reform. Until December of that year, the three major political parties seemed to favor strategies of limited cooperation for the negotiation of new electoral rules. However, the much publicized National Political Accord announced by the minister of the interior in January 1995 was stillborn when members of the PRI from the state of Tabasco rebelled against an alleged secret agreement between the PRD and the government to remove the newly elected governor whose victory was contested.

From this point forward, a dialogue began in the Ministry of the Interior between the government and the parties represented in Congress to negotiate the content of the definitive electoral reform. These negotiations, which one month earlier everyone had believed would be swift, lasted 18 months. The apparent weakness of the president was shown mostly in his relationship with his own party, the PRI, in an inability to control the actions of the PRI leaders at the state and local levels. This led the PRD and the PAN to successively abandon the negotiations. Once again, negotiations over the rules for electoral competition were intertwined with party competition.

In the summer of 1996, however, representatives of the political parties in the Congress voted unanimously for constitutional reforms that paved the way for the approval of a new electoral law. Discussions concerning such a law were held during the fall of 1996, but the expected consensual agreement among the three main political parties ultimately broke down at the last minute over details linked to party financing and political coalitions. For tactical reasons, the PAN refused to endorse the increase in the overall amount of public financing for all political parties. For several days, it seemed that the new law would be approved by the PRI and PRD. At the last moment, the negotiations between these two parties were aborted over the issues of public financing and electoral coalitions. According to accounts of the negotiations published in the national press, up until the moment of the vote, negotiators from the PRD thought they could get more in exchange for their support of the law. Their calculation failed. In the end, the reform was approved with the sole majority vote of the PRI. However, it must be stressed that most of the dispositions of the new law were the result of a consensual agreement among all the political parties.[37] Despite the difficulties inherent in such negotiations, a pattern of limited cooperation prevailed in the party system. This was made more evident after the July 1997 legislative election when all political parties opted for processing their electoral claims through the established institutional channels. This does not represent the end of electoral reforms in Mexico. Rather, it is the beginning of a basic agreement upon stable rules for electoral competition.

The result of the 1997 election had another significant effect on the process described in this chapter. For the first time since the consoli-

---

37. Representatives from the main political parties acknowledged in the months following the approval of the electoral reform that they all agreed upon most of the dispositions of the law. As an example of this, it is worth quoting what the PRD's leading negotiator, Porfirio Muñoz Ledo, said during the electoral reform about the reform a few days after the 6 July 1997

dation of a hegemonic party system in Mexico, the party in government will not have full control in the Chamber of Deputies. With 39 percent of the vote and 239 seats, the PRI is going to be twelve seats short of an absolute majority. Among the few exclusive powers of the lower house in Mexico is the yearly discussion and approval of the executive's budget proposal. At the moment of this writing, there are strong indications that opposition parties are going to take the opportunity to question the fiscal policy of the government (more specifically the value-added tax that was increased in 1995). Given the actual configuration of interests among political parties, it is doubtful that there will be major changes in the orientation of economic policy. However, it will surely stimulate public discussion over such policy and help to reestablish the broken link between the political and economic spheres of interest representation. Through their legislative action, political parties will have the opportunity to articulate economic interests. It remains to be seen how they will assume their new role.

Conclusion

Mexico has been experiencing two parallel processes of transformation that are characterized first, in the economic sphere, by the implementation of adjustment policies and second, in the political sphere, by pressures for the liberalization of the system of interest representation. In this chapter, my interest was in ascertaining the effects of both of these changes on one particular aspect of the system of interest representation: the party system. In this way, I attempted to explore the middle ground between "society-centered" and "state-centered" theories dealing with economic adjustment and democratization.

Behind the processes of transformation already mentioned, there is the outline of a more general problem: cooperation among actors and, more specifically, the consolidation of an efficient and long-lasting model of cooperation for those actors. Until the end of the 1970s, it was possible to identify both a model of development and a system of interest representation that were self-reinforcing and that maintained a stable model of

---

legislative election: "We put our proposal on the bargaining table. We discussed, we negotiated. With only 5 per cent of the senators and 10% of the deputies, the PRD got 80 per cent of its proposals included in the law" (*Reforma*, 9 July 1997).

cooperation. The 1980s were noteworthy for the rupture that took place in both spheres and for the attempts to reconfigure cooperative relations. A process of "centrifugal diversification" arose in which autonomous actors and potential options for cooperation multiplied. These options were not necessarily compatible with each other, and certainly were not leading to the establishment of a stable set of rules of the game. Although the model of cooperation between productive economic agents was repaired by the end of the 1980s, the same success did not occur in the party system. This confirms the existence of a widening gap between the representation of economic and political interests. The latter's internal dynamic was permeated by an alternation between strategies of cooperation and confrontation in which negotiations of the rules of the game were confused with strategies for attaining power. In this context, the party system tended to generate incentives for the use of extrainstitutional resources for purposes of conflict resolution. Only when an external threat to the survival of the party system as a way of participating in politics (the Chiapas rebellion) appeared at the beginning of 1994 did political parties feel obliged to install a model of limited cooperation.

The financial collapse of December 1994 demonstrated the fragility of the pattern of cooperation that had operated in the economic sphere since 1987. However, after a few months of disagreement among the main economic actors, the concertation formula of economic policy making was reestablished. The main features of the policy framework prior to the crisis were restored and, more important, no serious economic-policy alternative has emerged—at least until now. The party system also moved toward a fragile model of cooperation according to which parties at last seemed able to agree on rules of competition. However, here again, the long period of negotiations over electoral rules and the latter's vulnerability to what was really happening in terms of party competition showed the fragility of the model. The outcome of the 6 July 1997 election laid the ground for optimism in terms of the existence of a basic agreement on the rules for electoral competition. At last, electoral institutions and procedures served to process political conflict among parties. The eventual consolidation of stable political rules will help diminish the negative effects of politics on what takes place in the economic sphere.

The question of why no alternative economic policy can be articulated remains to be addressed. The answer appears to be more complex and to go far beyond the mere effects of current economic policy in limiting the potential of organized interests of civil society. Other factors such as the nature of social bonds and political structure have to be taken into account. Regarding social bonds, it would be a mistake to confuse real societies with an ideal model of Hegelian civil society in which pure interests would express themselves at the political level. Given that social bonds are deeply rooted in culture, the problem is not just of civil society being allowed to express itself politically. Many of the obstacles to democracy find their origin partly in civil society. Phenomena such as clientelism, corporatism, and subservience to hierarchical structures have a lot to do with the way people perceive their place in a social order. That perception does not necessarily lead to opposition to economic policies which are objectively adverse to the lower classes. Most electoral surveys in Mexico show that the strongest base of support of the PRI can be found in those strata that are most affected by the government's economic policy. The results of the July 1997 election, in which the center-left PRD had a surprisingly strong showing (26.6 percent of the vote) and the PRI was punished partly because of the immediate negative effects of adjustment policies on the electorate may indicate a change in the future. Still, it is a big step from a protest vote to support for an alternative economic project.

As I have shown, the actors involved in the political process, the nature of their opposition, and the way such opposition is linked to the issue of economic policy making are also important in explaining the existence or lack of alternative economic projects. Why in times of economic austerity do issues such as corruption, accountability, or electoral democracy prevail in the political debate over issues more directly linked to the government's economic policy? A big part of the answer to that question can be found in the way the political arena is shaped, with its different actors, their distinct strategies, and their mutual interactions. Retrieving concepts such as political actors and strategies allows us to go further in explaining the lack of alternatives to existing economic policies in Mexico. Among other things, it permits the introduction of simple ideas such as political imagination and innovation that lately have been lacking among the opponents of the current economic-policy orientation. Though it is true that part of the recent electoral success of the PRD can be attributed to its critique of "neoliberalism," the policy dimension of its economic program is remarkably poor.

As a concluding remark, an emphasis on the problem of cooperation may appear to leave aside the questions of political integration and participation that are, as it has been stressed by the editors in the introduction to this book, very important in the definition of the quality of democracy. However, cooperation is also fundamental in upgrading the quality of democracy. It helps to civilize political relations and, thereby, civil society. One of the great lessons from the theorists of natural rights must be remembered: society has to be civilized through institution building in order for democracy to prosper.

III

Hybrid Regimes and Neopluralist Politics

9

Is the Century of Corporatism Over?

Neoliberalism and the Rise of Neopluralism

Philip Oxhorn

Almost 25 years ago, in a seminal article of unusual influence, Philippe Schmitter boldly defended Mihaïl Manoïlesco's prediction that "the twentieth century will be the century of corporatism just as the nineteenth was the century of liberalism" (1974: 85). Disentangling the concept from its largely pejorative ideological and cultural baggage, Schmitter argued that corporatism was best understood as a system of interest intermediation, "a particular modal or ideal-typical arrangement for linking the associationally organized interests of civil society with the decisional structures of the state" (1974: 86). The imperatives of capitalist accumulation in the twentieth century, he argued, were forcing core and peripheral countries alike to turn to corporatist modes of interest representation in order to deal with various social tensions generated by modern capitalist development. Pluralism, it would seem, was an increasingly atavistic holdover

I would like to thank Carmen Sorger for her help in completing the research for this chapter. I would also like to thank Philippe Schmitter, Peter Kingstone, and Francis Hagopian for their comments on an earlier draft.

from nineteenth century liberalism—to the extent that it even continued to exist as a mode of interest intermediation in Latin America.

As Latin America prepares to enter the twenty-first century, it almost seems simplistic to ask if the "century of corporatism" is coming to an end. Yet the region as a whole has experienced tremendous socio-economic and political change since 1974, let alone the 1930s and 1940s, when corporatist modes of interest intermediation were first imposed. More specifically, the imperatives of capitalist accumulation in the late twentieth century are very different compared with the middle or early part of the century. The success and ultimate collapse of one develop-ment model (import-substituting industrialization [ISI] and the so-called crisis of the developmentalist state); the gradual (and still incomplete) emergence of a new, outward-oriented, neoliberal development model; and the resurgence of political democracy in Latin America suggest (at a minimum) that corporatist institutions will have to be adapted to fit the needs of a radically different context.[1]

This chapter argues that much more is happening than the mere adaptation of corporatist institutions to a new political and economic environment. A new mode of interest intermediation, *neopluralism*, is emerging that reflects the imperatives of the new development model in a situation of increasing social heterogeneity and political democrati-zation. While it remains to be seen if neopluralism will be as "successful" as its corporatist predecessor in maintaining social peace and stimulating capitalist development, it does reflect socioeconomic trends that will be difficult to reverse. Moreover, the relationship between neopluralism and political democracy remains ambiguous. For some, the basic charac-teristics of neopluralism suggest that an entirely new category of political democracy is emerging in Latin America—what O'Donnell (1994) calls "delegative democracy." At the same time, neopluralism is characterized by important authoritarian tendencies that (at best) severely limit its "democratic" qualities and (at worst) threaten to undermine existing democratic institutions in favor of new forms of authoritarian rule (Ducatenzeiler and Oxhorn 1994).

This chapter is divided into four sections. The first explores the relation-ship between corporatism as a mode of interest representation and capitalist development in Latin America, and argues that although there has been an elective affinity between corporatism and capitalist development,

---

1. It is worth pointing out that to his credit, Schmitter also noted that the "century" of corporatism would likely be a very short one!

this was due more to the nature of the ISI development model than to the imperatives of capital accumulation per se. The second section explores the relationship between a neoliberal development model and neopluralism, while the implications of neopluralism for democratization and improved social equity are considered in the third section. Finally, some speculations about what might actually happen in the twenty-first century will be tentatively offered in the concluding section.

Import-Substituting Industrialization and the Corporatist Imperative

Schmitter (1974) makes an important distinction between the kinds of corporatist institutions that are likely to be established in relatively advanced capitalist countries ("societal corporatism") and countries suffering from delayed dependent capitalist development ("state corporatism"). It is the latter, state corporatist model that concerns us here. Recognizing their respective country's disadvantaged position in an unequal international system of exchange and the need for a "defensive, nationalistic modernization from above" (119), elites in control of the state in many Latin American countries saw corporatist institutions as the solution to their developmental problems: "the abrupt demise of incipient pluralism and its dramatic and forceful replacement by state corporatism . . . [was] closely associated with the necessity to enforce 'social peace,' not by co-opting and incorporating, but by repressing and excluding the autonomous articulation of subordinate class demands in a situation where the bourgeoisie is too weak, internally divided, externally dependent and/or short of resources to respond effectively and legitimately to these demands within the framework of the liberal democratic state" (108). More specifically, state corporatism "definitively undermined the cohesion and capacity to act of the proletariat and even of the bourgeoisie with respect to general policy issues." It led to "an expansion in the role of technocratic expertise and impersonal (if not to say faceless) leadership styles" (125).

Development models affect how interests are organized and how representatives of different interests seek to influence policy outcomes. Similarly, alternative development models affect how a state will attempt to organize interests and limit their policy influence. It is important to emphasize that Latin American corporatism was invariably associated with a specific development model that was imposed throughout the region more or less simultaneously with corporatist institutions: ISI. The international capitalist economy was contracting as the core countries focused first on their own internal problems relating to the Great Depression of the 1930s, and then on one another during World War II. The vulnerability and relative backwardness of Latin American economies (and economic elites) to the vagaries of the international economy were dramatically highlighted by external events over which domestic elites had no control. Import-substituting industrialization can be seen as a reactive response during a particular phase in the international capitalist economy's development.

State corporatism both facilitated the switch to ISI and benefited from the economic prosperity ISI helped to create for roughly a generation. Populist coalitions uniting a weak national bourgeoisie with a developmentalist state relied on state corporatist institutions to win the allegiance of the growing working class. This was accomplished through hierarchical labor institutions that could effectively moderate workers' demands for social welfare benefits and greater social equity. As such, state corporatism became a fundamental component of processes of *controlled inclusion* (Oxhorn 1995a). Production for internal consumption required markets, and the "inward" orientation of development removed many external constraints to rising worker incomes in the modern, technologically advanced sectors of the economy. Sustained economic growth led to a doubling of per capita income in the region between 1960 and 1980 alone. This, in turn, resulted in upward social mobility for approximately one-fourth of the economically active population. It also created realistic expectations for social mobility among the rest of the population, particularly the young (CEPAL 1989b). At the same time, people outside the modern industrial sector of the economy were generally denied economic and political power. Organized labor became a relatively privileged group within Latin America's popular sectors, at the same time that its own interests were always subordinated to those of the dominant classes.[2]

Schmitter was correct in distinguishing types of corporatism according to levels of capitalist development, and in recognizing state corporatism's central role in promoting "modernization from above." But it could only

2. It is important to emphasize that this is in no way meant to be a "romantic" view of organized labor's earlier history. The ultimate subordination of its interests to those of the dominant classes must be stressed. Whenever organized labor challenged that subordination, the result was invariably repression in one form or another.

have done so to the extent that the development model allowed for a certain threshold of economic redistribution to the working class, at least during its early institutionalization.[3] These real gains (however limited in absolute terms or over time) provided the necessary initial legitimation of state corporatist institutions to allow them to survive for decades.[4]

This close relationship between state corporatism and ISI became clearest, ironically, as the development model began to show signs of its ultimate demise in the late 1960s. The viability of the ISI model required growing domestic markets. Ultimately, this led to growing demands by the lower classes that Latin American economies were increasingly strained to meet (CEPAL 1989b). By the 1970s, for example, the capacity of education to provide an avenue for social mobility was nearing exhaustion as the creation of new high-paying employment opportunities failed to keep pace with the expansion of educational levels in the workforce. This led to growing frustration, as new generations of young people were unable to realize the level of social mobility that earlier generations had enjoyed. High levels of income concentration, capital flight, and speculative investments further constrained the growth of productive employment. Protectionism, as well as the patronage and corruption associated with state corporatism and controlled inclusion, exacerbated problems of inefficiency and waste. Upward social mobility was barely sufficient to allow for a gradual decrease in the relative level of poverty, while the actual number of people living in poverty increased by 16 percent during the 1970s alone (CEPAL 1989b: 55).

These developmental problems culminated in the debt crisis and regional recession of the 1980s. As the region's per capita GDP declined by almost 10 percent during the 1980s, the already disadvantaged and the least organized were affected disproportionately. Open unemployment for the region as a whole rose from an average of 6 percent of the urban economically active population in 1974 to 14 percent in 1984, and the relative level of poverty again began to rise. By 1989, 183 million people lived in poverty—71 million more than in 1970 (CEPAL 1990).

An immediate consequence of the economic crisis and the predominant policy response to it has been the weakening of state corporatist

3. For the Mexican case, see Hamilton 1985; on Argentina, see Waisman 1987; for Brazil, see Skidmore 1967.

4. So strong was this legitimation that organized labor's allegiance to Peronism in Argentina and the PRI in Mexico, for example, was not undermined to any significant degree when both parties adopted ideological positions that in many respects were the exact opposite of those adopted in the 1930s and 1940s.

institutions, particularly organized labor. With the passing of the old development model and the introduction of a new neoliberal development model, the centrality of organized labor as a political actor in Latin American politics has been undermined. While it is still an important actor, it frequently remains a passive one in the face of economic policies and trends that further weaken labor's collective strength and well-being.

From State Corporatism to Neopluralism

The demise of ISI has coincided with a variety of other factors to favor the emergence of an alternative mode of interest intermediation: *neopluralism*. These factors include a radically different international context compared with that of the 1930s and 1940s, the nature of Latin American social structures in the 1980s, the dynamics of political liberalization and democratic transition, as well as the predominant policy prescriptions for constructing an alternative development model. But before the reason for the emergence of this particular mode of interest representation is explained, it is necessary to specify what it actually entails.

Neopluralism replaces the state-centered pattern of incorporating subordinate classes associated with state corporatism and processes of controlled inclusion with a market-centered pattern of lower-class incorporation. Its pluralist aspect comes from the multiplicity of forms of participation that neopluralism entails, as well as the absence of the state-imposed representational monopolies characteristic of corporatism. Organized labor becomes one actor among many, albeit weaker, with fewer privileges and in a less-unified form than in the past. Because neopluralism follows the demise of ISI, it necessarily entails removing collective rights and privileges previously authorized by the state to key actors as part of the coalition supporting ISI policies. This is particularly true for organized labor.[5] Moreover, neopluralism is characterized by its mix of both democratic and authoritarian forms of participation, which can include clientelism, plebiscitary forms of politics (perhaps best typified by Fujimori in Peru), as well as the remnants of state corporatist institutions imposed in the previous period. In many cases, important

5. It is important to emphasize that neopluralism does not emerge only in the aftermath of state corporatism. It does, however, represent the loss of organizational and political power on the part of organized labor. For this reason, Chile currently exhibits many of the characteristics of neopluralism despite the almost complete absence of state corporatism prior to the military coup.

authoritarian elements in neopluralism reflect the legacies of recent experiences of authoritarian rule (Hagopian 1993). Neopluralism is not incompatible with the institutionalization of extensive military participation in government or, as we shall see below, the hegemony of a single political party such as the Institutional Revolutionary Party (PRI, *Partido Revolucionario Institucional*) in Mexico.[6]

This strong authoritarian bent to neopluralism in Latin America is an important factor distinguishing it from pluralism in core countries. Similarly, the extreme social stratification of Latin America has contributed to an acute fragmentation of organized interests and the marginalization of large segments of the population that is much greater than what is typically the case in core countries. This fragmentation is only exacerbated by the weakness of political-party systems, and civil society more generally, in most of Latin America (Oxhorn 1995a; Mainwaring and Scully 1995).

Neopluralism is also characterized by a strong technocratic element, due largely to the necessity of avoiding the fiscal excesses of "economic populism" (Dornbusch and Edwards 1991) associated with the previous development model and mode of interest intermediation.[7] There is an explicitly antipolitical tone to neopluralism that seeks to replace political mechanisms for mediating conflicting interests with market-oriented ones based on economic efficiency.

As a mode of interest intermediation, neopluralism shares with its pluralist antecedent the belief that the best balance of interests and values within a given polity is produced by some form (however limited) of free competition among individuals in the rational pursuit of their self-interest. In much the same way that the market is characterized in liberal economics, the rational maximization of individual interests (which are reconciled through the mechanism of the market when they conflict) is portrayed as the driving force behind progress. Individual freedom is valued above all, and this requires respect for private property and (ideally, at least) the rule of law.[8]

6. In these areas, as well as in other respects, neopluralism does not represent a significant change from past patterns of political participation, because a phenomenon such as clientelism can exist within a variety of modes of interest intermediation. What is important is the new dynamic that clientelism, for example, assumes when neopluralism is the dominant mode of interest intermediation.

7. There is a certain irony here given that state corporatism was originally justified by Manoïlesco to help expand the role of technocratic expertise in policy making (see Schmitter 1974).

8. In a similar fashion, both neopluralism and pluralism tend to ignore or downplay the effects of socioeconomic inequalities on political outcomes. The significance of this omission

Not surprisingly, neopluralism is closely associated with the new development model that is quickly establishing its predominance within Latin America. As a result of the demise of ISI and the ensuing economic crisis, "a profound movement of policy reform is underway in Latin America" (Williamson 1990: 420).[9] This reform movement reflects the emergence in the 1980s of a new neoliberal policy consensus, or "universal convergence," among policy makers (both within and outside of the region) concerning the basic elements of a new development model. This alternative, neoliberal model is predicated on the need for market-based (as opposed to "state authoritarian" or statist), outward-oriented economic policies. The model's central elements include fiscal discipline, trade liberalization, competitive exchange rates, and the desirability of attracting direct foreign investment—virtually the mirror image of the ISI model it is replacing. Whereas ISI was initially a negative reaction to Latin America's unequal position within the international capitalist economy, the new model represents a positive reappraisal of the opportunities that a fuller insertion in the international economy offers. Rather than being shunned by core countries preoccupied with their own problems in the midst of a contracting world economy, the "Washington consensus" (Williamson 1990) emerged during the expansionary 1980s, as core countries and most international financial institutions actively encouraged the adoption of neoliberal economic reforms. Technical criteria of economic efficiency and competitiveness provide a rigid framework for state policy making, circumscribing the role of the state in the economy and in society to a minimum. This has had inescapable consequences for the mode of interest intermediation and the state's capacity to interact with different societal actors. Increasingly, the result has been the emergence of neopluralism as the predominant mode of interest intermediation. We can see this by looking at three sectors of society: the bourgeoisie, the organized working class, and the popular sectors more generally.[10]

---

for Latin America, where inequalities are much greater than is typical of the pluralist core, will be discussed in detail below.

9. It should be pointed out that when the Williamson volume went to print, the two principal exceptions to this trend were Brazil and Peru. Since then, after the election of Fernando Collor de Mello in Brazil in November 1989, followed by Fernando Henrique Cardoso's electoral victory in 1994, and the election of Alberto Fujimori in Peru in June 1990, the trend seems to have only intensified.

10. The organized working class is one component of the popular sectors. As a sociological category, the "popular sectors" are the disadvantaged groups in highly segmented, unequal societies. They are characterized by their limited life chances and consumption possibilities. In urban areas, the popular sectors include both organized and unorganized workers in the formal

As Schmitter (1974) highlighted, an important factor contributing to the emergence of ISI as a development model was the relative weakness of the national bourgeoisie. Perhaps the inevitable result of the ensuing decades of industrialization was the strengthening of this class to the extent that it would be less dependent on the state's protection and largesse.[11] A new, "modernized" bourgeoisie has emerged in much of Latin America that is capable of competing internationally. This group, in turn, has been a pillar of support for the new development model.[12] At the same time, it has become increasingly less dependent on state corporatist structures (to the extent that they even exist) for interest intermediation. Instead, access to policy makers has been sought through a variety of channels, both democratic and undemocratic (Gibson 1992). The bourgeoisie has also not been immune to neopluralism's tendency to fragment interest representation, and there has an been almost a natural tendency for business associations of various types and sizes to proliferate (Moore and Hamalai 1993).

The bourgeoisie has benefited from the current socioeconomic context in Latin America in ways that further accentuate trends toward neopluralism and away from corporatism (Gibson 1992; Bartell and Payne 1995; Oxhorn and Ducatenzeiler 1998). The liberal Right is the only political force that historically has been linked to alternatives to both state-centered development and the traditional political class and parties. Its electoral strength throughout Latin America reflects the decreased salience of social class as a basis for organizing collective identities, which has contributed to further fragmenting of working-class political influence. This has been exacerbated in that an important part of the Right's electoral appeal is based on its open antagonism toward organized labor.

economy, the unemployed who are seeking employment, people working in the informal economy, and the lumpen proletariat who are largely outside the formal and informal economies (see Oxhorn 1995a).

11. This is not to suggest that the entire bourgeois class is equally independent of state support. Liberalization of highly protected economies inevitably entails heavy losses for that sector of the bourgeoisie that was most heavily subsidized, directly or indirectly, by state policies of ISI. For this reason, widespread bankruptcies have been a major consequence of rapid structural adjustment, and this segment of the bourgeoisie has often opposed structural adjustment. Military regimes and economic crises have been important factors in weakening such opposition.

12. For Mexico, see Heredia 1992, and Loaeza 1992. For Argentina, see Ducatenzeiler and Oxhorn 1994 and Oxhorn and Ducatenzeiler 1994. For Chile, see Silva 1996; Barrera, Chapter 6 of this volume; and Campero 1984. For Brazil, see Tavares de Almeida 1994 and Cardoso 1986 and 1989. See also Bartell and Payne 1995.

Import-substituting industrialization similarly has contributed to growing working-class strength, but its dramatic demise and replacement by a neoliberal alternative have severely undermined the political and economic power of organized labor. As policies intended to create more open, outward-oriented economies are being implemented, there appears to be a clear trade-off between structural adjustment and increases in poverty (World Bank 1990: 55). This has only exacerbated preexisting problems caused by the collapse of ISI and the economic crisis that preceded the adjustment. Growing unemployment and legislative changes designed to ensure greater labor market flexibility have significantly diminished the bargaining strength of organized labor.[13] A principal mechanism for achieving international competitiveness in Latin America has been through wage suppression, which has further limited labor's bargaining strength (Hershberg 1997).[14] The neoliberal development model's overriding emphasis on maintaining trade balances (or surpluses), low inflation, and competitive exchange rates has virtually forestalled any possibility of distributional (let alone redistributional) concessions to organized labor (Notermans 1993). Rising levels of employment in the informal sector and the generally more precarious insertion of individual workers in the labor market suggest that it will be much more difficult to successfully organize labor in the future than was the case in the past during the reign of ISI (Barrera, Chapter 6 of this volume; Cameron 1994).

Finally, with regard to organized labor an important paradox must be noted: the government's ability to force organized labor's acquiescence was essential for implementing structural adjustment policies at the same time that those policies deliberately undermined traditional corporatist institutions that made such control possible in the first place (Oxhorn and Ducatenzeiler 1994; Ducatenzeiler and Oxhorn 1994; Murillo 1997; Zapata, Chapter 7 of this volume).[15] Several factors contributed to this, including organized labor's inability to resist in the face of the economic

13. These negative consequences of neoliberal economic policies for organized labor (and the working class more generally) are by no means limited to Latin America. The same effects can be seen in the core countries. For example, see McIlroy 1991; Marsh 1992; Shulman 1984; and Moller 1989. Similar experiences in various Asian countries were reviewed in Edgren 1990. See also Portes 1994.

14. In this regard, it is interesting to note that the threat of international competition has already been used in Mexico to force union concessions—even before the passage of the North American Free Trade Agreement. See Zapata, Chapter 7 of this volume.

15. Chile largely avoided this paradox because economic restructuring was carried out by a military regime.

crisis and the lack of any clear alternatives. In a number of countries, particularly Chile, the impact of repression against labor leaders also played an important role. The inevitable result, from the perspective of neopluralism, has been a growing distance between labor rank and file and labor union elites. The latter group, in exchange for their acquiescence to structural adjustment, has bargained for concessions intended to preserve their own status and institutional structures. Rather than retaining state corporatism's historical mechanisms for reproduction and social legitimation through even limited distributive policies, government strategies seem to have been designed to buy off increasingly anachronistic labor elites.[16] Organized labor has been reduced to an even more narrowly self-interested actor. Compared with the role formerly played by organized labor as a mechanism of controlled inclusion, it has become much more exclusionary than ever. The labor movement's ability to serve as an exclusive axis of representation for the popular sectors is highly questionable, not least because the gravest threat to organized labor's employment and earnings stability comes from within the popular sectors themselves as informality and unemployment grow (Oxhorn 1995b). Even organized labor's representational monopoly has come under increasing strain in almost every country as movements become more and more fragmented.

The particular manner in which the state relates to the popular sectors in general is an important aspect of neopluralism. This relationship between the state and the popular sectors has been defined by the emergence of a new policy approach for dealing with poverty: targeted assistance. Not surprisingly, targeted assistance is based on many of the same assumptions undergirding the neoliberal development model,[17] that is, the solution to poverty is to be found at the microlevel, by channeling minimal state welfare provisions to those most in need. Direct aid to the poor and most vulnerable in society is seen as allowing

16. It is important to note that this problem of social legitimation has not always been ignored. In Mexico, however, such concern has been more rhetorical than substantive, as agreements that undermined organized labor's historical sources of strength have been publicly pronounced to be examples of successful union negotiation (see Zapata, Chapter 7 of this volume).

17. Ironically, the social welfare polices of the Pinochet regime have become a model for Latin America. This is because of their consistency with neoliberal assumptions, as well as because of the comprehensiveness of social policy reforms in Chile and their apparent success in key areas. For an excellent and sympathetic analysis of Chilean social policies, see Castañeda 1990. Also see Oxhorn and Ducatenzeiler 1994; Graham 1994; Ward 1993; Dresser 1994; and Bresser Pereira and Nakano, Chapter 2 of this volume.

individuals to overcome any obstacles preventing their full participation in the market. The emphasis is on short-term solutions that will allow these people to become self-supporting through their participation in the labor market.

Reliance on the market for determining the best allocation of resources and opportunities for the poor is complemented by the state in its subsidiary role of providing certain public goods and income transfers targeted directly at those most in need of assistance. General subsidies and nonuniform, overly bureaucratic welfare policies are replaced by strictly needs-based direct payments (to users or service providers) in areas such as health care, education, nutrition, employment, and housing.[18] The efficiency of social welfare expenditures is increased by limiting the amount of "leakage" to middle- and upper-class groups. In the area of health care, for example, the state's role is minimized by making it the provider of last resort. Only the indigent and poor who cannot afford private health insurance will be channeled into a supposedly more efficient, streamlined public health service. Similarly, in the area of low-cost housing, the state's role is reduced to providing direct subsidies and screening for eligibility, leaving the market to ensure an adequate supply of low-cost housing once the "demand" from low-income groups has been guaranteed by the state.

The success of targeted assistance depends on decentralizing the administration of social welfare services. Implementation at the community level is portrayed as allowing for greater efficiency. Specific local interests and needs are said to determine the exact mix of services and benefits, making targeted assistance a demand-driven approach to overcoming poverty. Municipal governments, nongovernmental agencies, and in many instances popular organizations formed by the poor play important roles in designing services and determining the allocation of funds. Paradoxically (since targeted assistance has been most successfully implemented by nondemocratic regimes in Chile and Mexico), these policies can provide new spaces for democratic participation at the grassroots level.

Mexico is particularly interesting in this regard. The PRI's political hegemony has given state institutions a particular kind of politicization that historically has locked out alternative parties. Mexico began implementing programs of targeted assistance in the late 1970s, as part of its

---

18. It should be noted that these reforms often reflect the deliberate dismantling of the central mechanisms for institutionalizing state corporatism.

effort to contain the political consequences of its emerging socio-economic problems (Ward 1993). This culminated after the narrow election of Carlos Salinas in 1988, with the creation of the National Solidarity Program (PRONASOL). Despite any lack of consensus on PRONASOL's relation to the PRI and Mexico's clientelistic political process more generally,[19] PRONASOL has achieved a level of institution-alization that suggested it might form the basis of a new ruling coalition based on the support of the popular sectors (Dresser 1994). This would foreclose the necessity for greater political liberalization, at the same time that the importance of traditional corporatist labor institutions would be diminished.[20]

Before proceeding, it is important to note that neopluralism is inextricably associated with the dynamics of political liberalization and democratic transition, which have also swept the region over the past decade. Neopluralism, at a minimum, seems to require some form of electoral legitimation of executive authority. Such legitimation is con-sistent with Chile's relatively consolidated democratic regime. Yet it is also consistent with the kind of authoritarian concentration of executive authority that O'Donnell (1994) has labeled "delegative democracy" but which might more appropriately be called "hyper-presidentialism" (Ducatenzeiler and Oxhorn 1994).[21] Indeed, this is a central aspect of neopluralism: the combination of explicitly authoritarian and democratic forms of participation.

The acute fragmentation of interests associated with neopluralism may also be a reflection of this dynamic of democratization (Oxhorn 1995b; O'Donnell and Schmitter 1986; Canel 1992). The mobilization of the popular sectors has been of critical importance in recent transitions, as part

19. For example, Dresser (1994) argued that PRONASOL is nothing more than "neo-populism." As such, it represents a return to traditional practices of placing partisan interests ahead of the technical criteria for providing social assistance associated with targeted assistance. Ward (1993) argued that it is still premature to draw such a conclusion, while Fox (1994) suggested that PRONASOL has opened up important new spaces for popular sector participation in policy making. This very ambiguity is perhaps just another example of the complex mix of participatory forms characteristic of neopluralism.

20. PRONASOL was disbanded after Salinas left office in late 1994, suggesting its success was less than some had expected. However, it is unlikely the Mexican government will abandon targeted assistance as its principal strategy for dealing with poverty.

21. The best-known examples of this phenomenon include Menem in Argentina, Collor de Mello in Brazil, and Fujimori in Peru. More generally, hyper-presidentialism is typical of recent political processes in countries as diverse as Ecuador, Bolivia, and Mexico, to name but a few. We will return to the significance of this phenomenon in the concluding chapter of this volume.

of what O'Donnell and Schmitter call the "resurrection of civil society." Once elections are called, however, there is a dramatic demobilization of the popular sectors, as political parties come to dominate the political process. Intermediate levels of autonomous popular sector representation are disarticulated. The popular organizations that emerged throughout Latin America in recent years to help cope with unprecedented economic dislocations and demand greater political liberalization have ultimately remained confined to the community level after the initial impetus for political liberalization has run its course. Paradoxically, this suggests that the political significance of the popular sectors might actually be greater under authoritarian regimes than democratic ones (Oxhorn 1994). After a very public role is played by the popular sectors in struggles to topple repressive authoritarian regimes, the return of generally less-repressive democratic politics appears to push them out of the limelight, as their organizational presence on the national scene more-or-less disappears.[22] This paradox further serves to highlight the ambiguous relationship between neopluralism and democracy, an issue to which we now turn.

Neopluralism, Political Democracy, and the Politics of Power

Like its pluralist antecedent, the Achilles' heel of neopluralism is its inability to correct for the undemocratic consequences of an unequal distribution of power resources within society. This "elitist" critique of liberal, pluralist democracy in the core countries is by now well known (e.g., Bachrach 1967). The classic pluralist response, however, is perhaps more relevant for understanding the democratic implications of neopluralism in Latin America.

The pluralist response to its elitist critics is most articulately expressed in Robert Dahl's seminal study of local politics, *Who Governs: Democracy*

---

22. This is not meant to imply that the popular sectors do not periodically reemerge onto the public scene during specific periods of political and/or economic crisis. The overwhelming support among the popular sectors for Fujimori's suspension of the constitution is one example that is perhaps typical of neopluralist politics (see Roberts 1995). Similarly, the popular sectors played an important role in ultimately forcing the 1992 resignation of Collor de Mello in Brazil (see Weyland 1993). A hallmark of such a public presence in the context of neopluralism is that is both short lived and characterized by a spontaneity that belies any strong organizational foundations.

and Power in an American City (1961). Modernization, with its concomitant socioeconomic heterogeneity, was the source of a gradual evolution of New Haven, Connecticut, city politics from an oligarchic system dominated by a small group of "patricians," to a remarkably pluralist one in which the average citizen is able to compensate for disparities in wealth and social status through voting in competitive elections. Dispelling what he calls "the myth of the primacy of politics in the lives of citizens" (280), Dahl noted that the average citizen was in fact quite apathetic. The effectiveness of pluralist politics suggests that this is not only normal but good. In affluent societies, according to Dahl, participation is low because people can exercise their political influence indirectly through the electoral process, and they tend to act only when there is some perceived threat to their interests. A vague societal consensus on the appropriateness of democratic norms (what Dahl refers to as a "democratic creed") and this possibility that the average voter will use his/her normally underutilized political resources provide the necessary check against the potential abuse of authority that such a system might otherwise invite.

It is important to emphasize that this evolution from oligarchic to pluralist politics reflects the impact of socioeconomic modernization on available political resources. Industrialization and growing levels of social mobility among the lower classes effectively transformed the nature of political resources so that they became increasingly noncumulative in the era of pluralist politics. Ultimately, "numbers" as a political resource were able to compensate for the disparities in wealth and social status that had made political resources cumulative during the oligarchic period. So important was this transformation of political resources from cumulative to noncumulative that Dahl argues the evolution from oligarchic to pluralist politics actually preceded any institutional changes in the formal structures of government. Just as the market generates maximum well-being in the economic sphere, it would seem that the market's expansion and development will ultimately generate maximum well-being in the political sphere as well.

Turning to Latin America, political resources have only rarely been noncumulative in nature. Despite impressive economic growth and industrialization throughout much of the region during the reign of ISI and state corporatism, Latin America's extreme social stratification and inequality were only marginally reduced (CEPAL 1989b). The economic dislocations associated with the crisis of ISI and the imposition of an alternative neoliberal model of development have (at least in the short to medium term) reversed even this limited improvement in relative social equity, at the same time that absolute levels of poverty have increased.[23]

Moreover, "numbers" have generally not empowered the popular sectors the way pluralists predicted. Whenever mass-based actors have attained political ascendancy over traditionally dominant classes, the result has been the breakdown of democracy and the imposition of some form of nondemocratic rule (Karl 1990). More common has been the manipulation of the popular sectors by aspiring populist elites in pursuit of political power, with the most obvious examples including Cárdenas in Mexico,[24] Vargas in Brazil, and Perón in Argentina—which also happen to be the cases of the most advanced forms of state corporatism. While the short-term gains for the popular sectors, particularly organized labor, were often significant, they were invariably eroded by the economic and political instability that this particular form of mass mobilization has entailed in Latin America (Oxhorn 1995a; Dornbusch and Edwards 1991).

Neopluralism, as well as the neoliberal development model that undergirds it, have exacerbated the historical problem of turning numbers into political power in Latin America. This is true despite the unprecedented number of democratic political regimes in the region. One reason reflects limits to social mobility created by the new development model that, for example, has been a clear result of the privatization of services formally provided by the state, which has exacerbated the exclusionary effects of the neoliberal development model (CEPAL 1988). In selling off state enterprises that provide the infrastructure for development (energy, transportation, communications, etc.), the tendency toward excessive concentration of economic resources is reinforced as such services become more oriented toward satisfying the demand of the wealthiest economic actors. Similarly, the privatization of key social services such as social security, health care, and housing favors the middle and upper classes, which have the necessary incomes to pay prices that are profitable. But perhaps the most dramatic change has come in the area of

23. The Chilean experience is quite revealing in this regard. After peaking at 46.6 percent of the population in 1987, sustained economic growth was able to bring the poverty rate down to just over 30 percent by the end of 1993. Despite this dramatic drop in the poverty rate (which meant that approximately 1.5 million people were able to escape from poverty) and unprecedented economic performance in terms of growth and the control of inflation, there was no significant improvement in income distribution during the period (see Ruiz-Tagle 1993). Moreover, both the level of poverty and income inequality were still significantly higher in 1991 than they had been *before* Allende assumed office in 1970 (see Barrera, Chapter 7 of this volume).

24. During the 1930s.

education: "With respect to private services tied to . . . education and professional training, the fact is widely known that today, to a great extent, they fulfil less a function of social mobility—as was traditional in Latin America—and instead act as a mechanism for the reproduction of social inequality and the introduction of new elitist forms in society" (12).

Targeted assistance has generally had a similar effect. The effectiveness of targeted assistance for dealing with the immediate needs of the poor can be quite dramatic, as it was in the case of Chile under the military regime (Castañeda 1990). Yet the evidence from both Chile and Mexico, the two countries where the development of targeted assistance has been the most advanced, suggests that the structure of poverty itself has not been changed significantly.[25] Moreover, targeted assistance's demand-based nature implies (implicitly if not explicitly) competition among grassroots organizations and local communities. State agencies can play popular organizations off against each other in a competitive scramble for limited resources (Gay 1990; Cardoso 1992; Piester 1994; Eckstein 1988). Decentralization of social welfare services, moreover, can further fragment potential popular social movements, restricting popular sector organizational activity to narrowly circumscribed communities. Popular organizations often remain small, atomized, and dependent on state largesse. The emphasis of targeted assistance on helping people participate in the market can also generate political apathy. As people's efforts are devoted to participating in the market, there is less time and perceived need to become politically active. People become more complacent, at least as long as the economy seems to be on track. Even in Mexico, the limited nature of recent political reforms has met with only sporadic opposition. The pressure for further democratization clearly has abated since Salinas's narrow electoral victory in 1988, and PRONASOL is one important factor.[26]

While apathy may be seen as a sign of a healthy democracy in the pluralist core, in the neopluralist periphery it is often an indicator of growing social frustration, socioeconomic exclusion, or both. Like state corporatism, neopluralism seems to be a phenomenon closely associated with late, dependent capitalist development. Under these circumstances, the excessive fragmentation of interests associated with neopluralism

---

25. On the Chilean case, see Ruiz-Tagle 1993; Oxhorn and Ducatenzeiler 1994; and those in footnote 23. On Mexico, see Ward 1993 and Dresser 1994.

26. The peasant uprising in Chiapas may represent an important turning point. Not only is greater democratization a primary demand of the insurgents, but Chiapas was a major recipient of PRONASOL funds. Renewed pressures for democratic reform have also been fed by various political crises within the PRI, beginning with the assassination of its 1994 presidential candidate.

becomes self-defeating from the perspective of the popular sectors, yet there seems to be little alternative. Vast disparities in political resources give democratic regimes in much of Latin American a "schizophrenic" character that reflects the "angry atomization of society" (O'Donnell 1993: 1360, 1365). The fragile nature of most democratic regimes in the region is no surprise, while the socially atomizing effects of neopluralism help explain why they seem to last so long.[27] Neopluralism contributes directly to what O'Donnell has called "low-intensity citizenship": "the components of legality and, hence, of publicness and citizenship, fade away at the frontiers of various regions and class, gender and ethnic relations. . . . [T]he democratic participatory rights of polyarchy are respected. But the liberal component of democracy is systematically violated. A situation in which one can vote freely, but cannot expect proper treatment from the police or the courts" (O'Donnell 1993: 1361).

In this context, the ideal of citizenship becomes disembodied. Individuals enjoy certain rights, yet as people they have little or no influence over their lives. The rights and freedoms so cherished by the pluralists often ring hollow for many in the popular sectors when neopluralism is the principal mode of interest intermediation. Perhaps the greatest threat to democratic stability is that it is becoming "irrelevant" to the resolution of the popular sectors' most immediate problems (Garretón, 1998).

At the same time, however, the situation is not necessarily entirely so bleak. Liberal democracy offers a potential for change that its alternatives seem to lack in Latin America. The demand-based nature of directed assistance and the revitalization of local levels of government can create important new democratic spaces (Graham 1994; Fox 1994). Civil society, at least at the grassroots level, can be strengthened by incorporating social organizations and local governments into the policy-making process. The decentralized and technical nature of targeted assistance can also limit the scope for manipulation by old-style clientelistic elites and institutions. Even in a country such as Bolivia, with weak institutions and a long history of political clientelism, targeted-assistance programs were able to retain a remarkable level of transparency (Graham 1994). Moreover, social welfare policy is becoming an arena for pluralist political-party competition, even in Mexico (Ward 1993). This too can open up more space for citizen involvement.

---

27. For example, Brazil's transition to democracy ended almost 10 years ago, and it just completed its third democratic presidential election. Argentina's democratic regime is even older, while Mexico's political liberalization (Chiapas not withstanding) seems to have stalled.

As the example of Chile demonstrates, the difference between despair and hope rests on the strength of state institutions and the ability of popular sector interests to achieve some national projection. Strengthening the institutions of the state to avoid their excessive politicization and strengthening civil society, particularly political parties, can at least attenuate the most negative consequences of neopluralism. The popular sectors in Chile remain atomized, lacking any autonomous political projection of their interests (Oxhorn 1995b). Organized labor is also organizationally and structurally weak (see Barrera, Chapter 6 of this volume). Yet Chile enjoys an institutionalized political-party system with real ties to civil society that spans the entire political spectrum. This provides at least the potential for effectively aggregating and representing all major societal interests at the national level. At the same time, the strength of state institutions allows for the possibility that effective reforms will help mitigate the worst consequences of both neopluralism and the neoliberal economic model from the perspective of greater social equity and more complete citizenship for the popular sectors.[28] Not surprisingly, Chile's democratic regime is also among the most consolidated in Latin America. Whether other countries will be able to follow Chile's example remains in doubt, and even Chilean "democracy" suffers from serious limitations.[29]

Conclusion: The Century of Neopluralism?

Lasting somewhat less than a hundred years, the predominance of state corporatism as a mode of interest representation in Latin America corresponded to periods of significant economic growth and decline. In terms of ensuring "social peace," state corporatism has been associated with violent military regimes in both Argentina and Brazil. In fact, state

28. For example, Chile is one of the few countries in Latin America to have resolved the fiscal crisis of the state (Bresser Pereira 1993). Similarly, social programs under the democratic regime have enjoyed significant increases in funding, and efforts have been made to democratize the now more powerful local levels of government (see Oxhorn 1995a).

29. The so-called authoritarian legacies that seriously limited the scope of democratic processes are discussed in Garretón 1995, 1994 and Scully 1996. Significantly, the latter author noted the various ways in which the limits placed on Chile's democratic regime by the outgoing military regime have actually been conducive to the country's successful economic performance after the transition. Once again, the relationship between neopluralism and the new development model should be clear.

corporatism seems to have led to political stability only in authoritarian Mexico. To the extent that state corporatism (ideally, according to Manoïlesco) was to result in a political system in which "the past century's ideals of individual equality and liberty would be replaced by new collective goals of *social justice*" (Schmitter 1974: 122), it seems that such hopes could not be further removed from reality. State corporatism has only exacerbated historic problems of inequality (even while helping Latin American economies to generate considerable wealth through industrialization). It certainly has been no better at ensuring "social justice" than its predecessors. Arguably, state corporatism has actually been less effective compared with the distinctly noncorporatist experiences of countries such as Chile and Uruguay, where political parties have traditionally been much stronger. How is neopluralism likely to measure up?

As suggested above, the long-term consequences of neopluralism will be mitigated by various other factors, particularly the type and strength of state institutions and political-party systems. Politicized states with weak institutions will be hard pressed to solve fundamental problems of policy-making capacity, particularly the fiscal crisis of the state (Bresser Pereira 1993; Ducatenzeiler and Oxhorn 1994). Similarly, the authoritarian nature of state institutions in countries such as Mexico and Brazil suggests that the nondemocratic aspects of neopluralism will tend to predominant (Dresser 1994; Hagopian 1993, 1990). This problem is only exacerbated by the weakness of political-party systems in both countries, which prevents the effective representation of popular sector interests at the national (or even subnational) level (Mainwaring and Scully 1995). In contrast, the strength of state institutions and political parties in Chile has helped to partially mitigate the authoritarian legacy of the military regime and its 1980 constitution. Moreover, the worst of the socioeconomic consequences associated with neopluralism seem to have been moderated: sustained economic growth and renewed social spending have contributed to a dramatic decline in poverty, while tendencies toward increasing inequality and social stratification have at least been halted.[30]

---

30. It is important to emphasize that the bulk of the reduction in the poverty rate in Chile resulted from economic growth and the decline in the unemployment rate. This suggests that further reductions in poverty from the current level of 30 percent will be much more difficult to realize, even if Chile's unprecedented period of economic growth (averaging 7 percent per year since 1987) continues (Ruiz-Tagle 1993). Moreover, it is not clear that other countries will be as fortunate in terms of sustained economic growth. Mexico's recent economic crisis, with its economic repercussions throughout Latin America, is a case in point.

The importance of these mitigating factors also underscores the significance of authoritarian legacies in understanding the nature of neopluralism. While I have emphasized the relationship between a new economic model and the emergence of neopluralism (in part to underscore that authoritarian regimes are not a prerequisite for neopluralism, just as they are not necessary for the enactment of neoliberal economic reforms), prolonged authoritarian rule can help lay the foundation for neopluralism. Repression not only weakens important actors within civil society (particularly leftist parties and organized labor) but also contributes to the fragmentation of civil society in a number of ways (Corradi, Fagen, and Garretón 1992). Political-party systems in many cases have been weakened, and their relationship to civil society has been affected by the cessation of normal political activity during the duration of the authoritarian regime. In most cases, historical problems relating to the region's notoriously weak political-party systems have been left unchanged, if not exacerbated (Mainwaring and Scully 1995; Hagopian 1993). Authoritarian "enclaves" further concentrate executive authority, at the same time that they give militaries unprecedented institutionalized political influence and prerogatives. Indeed, one of the most important "interest groups" in neopluralist politics is the military. Ironically, the lawlessness, rising crime rates, and corruption associated with neopluralism are generating pressures (both international and national) for a greater role for the military in Latin American societies.[31]

The return to an emphasis on ideals of individual equality and liberty (a possibility that Manoïlesco seemed to have relegated to the "dustbin of history") embodied in neoliberalism has some rather paradoxical implications for the stability of neopluralism as a mode of interest intermediation. Whereas state corporatism (ideally) sought to deal with the problem of maintaining social peace by collectively organizing society to neutralize potentially contradictory class interests, neopluralism seeks the same result through the atomization and fragmentation of social organization, particularly among the popular sectors. Targeted assistance, for example, is an explicit effort to help individuals deal with what are essentially characterized as market imperfections. This emphasis on participating in

31. See Millet and Gold-Bliss 1996. In many ways, the military is returning to its historical role as power broker, as opposed to the various instances in which the military as an institution took power for indefinite periods in the 1960s and 1970s. This "new" role is perhaps clearest in the military's decisive backing of Fujimori's suspension of the constitution in Peru in 1994 (Mauceri 1995), as well as in the manner in which the military effectively resolved Ecuador's constitutional crisis in early 1997.

the market, in turn, complements social fragmentation by encouraging political apathy. The result is a muting of social pressures for change—and relative political stability.[32]

A good example of this is the changing significance of organized labor as a political actor. While obviously still important, labor is much less central to Latin American political processes than in the past. In recent years, organized labor has perhaps been most notable for its acquiescence in policy decisions related to structural adjustment than for any positive role it may have played in fundamentally altering those policies. This compares with its past role, when organized labor was the primary determinant of the evolution of social welfare policies in the region (Mesa Lago 1978), and perhaps even the evolution of entire political systems (Collier and Collier 1991).[33] Whereas state corporatism assigned organized labor a central role in reinforcing social stratification by recognizing it as a privileged actor among the popular sectors, neopluralism accomplishes much the same goal by weakening labor's collective bargaining strength and further fragmenting the representation of popular sector interests. Even the pretense of representing an entire class is lost as organized labor turns increasingly to matters affecting the immediate interests of union members (and union leaders in particular). In this way, the labor movement becomes a quintessential "interest group" within a neopluralist system of interest intermediation.[34]

Just as Mexico and Brazil were archetypical examples of state corporatism in Latin America, they are rapidly becoming archetypical examples of neopluralism. Increasing social fragmentation exists within an overall social structure that is highly segmented. The fact that the two cases represent differing levels of respect for democratic participatory rights highlights the ambiguous relationship between neopluralism and political democracy. Yet both exhibit the kind of disembodied, low-intensity citizenship that characterizes the most negative aspects of neopluralism. As already noted, Chile represents the opposite extreme, in which a dynamic economy and a relatively consolidated democratic

32. An important contributing factor is the weakness of any alternatives, particularly from the Left.

33. Indeed, labor's political influence played an important role in ushering in military regimes in a number of countries in the 1960s and 1970s (see O'Donnell 1979; Collier 1979; and Garretón 1989). One result was the extreme repression of labor movements in these countries, which further weakened the collective strength of labor organizations at the onset of neoliberal reforms.

34. As such, it only seems more improbable that organized labor will be able to effectively act on behalf of all members of the popular sectors.

regime can help attenuate some of the worst aspects of neopluralism, despite high levels of social atomization among the popular sectors. Other countries, such as Argentina, Bolivia, Colombia, and Venezuela, appear to fall somewhere in between, striving to be like Chile yet somehow falling short in various ways.

Only time will tell if neopluralism will prove to be as durable a mode of interest intermediation as state corporatism. Perhaps the greatest threat to its predominance is that the vast mass that makes up the disembodied citizenry of Latin America will become a readily available social base for new populist leaders appealing to their sense of frustration and limited hopes. There is already ample evidence that this is happening, as a new form of "neopopulism" that is intimately linked with neoliberal economic reforms begins to emerge in countries as diverse as Argentina, Brazil, Ecuador, and Peru (Roberts 1995; Weyland 1996). Yet populism in all of its various guises is another historical problem in Latin America. It is a problem that may be beyond the ability of neopluralism to resolve; it certainly is beyond the scope of this chapter.

10

New Democracies and Economic Crisis in Latin America

Francisco C. Weffort

The central argument of this chapter is that the "new democracies" in Latin America are democracies in the making. They are being constructed within the political context of a transition process that inevitably made them merge with important legacies from the authoritarian past. They are also being constructed during a social and economic crisis that accentuates the impact of extreme social inequalities from the past and newly emerging social inequalities. Under such conditions, they are taking on a peculiar institutional shape that places more emphasis on delegation than representation (or participation). In a similar vein, I will suggest that leadership (as well as related institutions and attributes such as political craftsmanship) matters for the consolidation of democracy, and we should be prepared to admit that the consolidation of new democracies is much more fraught with difficulties than was the process of transition.

If, during the 1960s and 1970s, Latin America offered a number of examples of authoritarian regimes, in the 1980s, it provided multitude examples of new democracies. Some of these, particularly those in Argentina, Brazil, Peru, and Guatemala, are seen here as paradigmatic cases. Although my argument mainly references Latin American cases, this does not mean that we cannot find examples in other parts of the world, and some comparison with East European countries would be desirable. Unfortunately, this is beyond the scope of this chapter.

Institutions: Hybrid Regimes

New democracies are "hybrid regimes," but what kind of hybrids are they? The blending of institutional mechanisms is not new in political systems but on the contrary is quite common. Most real political regimes are hybrids in at least some measure. In fact, some of the most modern representative systems have been combined with mechanisms for direct participation, with corporatist mechanisms, or with both. In a more general sense, we could say that liberal democracy itself is an institutional hybrid—one that took a long time to evolve into the form we know today.

But my point here does not concern the contrast between hybrids and nonhybrids. Rather it is that "new democracies" represent a particular kind of hybrid. What kind of hybrid? To answer this question, I will draw on Philippe Schmitter's suggestion that if we want to understand the chances for consolidation in the present (or in the future), we must look at the past, that is, at the transition (1991). My general hypothesis is that new democracies are political regimes in which the transition entailed the merging of democratic institutions with important legacies from a recent authoritarian past.

Among such legacies are the following: first, the relative continuity in state structures inherited from the authoritarian past, and second, the relative persistence of leaders from the previous regime. The first set of legacies refers to institutions such as the armed forces (including the intelligence community), state-owned banks, and other public enterprises, as well as all sorts of institutions geared toward economic intervention. These institutions assert the primacy of chief executives over parliaments and preserve the subordination of associations in civil society to the state apparatus. The second set of legacies refers to leaders (and related institutions), a subject to which I will return.

To illustrate the point, let me examine a specific and well-known example of an institutional hybrid: the historical subordination of trade unions to the state in Brazil, which persisted through the periods of populist democracy (1945–64) and new democracy (since 1984). This subordination was not only a matter of the dependent behavior of workers vis-à-vis the state but was also a question of institutional constraint resulting from a complex structure built after 1945, to preserve the legacy of the *Estado Novo* dictatorship (1937–45). The latter created a specific set of legal institutions in order to encapsulate unions and workers, including constitutional restrictions, a labor ministry, social security institutions, an official union structure, and a "union tax" collected by the state for the specific purpose of financing union activities (Moraes Filho 1962; Simão 1966; Rodrigues 1968; Rodrigues 1966; Schmitter 1971; Erickson 1977). Relying on fascist assumptions, this complex union structure functioned for two decades inside a democratic framework (1945–64) and then during the military dictatorship. It was revived again in the new democracy, beginning in 1984.

Again referring to Brazil, the 1988 constitution (which provides the main institutional framework for Brazil's current democracy) preserved most of these authoritarian institutions. In addition, it preserved some of the structures, mainly in the economic sphere, that were created during military dictatorship. But it also introduced some significant democratic changes: the right to strike, the independence of unions from the labor ministry, and recognition of independent national workers' confederations. At first sight, these changes were considered to be limited in scope by left-wing politicians, but those views have changed somewhat. Today, some people find it difficult to deny that these changes have also meant real improvements in the autonomy of a specific segment of civil society vis-à-vis the state. Criticisms are more frequent today with respect to liberal and conservative trends, as well as with respect to parties that pressure for a "revisionist movement" in Congress. The latter want to change the constitution according to a more liberal (or conservative?) bent, focusing mainly on economic matters. The main points of contention are state monopolies (oil and communication, for example), social laws protecting corporatist labor groups, and the structure and distribution of taxes to provincial states and cities.

Leadership: Continuismo and "Conversion"

It should be emphasized that this second point interacts with the first one dealing with political institutions, at least in the following sense: the most eloquent moment for a democratic leadership lies in the building of democratic institutions. For the purposes of this chapter, I would say that part of the problem of creating a new democratic leadership turns on the matter of creating (and consolidating) new democratic institutions.

The significance of the reform strategies of democratic leaders should be underlined, for this is an area in which new democracies have achieved considerable success. I am referring to institutional reforms such as constitutional revisions as well as to the establishment of new laws governing elections, the formation of political parties, the activities of associations, and so on. Even if such questions have not been fully resolved in countries like Brazil, Chile, and Argentina, this is the area in which the most important achievements have been made. I cannot say the same about the sphere of economic and social reforms. Failures on this front have undermined political institutions and delegitimized political leaders.

The "democratic assumption" underlying these reflections is that leadership (and related institutions) plays a part in the consolidation of democracy. First, the chances for democratic consolidation are greater if leaders are democratically self-conscious. Second, and conversely, the prospects for consolidation are slimmer if leaders are authoritarian. Third, the chances for democratic consolidation are only slightly better if otherwise democratic leaders are not conscious of the role they play, or if they form part of a diffuse agglomerate playing personal or sectoral "games." I would say, beginning with the case of Brazil, that the leadership of new democracies falls in the second and third categories more than in the first.

Nevertheless, one function of political theory is to remind us that the scenarios for democratic consolidation are not necessarily clean or clearcut. Even when theory reveals that progress toward freedom and popular participation is a general trend, most democratic transitions were led by people who were not "born" democratic. Democracies are born of conflict and violence, and most of their leaders are born of dictatorship. In this sense, Latin America's new democracies have a better beginning compared with East European countries. The presence of democratic leaders such as Alfonsín and Menem, Patricio Aylwin and Ricardo Lagos, Ulysses Guimaraes and Luiz Inacio Lula da Silva was perhaps more central in Latin America than it was in Eastern Europe, even if we cannot forget leaders like Walesa and Havel. Some of the Latin American leaders were holdovers from previous democratic regimes or individuals who took advantage of political opportunities within the "limited pluralism" (J. Linz) of authoritarian regimes. Eastern Europe experienced a longer period of nondemocratic rule, during most of which no space was permitted for any sort of pluralism. That is the reason for a greater number of "conversions" among European leaders. (On the concept of conversion, see Elemer Hankiss 1991: chap. 9.)

In the Latin American transitions, "*continuismo*" is more striking than "conversion." In Brazil, for example, *continuismo* resulted not only from imposition by the military groups leaving power but also from choices made by most of the democratic forces. The choices involved a compromise among moderates that expressed the prevailing power realities in the country. This compromise embodies the essential characteristics of Brazil's new democracy, namely, that is a product of a "conservative transition."

Political Democracy and Social Inequalities

Why do we call this hybrid regime that we have had in Brazil since 1984 a democracy? It is because, in spite of all kinds of continuities, conversions of leaders, and other possible elements of hybridization, Brazilian leaders during this period experienced the "institutionalization of uncertainty" (Przeworski 1986) that is the cornerstone of representative democracy. The same could be said about Brazil's earlier "populist democracy" (1945–64). It was an "unstable democracy" (Lipset 1959) marked by intermittent military intervention. It was, as the current one is, a weak democracy. But it was, by any reasonable interpretation, a democracy.

The statement above implies a "minimal definition" of democracy. But despite its analytical utility, this minimal definition requires some further elaboration. I would say that the minimal procedural functioning of a political democracy implies certain minimal social conditions. It seems clear to me that this argument was developed in the late 1950s by political scientists such as Dahl and Lipset—only to be forgotten by many people studying transitions (and consolidations) in the 1980s. Most of the latter accept the minimal definition of democracy as if the "rules of the game" (Bobbio 1987) were mere forms (we might say empty forms) bereft of any social content.

The assumption that rules always have some social content seems especially appropriate for the study of transitions, particularly when we consider societies characterized by strong social pressures. Countries like Brazil, Guatemala, and Peru have traditionally been marked by deep social inequalities. Other countries historically characterized by more modest concentrations of wealth, such as Argentina, are currently experiencing the rise of unprecedented new social inequalities through a process known as "unequalization" (O'Donnell 1994). It seems reasonable to assume that in either case, new democracies also face the added burden of prolonged economic stagnation.

When we speak of the minimal conception of democracy, we are referring to citizens in the context of a modern nation-state (Valenzuela 1992). People are considered to be citizens because they are presumed to be able to make use of the minimal rules of democratic participation. This means that they are assumed to possess the basic social attributes that define personhood. Distinct from the city-state of ancient times and a political regime of the Middle Ages, citizenship in the modern nation-state is a political reality, separate from the social reality of personhood. But the political reality of citizenship rests on the social foundation of personhood or the social foundation of the individual. What happens in situations in which this foundation is missing?

Theories of democratic development should not neglect theories of societal development. We cannot be so formalistic as to think that the minimal definition of democracy would be operative in any kind of context, as if democracy were entirely independent of certain basic variations in social context. Insofar as the democratic equality of citizens depends on some level of social equality among individuals, a theory of democracy requires a theory of society.

I am referring here to social equality not in the Marxian, but in the Tocquevillean sense. Even when Tocqueville thinks of democracy as a type of society (as opposed, for example, to aristocracy), the nearly universal personhood that is characteristic of modern societies is a necessary condition for the proper working of political democracy. Sartori's definition of "social equality" goes right to the point: "social equality, understood as equality of status and of consideration, thus implying that class and wealth distinctions carry no distinction" (1987). Tocqueville's idea of social equality is that of *égalité de condition*, that is, the opportunity for an individual to be treated as an individual by others, in contrast to situations in which *diférence* is the predominant feature of social behavior. Modern society, in this sense, contrasts with aristocratic society (twelfth-century France, for example), as well as with hierarchic society (India or traditional China). It also contrasts with situations of extreme social inequality (north and northeast of Brazil) or newly emerging social inequalities ("unequalization").

The fact is that the above minimal social conditions are absent in many new democracies. As for these countries' pasts, this absence can help explain their characteristic democratic instability and some of their typical political experiences and legacies: Vargas (and the Vargas tradition) in Brazil, Perón (and the Peronista tradition) in Argentina, the Mexican regime based on the dominant role of the PRI, the leadership of Haya de la Torre and the Alianza Popular Revolucionaria Americana, as well as the reformist experiment led by General Velasco Alvarado in Peru, and so on.

Yet the political consequences of extreme social inequality make today's situation rather complicated. I do not think that the new democracies will repeat the populist experiences of the past. Populist experiments were always nurtured by an important burst of economic growth (Argentina from 1945 to 1955, for example) or by an entire period of economic growth (Brazil after 1930 and up to 1960). This is also the case of Mexico, and to a lesser extent, the same argument fits Peru and other Latin American countries through the 1960s. Thus, most people have associated populist regimes with their ability to provide for more individual independence at the social level, even if individuals remained politically dependent.

In the 1980s, countries underwent political democratization at the same time that they were afflicted by a profound and prolonged economic crisis that generated social exclusion and massive poverty, diminishing the individual's basic sense of independence. In turn, the basic assumption of a minimal level of social equality among individuals was also undermined, with serious effects for the functioning of political democracy. Some of these countries are building political democracy over a minefield of social exclusion. Others, such as Argentina, are undertaking the construction of political democracy within the context of newly emerging social inequalities.

Conclusion

To sum up my arguments, I will address two basic questions. First, is political democracy possible in societies marked by high degrees of inequality (Brazil, Peru) or by newly emerging social inequalities (Argentina)? My answer is yes, but I would also say that there is a contradiction between a system based on the political equality of citizens and societies based on such extreme inequalities. That contradiction opens the way for tensions, institutional distortions, instability, recurrent violence, and so on. Extreme inequalities do not nullify the prospects for political democracy, but they make a difference.

The second relevant question is this: Under such conditions, is the consolidation of democracy possible? My answer is no. The characteristics of the Brazilian case seem clear to me: low levels of party institutionalization, intermittent stalemates between the executive and legislative branches, and the persistence of *decretismo* as a way of overcoming a permanent crisis of governability. Those are some of the institutional features of the kind of democracy that is possible in a situation of "social apartheid."

And, finally, a concluding note. What kind of democracy can grow under such conditions? I think the best answer, for the moment, was given by O'Donnell in his definition of "delegative democracy": "Delegative democracies rest on the premise that whoever wins election to the presidency is thereby entitled to govern as he or she sees fit. . . . The president is taken to be the embodiment of the nation and the main custodian and definer of its interests" (1994: 59–60). If representative democracy is thought to be a system based on equal, independent individuals able to represent themselves, then "delegative democracy" is a system based on unequal, dependent individuals unable to represent themselves.

11

Conclusions

What Kind of Democracy? What Kind of Market?

Philip Oxhorn and Graciela Ducatenzeiler

For better or worse (and we invariably believe it has been for the better),
Latin America has now completed its transitions to democratic regimes,
with the noticeable exception of Mexico (and Cuba). The rich literature
on transitions has already given way to a new literature focusing on the
consolidation of those democratic regimes, often by the same authors.[1]
While we believe that this literature has made numerable invaluable
contributions to understanding the processes of democratization in the
region, we also think its emphasis on "consolidation" has been somewhat misplaced. The growing threats to democracy in Venezuela and
Colombia (two of the region's oldest democracies), the collapse of
Uruguayan and Chilean democracies in the early 1970s (historically the
region's most stable democratic regimes, rivaling or even surpassing the
experience of many European regimes), and the persistence of all the

---

1. Among the numerous contributions to this literature, see Gunther, Puhle, and
Diamandouros 1995; Linz and Stepan 1996a, 1996b; Schmitter 1995; and Mainwaring, O'Donnell,
and Valenzuela 1992.

newly created democracies of the past quarter century despite their undeniable fragility (with the partial exceptions of Haiti and Peru, both of which experienced relatively short periods of unconstitutional rule in the 1990s) underscore how ambiguous and ephemeral any concept of "consolidation" in the Latin American context necessarily is. Just as Przeworski (1986) noted that illegitimate political regimes can survive for long periods in the absence of viable alternatives, "unconsolidated" democracies in Latin America also have experienced an impressive staying power in recent decades, even when apparently consolidated regimes in the 1970s did not. Indeed, what may be more important are the ways in which existing democratic regimes encourage or block the emergence of alternatives that are perceived to be both preferable and viable.

Whether alternatives will emerge that are widely perceived to be both viable and preferable to Latin America's existing democracies will depend in large part on the specific characteristics of those regimes or, as we suggested in the book's introductory chapter, their quality. Determining this will involve an examination of their institutional characteristics and how they both reflect and shape the particular contours of each country's civil society. Moreover, an explicit discussion of their normative dimension in terms of governmental accountability and broad citizen participation will be required. Ultimately, this focus on democratic quality will offer many of the same insights as a focus on the consolidation of existing democracies, but it will do so in a less ambiguous fashion. Instead of analyzing what democracies might become (i.e., consolidated), we will focus on what they actually are.

Similarly, there has been considerable progress in implementing neoliberal economic reforms in the region. In this regard, the ambiguity is less the result of the conceptual tools we apply to the matter than of the fact that the economic success of such reforms has at best been only partial. Still, the chapters in this volume suggest that certain clear patterns are emerging in how markets are functioning, patterns that are often most apparent in the actual behavior of important political and social actors, as well as in the consequences market reforms have had for specific societies. Obviously this has important implications for the quality of democracy in those countries, and for this reason we will attempt to highlight some defining characteristics of the kind of markets that prevail in Latin America today, before turning to the question of the kind of democracy that appears to be accompanying it.

What Kind of Market?

The reduction of the state's role and its replacement with regulation by the market occupy the principal position on the economic agenda of Latin American governments. Implicitly, it is assumed that a dramatically smaller state would allow for the emergence of a type of capitalism that would be independent of the public sector and capable of combining economic expansion with fiscal equilibrium.[2]

The first tool used by the majority of the countries in the region to achieve this objective consisted of the emergency programs that translated into a reduction in public expenditures through the freezing of public-sector salaries, as well as decreases in subsidies to the private sector and public investment. The consolidation of a climate of confidence as a result of economic stabilization, accompanied by institutional changes and changes in the rules of the game, would permit, according to the authors and ideologues of these policies, the emergence of a private capitalism— Weberian entrepreneurs, capable and motivated, who could replace state capitalism. Private business interests would be responsible for productive investment, while the state would concentrate on public goods and relief for those social sectors most affected by the economic crisis and the adjustment process. Logically, the next steps were the privatizations and commercial liberalization. The former would allow for the substitution of public investment by national and foreign private investment. The latter would mean "exposure to the marketplace as disciplinarian and enforcer of maximum efficiency" (Gerchunoff and Torre 1992: 270).

This emerging neoliberal development model, based on fiscal and monetary discipline, free trade and open markets, and a minimal role for the state in directing economic activity, has brought with it economic changes of a magnitude that are unprecedented in most countries since the Great Depression. These changes, however, did not always produce the results that their authors had predicted. Rational entrepreneurs did not appear (except in those countries where they had already existed, independently of the influence of the new model, as in Chile and Brazil), public and private investment declined (with the exception of speculative

2. It must be emphasized that a "small" state is not necessarily a weak one (North 1981; Korzeniewicz and Smith 1997; Smith and Korzeniewicz 1996). As will be discussed below, neoliberal reforms may even (paradoxically) require a strengthening of the state. This strengthening of state institutions, in turn, could help insulate the state from interest groups and increase its capacity for regulating property rights, as well as macroeconomic and micro-economic behavior.

investment in the moments of high euphoria and confidence in these models), and the social situation experienced and continues to experience a strong process of deterioration with increases in inequalities, unemployment rates, and so on.

Many of these economic changes have clearly been for the better, given the magnitude and pervasiveness of the fiscal crisis, demonstrating the fragility of the state and its incapacity to respond to social demands. Even the most critical essays in this volume would agree. But what kind of market, or more generally, what kind of capitalism do these reforms appear to embody?

First, the limited role for the state in economic matters implies a market that is increasingly unregulated. "Free" markets in the most basic sense would seem to be an ideal guiding these policies.[3] This is true even at the level of regional economic integration, as Chapter 3 by Fuentes demonstrates.

The reduction of the role of the state does not relate only to a decrease in its direct participation in productive activities but also to a lack of state participation in the organization of the market. The importance of this is that there are few structures that mediate the power of economic resources in this kind of market, which threatens to undermine the very economic model whose implementation is being sought. Paradoxically, the neoliberal model requires a state that is smaller and less interventionist at the same time that it needs a state capable of organizing markets in such a way as to combine what is lucrative from the point of view of the private sector with what is desirable from the point of view of society as a whole. A new type of state intervention could therefore help achieve a better distribution of costs and benefits from privatization policies (Gerchunoff and Torre 1992; Schvarzer, Chapter 4 of this volume). Moreover, the reorganization of markets and of the relations between the state and society presupposes an institutional transformation that can only be attempted by a strong (even if small) state (Gerchunoff and Torre 1992). Yet this is what is most notably lacking in the kind of markets that are emerging in Latin America today.

As a result of this absence of state regulation, economic power comes to dominate in ways that are much more extreme than is customary in

---

3. It should be pointed out that this does not imply that there would be no regulations. In particular, the Chilean experience demonstrates the importance of regulating financial markets in order to avoid speculative and nonproductive investments in favor of more productive ones (see Silva 1996). Chapter 4 by Schvarzer emphasizes for the Argentine case the negative consequences of avoiding this kind of regulation.

other capitalist societies. This is clearest in Chapter 4 by Schvarzer (which focuses on the elite level in Argentina) and Chapters 6 and 9 by Barrera and Oxhorn (which, respectively, focus on the popular sectors in Chile and Latin America more generally). Even Mexico's corporatist structures, as shown by Zapata, have been remolded to the benefit of markets. In general, there has been an "informalization of the formal sector" of the economy as labor market regulation has increasingly been left to market forces (Portes 1994; see Barrera, Chapter 6 and Zapata, Chapter 7 of this volume). Actors who lack economic resources are quite literally at the mercy of the market. Moreover, as the chapters by Bresser Pereira and Nakano and Oxhorn show, targeted or compensatory social policies can help alleviate some of the worst short-term consequences of this. In the longer run, however, they cannot alter the structure of poverty, and instead reinforce a market logic in social relations that emphasizes individual social mobility through the economic opportunities growing markets can provide.

The flip side of this is the growing influence of business interests (especially those connected with international finance capital) in Latin American politics (Mahon 1996; Keohane and Milner 1996), due to their preponderance of economic resources, as well as their central role as the engine of economic growth replacing the state. To the extent that such influence takes institutionalized forms consistent with the maintenance of political democracy, this is not only positive but may represent an important change from the past. Chile may be a good example of this (Silva 1996). If, however, such influence is through less formal channels and/or undemocratic ones—as may be the case in a number of countries—the situation is much more ambiguous. As Mahon noted, "those who move markets may have no objection to formally unaccountable state power, as long as it is informally accountable to them" (1996: 200).

Perhaps an unexpected by-product of the dominance of economic resources in the new development model that is emerging is a concomitant decline in the political influence of actors who formerly enjoyed a lot of influence due to their control over symbolic/ideological resources (the church and even certain political parties). Perhaps more important are the actors who had enjoyed tremendous power through their control over access to the state (such as political parties); in particular, the state's coercive apparatus (i.e., the military) may have declined appreciably.[4]

4. Obviously economic change is only one—albeit important—factor in this shift in power resources. International factors (like the end of the Cold War and changes in the Catholic

The military, in particular, continues in most cases to suffer from the lack of control over its economic resources, which in turn helps circumscribe its political role to the more traditional one of power broker in times of crisis.[5]

As this particular type of market logic increasingly pervades Latin American societies, the exclusionary aspects of this kind of market become more and more evident. While job growth has contributed in some countries to dramatic falls in the poverty rate, its effects on income distribution have been extremely limited. To date, the empirical evidence demonstrates that (with very few exceptions) Latin America's historical problem of social inequality—exacerbated by the extent of the 1980s economic crisis—has not been effectively addressed by the new economic policies (Oxhorn, Chapter 9 and Barrera, Chapter 6 of this volume; Altimir 1995, 1993). This, in turn, reflects that reductions in poverty (which have often been substantial and are invariably positive) have been almost entirely the result of economic growth and not social policies (Helwege 1995; ECLAC 1994b). As the 1994–95 Mexican economic crisis reminds us, however, such jobs can be extremely precarious. Even in a "successful" economy like Chile's, the precariousness of employment for workers in general is an important characteristic of this kind of market development (Díaz 1991).

In sum, the markets that are emerging throughout the region are characterized by little regulation, a minimal state presence, and an accentuation of liberal individualism (as opposed to more collective or communitarian visions of society).[6] In addition, they are very much pro-business. Such markets, in turn, support a peculiar form of capitalism, one that we would call *predatory capitalism*. Its predatory nature is most clear in the chapters by Baer and Paiva, Schvarzer, and Barrera. It is a capitalism that preys on those without economic resources—the popular sectors, noncompetitive industries—deprives the state of resources through its policy prescriptions (Bresser Pereira, Maravall, and Przeworski 1993),

---

Church under the leadership of Pope John Paul II, among others), the discrediting of military rule in a number of countries throughout the region, and the pressures created by the fact that virtually all countries in the region now have political democracy, while pressures for further democratization may be growing in the obvious exceptions like Mexico, are also very important.

5. See Millet and Gold-Bliss 1996 and Hunter 1995. In this regard, the financial guarantees that the Chilean military enjoys would appear to be even more significant. On the nature of those guarantees, see Scully 1996.

6. See Walzer 1991 and Taylor 1990.

and, as the chapters by Weffort, Bresser Pereira and Nakano, and Baer and Paiva suggest, perhaps even undermines important aspects of the common good. It is a process that, as all of the chapters in this volume suggest in different ways, has its own dynamic and tends to disproportionately reward those who already exercise some form of power (particularly economic).

The severity of the socioeconomic dislocations caused by the rapid (re)introduction of market forces associated with predatory capitalism has led some to draw interesting parallels with the latter part of the nineteenth century through the 1920s (Korzeniewicz and Smith 1997; Smith and Korzeniewicz 1996). This was the last period during which economic liberalism dominated the region. Building on Karl Polanyi's characterization of that tumultuous period in Western history as the "great transformation," Korzeniewicz and Smith argued that Latin America is undergoing its second "great transformation" as a result of the neoliberal economic policies sweeping the region over the past several decades. From this perspective, the very predatory nature of capitalism makes it unlikely that it will be long lasting. Just as nineteenth-century economic liberalism led to the emergence of powerful labor movements and other actors that successfully struggled to reign in capitalism by ultimately erecting the modern welfare state, the current period is seen as one in which new actors, particularly women's movements, will work to erect new state institutions that can correct many, if not all, of predatory capitalism's most pernicious elements. Polanyi summarized the challenge that unregulated markets posed for society in the early twentieth century in a way that seems almost prophetic for Latin America in the 1990s: "the [nineteenth century] idea of a self-adjusting market implied a stark utopia. Such an institution could not exist for any length of time without annihilating the human and natural substance of society. . . . Inevitably, society took measures to protect itself" (1944: 3).

Regardless of whether such a counterreaction is equally inevitable in the current context (and we certainly hope that it is), the evidence presented in this volume suggests that it may be a long time in coming. The fragmentation and atomization of civil society, as well as the weakening of the same actors (organized labor and the political left) responsible for curbing the excesses of the market earlier in this century, make it difficult to identify any particular actor or actors that could effectively bring pressure for implementation of such changes. The social movements that were important in mobilizing against authoritarian regimes have had a particularly difficult time in adapting to the new political and economic context once transitions to democracy took place (Oxhorn 1996). Moreover, it is not apparent what such changes would even entail. The first great transformation coincided with a unique period of intellectual effervescence. The ideas of then contemporary thinkers such as Weber, Marx, and Keynes—to name but a few—served not only to delineate specific policy alternatives but to catalyze collective action in the pursuit of what were perhaps less stark utopias. Today, by contrast, the pre-requisite intellectual counterreaction is at best just beginning. Indeed, one of the objectives of this volume is to help contribute to such an intellectual endeavor. In the meantime, as the chapters by Barrera and Oxhorn suggest, the likely counterreaction appears limited to mirroring Chile's experience in the mid-1980s. The collapse of the Chilean economy in 1982 led to important changes in the radical neoliberal policies in place at the time, generating sustained economic growth and significant reductions in poverty. Yet the marginalization and social inequity associated with the neoliberal model remained largely unaffected.[7]

It is also important to remember that in Latin America, society was much less able to defend itself from the market in the aftermath of the first great transformation than Western Europe. While the market was effectively controlled by the state, the outcome was anything but the stable democracies and advanced welfare states Polanyi applauded. Under the current circumstances, a social consensus is even more difficult to establish. As Bresser Pereira and Nakano suggest in Chapter 2 of this volume, it may be impossible. Even where there appears to be an economic consensus, this generally excludes policy areas dealing specifically with distributional issues (Williamson 1990, 1993), and does not necessarily provide the basis for a clear political consensus (see Prud'homme, Chapter 8 of this volume). So what kind of democracies can survive in these circumstances?

What Kind of Democracy?

Throughout Latin America in recent years, there has been growing evidence of a trend toward the undemocratic concentration of political power as a result of misguided efforts to increase economic and political

---

7. Similarly, the Mexican economic crisis that began with the 1994 peso devaluation has not yet led to any substantive economic policy changes which could begin to reverse the most

efficacy, allegedly to safeguard and legitimate democratic institutions for the future. This is not only a possible prerequisite for the adoption of many neoliberal economic policies, it is a style of governance completely compatible with continued functioning of the model and therefore unlikely to change due to economic pressures alone (Mahon 1996).[8] Much of the work looking at this phenomenon seems even to accept the premise that this current drift toward authoritarian solutions to problems of governability represents a new form of democratic regime (Collier and Levitsky 1997). O'Donnell is the most systematic in the defense of this position and states at the onset that he is engaged in an attempt to "depict a 'new species,' a subtype of existing democracies that has yet to be theorized" (1994: 55).[9] Arguing that existing democratic theory focuses exclusively on the various subtypes of *representative democracy*, O'Donnell suggested that in Latin America and other regions, new democratic regimes are assuming a different set of characteristics that are more appropriately identified with what he calls *delegative democracy:* "Delegative democracies rest on the premise that whoever wins the election to the presidency is thereby entitled to govern as he or she sees fit, constrained only by the hard facts of existing power relations and by a constitutionally limited term of office. The president is taken to be the embodiment of the nation and the main custodian and definer of its interests. The policies of his government need bear no resemblance to

---

predatory aspects of its market economy. While this may change as a result of the 1997 elections, in which the ruling Institutional Revolutionary Party lost its majority in the lower house of the national legislature for the first time and the leftist Revolutionary Democratic Party's candidate won the mayoral race in Mexico City, there is little evidence to suggest that such reforms would go further than those already implemented in Chile in the 1980s (see Prud'homme, Chapter 8 of this volume).

8. This is consistent with our observation in Chapter 1 of this volume that regime type is increasingly seen by analysts as having only limited relevance for understanding successful economic reform. The dividing line between "authoritarian" and "democratic" regimes is becoming increasingly blurred. As a further illustration of the point, regime type was hardly discussed at all in a recent volume exploring the relationship between internationalization and domestic politics, except for the observation that authoritarian regimes might be able to resist the pressures created by increased internationalization of the world economy longer than democratic ones (see Keohane and Milner 1996).

9. Also see O'Donnell 1993, 1996a. While Weffort (Chapter 10 of this volume) adopts this terminology, he draws an important distinction that we will emphasize in what follows: the *hybrid nature* of democratic regimes in the region that combine elements of both authoritarian and democratic government. Karl (1995) developed a similar argument for understanding democratic regimes in Central America. Acuña and Smith (1994) also looked at the limited nature of democratic regimes without redefining the basic concept of political democracy in the process.

the promises of his campaign—has not the president been authorized to govern as he (or she) thinks best?" (59–60).

More generally, O'Donnell suggested this pattern reflects the lack of institutions that can aggregate and represent interests, as well as lengthen the time horizon of actors in order to avoid what he described as a "colossal prisoner's dilemma" in which individuals' short-term interests prevail. Swift, unilateral presidential action that can rise above this fray of naked self-interest to insulate technocratic policy makers is the solution. In a later article (1996a), O'Donnell argued that institutionalization is taking place, but that it is taking a different form compared with the kind of institutionalization characteristic of representative democracies. It is a type of institutionalization that cannot be understood in terms of the extension of citizenship or, in other words, the application of the democratic norms to civil society. Rather, it reflects a mixture of formal and informal institutional rules that current democratic theories do not help us understand. These informal institutional rules are constituted by what O'Donnell called particularism or clientelism. In other words, they are constituted by traditional politics.

To a certain extent, references to traditional political practices and styles, the historical recourse to strong, unilateral executive action, *caudillismo*, and so on, in much of O'Donnell's work is reminiscent of the large body of literature on Latin America's unique authoritarian political culture (Wiarda 1982, 1990). While the usefulness of political culture for determining the prospects for democracy is highly doubtful (Karl 1990), it is clear that Latin America has had a long history of authoritarian politics whose causes are found in the way in which interests are organized and expressed, as well as in the historical weakness of political institutions in many countries (Faucher, Ducatenzeiler, and Castro Rea 1993).

The latter point raises an important question: What makes these explicitly authoritarian tendencies democratic, let alone a new subtype of democratic regime? Obviously, the presidential elections that initially bring these leaders to power and allegedly grant them a virtual blank check in terms of their ultimate authority while in office are central to answering this question. As O'Donnell noted, these elections conform to the minimal requirements suggested by Dahl for characterizing polyarchy (Dahl 1982: 11), in that they generally exhibit few constraints on contestation and participation by the citizenry.

If these regimes can be characterized as democratic, they would seem to represent not something "new" in democratic theory but only the most obvious example of the kind of representative democracy championed by Joseph Schumpeter in his classic work, *Capitalism, Socialism, and Democracy* (1950). Schumpeter provides a minimalist definition that restricts democracy to electoral competition. For Schumpeter, democracy is—and should be—limited to a political method "in which individuals acquire the power to decide by means of a competitive struggle for the people's vote" (269). Citizens must be relatively free to run for elected office, but the democratic process starts with the periodic calling of elections and ends once the ballots are counted. Between elections, elected leaders alone are responsible for policy-making decisions, more or less insulated from any pressures other than those that may result from their competition with other elected leaders and supported by "a well-trained bureaucracy of good standing and tradition, endowed with a strong sense of duty and a no less strong *esprit de corps*" (293). This minimalist conception of democracy has recently been adopted by a number of authors, such as Huntington (1991). As noted by Diamond,[10] advocates of electoral democracy "commonly acknowledge the need for minimal levels of civil freedom in order for competition and participation to be meaningful. . . . [H]owever, they do not devote much attention to the basic freedom involved" (1996: 21).

All of the chapters in this volume (and even O'Donnell's own work), however, emphasize that Latin America's new (and old) democracies are, at best, ambiguously "democratic" but certainly not representative of a fundamentally new style of politics in the region. Rather, what we seem to be witnessing is a continuation of many of the most negative tendencies that contributed to political instability in the region during this century, if not longer. These regimes are not "predictable": there is no predictable relation between promises and actual policies. They are above political parties and are not accountable to any political institution. They also function on the basis of decrees (*decretismo*). Many of these same tendencies have been closely associated with presidential systems of government in Latin America (Linz 1990, Linz and Valenzuela 1994). Perhaps what is really "new," we would suggest, is the *hyper-presidentialism* caused by the unprecedented severity of the current economic crisis and the kind of market that is emerging in its wake.

Hyper-presidentialism reflects the extreme concentration of political authority in the office of the president. The person who occupies that

10. Diamond (1996: 23) distinguishes between electoral democracy and liberal democracy. The latter is characterized not only by universal suffrage and the existence of free and fair elections but also by horizontal and vertical accountability and extensive provisions for political and civil pluralism, as well as for individual and group freedoms.

office becomes a key political actor in mediating diverse conflicts within society but as a result is not by any means an autonomous actor. Rather, the president's power and how he (or occasionally she) exercises it reflect the nature of the social forces and other actors (particularly the military) who provide the president's basis of political support. Weak, isolated presidents are still vulnerable, as the fall of Collor de Mello suggests, just as presidents with stronger bases of support can survive scandals that their weaker brethren cannot, as is suggested by Carlos Menem's continued dominance of Argentine politics (Weyland 1993). This underscores how other actors still exercise tremendous importance, particularly during times of economic or political crisis, as Chapters 4 and 5 of this volume by Schvarzer and Baer and Paiva, respectively, suggest.

Hyper-presidentialism is a classic example of a hybrid regime. In the current period, as emphasized in Chapter 9 by Oxhorn, it is legitimized by electoral victory, but it is not limited to "democratic regimes." Pinochet's Chile and the Mexican presidency are also good examples.[11] Fujimori in Peru, particularly after his 1992 *autogolpe* and the enactment of a new constitution, is also another obvious example.[12] In this regard, hyper-presidentialism also has many characteristics similar to those associated with *neopopulism* in the current period (Roberts 1995; Castro Rea, Ducatenzeiler, and Faucher 1992).

The social fragmentation and inequality prevalent in this context of predatory capitalism and hyper-presidentialism undergirds both. Neo-pluralism and the sharp constraints on the emergence of alternatives suggest that the stability of this kind of democracy can be quite long lasting, as if through a species of social and political inertia. Indeed, as all the chapters in the present volume seem to suggest, political stability has been maintained precisely by accentuating many of these tendencies in each of the countries studied. What is the meaning of this stability? Is this proof that these democracies are becoming consolidated? Not necessarily. To understand the significance of such stability, it is important to conclude by returning to the normative dimensions of the kinds of democracies prevalent throughout the region. As all of the chapters suggest, particularly those by Oxhorn and Weffort, the hallmark of these hybrid democracies is their very shallow normative dimension. Governmental

11. On Chile, see Remmer 1989. Changes in the nature of the president's support coalition can have important consequences for the constraints imposed on presidential power (see Dresser 1994).

12. There are examples outside the region of this as well, particularly in Eastern Europe and Russia (see Frye 1997).

accountability and broad citizen participation are not only lacking in the present context, there is little evidence that policy makers are concerned by this lack. We feel this is perhaps the greatest danger to social peace in the coming years. While elections and the limited political rights associated with them in the political realm, along with economic growth and poverty reduction (in most countries), are in themselves good and should not be ignored or underappreciated, they are not panaceas. Indeed, as we suggested in the volume's introduction, the long-term viability of both really cannot be separated from this normative dimension of democracy. If democracy remains minimalist, it will be very difficult for it to become consolidated; the excluded cannot remain excluded forever. One could imagine that an "illiberal democracy"[13] could endure with all of its defects to the extent that there is no better alternative, but it could become consolidated only with great difficulty. Ultimately, economic and political efficiency will depend on the creation or maintenance of strong institutions for the representation and aggregation of interests, as well as on the mediation of economic power's influence. The region's leaders and policy makers ignore this only at their great peril.

13. Our use of this concept is similar to that found in Collier and Levitsky 1997 in terms of the weakness of civil liberties in Latin America. We differ, however, in emphasizing the hybrid nature of such regimes. For Collier and Levitsky, illiberal regimes are an example of what they call a "diminished subtype of democratic regimes." They argue that there are other kinds of diminished subtypes, depending on the particular attribute of the minimal procedural definition of democracy that is missing. As explained above, we choose to focus on the hybrid nature of these regimes in order to highlight both the authoritarian elements present in the region's systems of government and the detrimental effects this has on the normative dimension of democratic governance.

References

Acuña, C., ed., 1995. *La nueva matriz política argentina*. Buenos Aires: Nueva Visión-North-South Center.

Acuña, C., and W. Smith, 1994. "The Political Economy of Structural Adjustment: The Logic of Support and Opposition to Neoliberal Reform." In W. Smith, C. Acuña, and E. Gamarra, eds., *Latin American Political Economy in the Age of Neoliberal Reform*. New Brunswick: Transaction.

Afonso, J. R., F. Rezende, M. da C. Silva, and R. Varsano, 1989. "A Tributação e o Orçamento na Nova Constituição." In *Perspectivas da Economia Brasileira 1989*. Rio de Janeiro: IPEA.

Alesina, A., 1987. "Macroeconomic Policy in a Two-Party System as a Repeated Game." *Quarterly Journal of Economics* 102 (410).

Alesina, A., and A. Drazen, 1991. "Why Are Stabilizations Delayed?" *American Economic Review* 81 (5).

Alesina, A., and D. Rodrik, 1992. "Distribution, Political Conflict, and Economic Growth: A Simple Theory and Some Empirical Evidence." In A. Cukierman, Z. Hercowitz, and L. Leiderman, eds., *Political Economy, Growth, and Business Cycles*. Cambridge: MIT Press.

Alesina, A., and G. Tabellini, 1988. "Credibility and Politics." *European Economic Review* 32 (March).

Alesina, A., and J. Sachs, 1988. "Political Parties and the Business Cycle in the United States, 1948–1984." *Journal of Money, Credit, and Banking* 20 (1).

Altimir, O., 1993. *Income Distribution and Poverty Through Crisis and Adjustment*. United Nations working paper, September, CEPAL.

———. 1995. *Inequality, Employment, and Poverty in Latin America: An Overview*. Paper presented at the conference, Poverty in Latin America: Issues and New Responses, 30 September to 1 October, Kellogg Institute for International Studies, University of Notre Dame.

Amsden, A., 1989. *Asia's Next Giant: South Korea and Late Industrialization*. New York: Oxford University Press.

Arida, P., and A. L. Resende, 1984. "Inertial Inflation and Monetary Reform." In J. Williamson, ed., *Inflation and Indexation: Argentina, Brazil, and Israel*. Washington: Institute for International Economics.

Aujac, H., 1950. "L'influence du comportement des groupes sociaux sur le développement d'une inflation." *Économie apliquée*, no. 4.

Bachrach, P., 1967. *The Theory of Democratic Elitism: A Critique*. Boston: Little, Brown.

Baer, W., 1991. "Social Aspects of Latin American Inflation." In W. Baer, J. Petry, and M. Simpson, eds., *Latin America: The Crisis of the Eighties and the Opportunities of the Nineties.* Champaign: University of Illinois, Bureau of Economic and Business Research Publishers.

Baer, W., and A. V. Villela, 1994. "Privatization and the Changing Role of the State in Brazil." In W. Baer and M. Birch, eds., *Essays on Privatization in Latin America: The Changing Roles of Public and Private Sectors.* New York: Praeger.

Bailey, N., 1990. "Another Perspective on the Economist and Third World Debt." *International Economy* 3 (June–July).

Banco Central do Brasil, 1989. *Brasil: Programa Econômico,* no. 35 (December).

Banco Nacional de México, 1988. *Examen de la situación económica de México* (January).

Barrera, M., 1980. *Política laboral y movimiento sindical chileno durante el régimen militar.* Working paper, The Wilson Center, Washington, D.C.

———. 1989. "Capitalismo post-nacional y diversas lógicas de organización y acción sociales: ¿Nuevos actores sociales para la transición?" *Cauce, quincenario de política, economía y sociedad.* Santiago.

Bartell, E., and L. Payne, eds., 1995. *Business and Democracy in Latin America.* Pittsburgh: University of Pittsburgh Press.

Bates, R., and A. Krueger, 1993a. "Generalizations Arising from the Country Studies." In R. Bates and A. Krueger, eds., *Political and Economic Interactions in Economic Policy Reform.* Cambridge, Mass.: Basil Blackwell.

———. 1993b. *Political and Economic Interactions in Economic Policy Reform: Evidence from Eight Countries.* Cambridge, Mass.: Basil Blackwell.

Bazdrech, C., N. Bassai, N. Lustig, and S. Loaeza, eds., 1992. *México, auge, crisis y ajuste.* México, D.F.: El Trimestre Económico, Fondo de Cultura Económica.

Bizberg, I., 1990. "La crisis del corporativismo mexicano." *Foro Internacional* 30: 4.

———. 1994. "Restructuración productiva y transformación del modelo de relaciones industriales: 1988–1994." Paper presented at the conference, Mexico in 1994: A Balance of President Carlos Salinas de Gortari Administration, 2–4 November, Université Laval, Quebec.

Bobbio, N., 1979. "Il Modello Giusnaturalistico." In N. Bobbio and M. Bovero, eds., *Società e Stato nella Filosofia Politica Moderna.* Milan: Il Saggiatore.

———. 1987. *The Future of Democracy: A Defense of the Rules of the Game.* Minneapolis: University of Minnesota.

Bonelli R., and E. Landau, 1990. "Do Ajuste à Abertura: A Economia Brasileira em Transição para os Anos 90." *Texto para discussão,* no. 251. Rio de Janeiro: Pontifícia Universidade Católica do Rio de Janeiro, Departamento de Economia.

Bovero, M., 1979. *Società e Stato nella Filosofia Politica Moderna.* Milan: Il Saggiatore.

Bresser Pereira, L. C., 1985. *Pactos Políticos.* São Paulo: Brasiliense.

———. 1988. "Economic Reforms and the Cycles of the State." *World Development* 21 (8).

———. 1990. "As Incertezas do Plano Collor." In C. de Faro, ed., *Plano Collor: Avaliações e Perspectivas.* Sao Paulo: Livros Técnicos e Científicos Editora.

———. 1991a. *Economic Crisis in Latin America: Washington Consensus or Fiscal Crisis Approach?* Working paper no. 6, University of Chicago, Department of Political Science, East South Systems Transformations Project.

———. ed., 1991b. *Populismo Econômico.* São Paulo: Editora Nobel.

———. 1993. "Economic Reforms and Economic Growth: Efficiency and Politics in Latin America." In L. C. Bresser Pereira, J. M. Maravall, and A. Przeworski, *Eco-*

nomic Reforms in New Democracies: A Social-Democratic Approach. Cambridge: Cambridge University Press.

———. 1996. *Economic Crisis and the State Reform in Brazil*. Boulder: Lynne Rienner.

Bresser Pereira, L. C., and J. Abud, 1994. "Net and Total Transition Cost: The Timing of Economic Reform." *Texto para discussão*, no. 41. São Paulo: Fundação Getúlio Vargas, Departamento de Economia.

Bresser Pereira, L. C., and Y. Nakano, 1987. "The Theory of Inertial or Autonomous Inflation." In L. C. Bresser Pereira and Y. Nakano, *The Theory of Inertial Inflation*. Boulder: Lynne Rienner.

———. 1991. "Hyperinflation and Stabilization in Brazil: The First Collor Plan." P. Davidson and J. Kregel, eds., *Economic Problems of the 1990s: Europe, the Developing Countries, and the United States*. Aldershot, England: Elgar.

Bresser Pereira, L. C., J. M. Maravall, and A. Przeworski, 1993. *Economic Reforms in New Democracies: A Social-Democratic Approach*. Cambridge: Cambridge University Press.

Bruhn, K., 1997. *Taking on Goliath: The Emergence of a New Left Party and the Struggle for Democracy in Mexico*. University Park: Pennsylvania State University Press.

Bruno, M., S. Fischer, E. Helpman, and G. Liviatan, eds., 1991. *Lessons of Economic Stabilizations and Its Aftermath*. Cambridge: MIT Press.

Buchanan, J., and G. Tullock, 1962. *The Calculus of Consent*. Ann Arbor: University of Michigan Press.

Buchanan, J., and R. Tollison, eds., 1984. *The Theory of Public Choice II*. Ann Arbor: University of Michigan Press.

Buchanan, P. G., 1995. *State, Labor, Capital*. Pittsburgh: University of Pittsburgh Press.

Calderón, A., 1993. Inversión extranjera directa y la integración regional: La experiencia en América Latina y el Caribe. Unpublished manuscript, Joint ECLAC/UNCTAD Unit on Transnational Corporations, Santiago.

Cameron, M. A., 1994. "Political Parties and the Informal Sector in Peru." Paper presented at the conference, New Forms of Inequality and Popular Representation in Latin America, 3–6 March, Columbia University, New York.

Camou, A., 1992. "Gobernabilidad y democracia." *Nexos* 15: 170.

Campero, G., 1984. *Los gremios empresariales en el período 1970–1983: Comportamiento sociopolítico y orientaciones ideológicas*. Santiago: Instituto Latinoamericano de Estudios Transnacionales.

Canel, E., 1992. "Democratization and the Decline of Urban Social Movements in Uruguay: A Political-Institutional Account." In A. Escobar and S. Alvarez, eds., *The Making of Social Movements in Latin America: Identity, Strategy, and Democracy*. Boulder: Westview Press.

Canitrot, A., 1975. "La experiencia populista de redistribución del ingresso." *Desarrollo Económico*, no.15.

Canitrot, A., and S. Junco, 1993. *Apertura y condiciones macroeconómicas: El caso argentino*. Working document no. 108, Inter-American Development Bank, Washington, D.C.

Canitrot, A., and S. Sigal, 1995. "Economic Reform, Democracy, and the Crisis of the State in Argentina." In J. Nelson, ed., *Democracy and Economic Reforms in Latin America*, vol. 2. Washington, D.C.: International Center for Economic Growth and the Overseas Development Council.

Cardoso, F. H., 1986. "Entrepreneurs and the Transition Process: The Brazilian Case." In G. O'Donnell, P. C. Schmitter, and L. Whitehead, eds., *Transitions from Authoritarian Rule: Comparative Perspectives*. Baltimore: Johns Hopkins University Press.

―――. 1989. "Associated-Dependent Development and Democratic Theory." In A. Stepan, ed., *Democratic Brazil: Problems of Transition and Consolidation*. New York: Oxford University Press.

Cardoso, R. Correa Leite, 1992. "Popular Movements in the Context of the Consolidation of Democracy in Brazil." In A. Escobar and S. Alvarez, eds., *The Making of Social Movements in Latin America: Identity, Strategy, and Democracy*. Boulder: Westview Press.

CARI (Consejo Argentino para las Relaciones Internacionales), 1989. F. de la Balza, ed., *El financiamiento externo argentino durante la década de 1990*. Buenos Aires: Sudamericana.

Carneiro, D. D., and R. L. F. Werneck, 1992. "Public Savings and Private Investment Requirements." Working papers series 100, March, Inter-American Development Bank.

Casar, J. I., 1993. "La gran promesa: Macroeconomía, competitividad industrial y el futuro de la economía mexicana." Unpublished manuscript, March, Instituto Latinoamericano de Estudios Transnacionales, Mexico, D.F.

Castañeda, T., 1990. *Para combatir la pobreza: Política social y descentralización en Chile durante los '80*. Santiago: Centro de Estudios Públicos.

Castro Rea, J., G. Ducatenzeiler, and P. Faucher, 1992. "Back to Populism: Latin America's Alternative to Democracy." In A. R. M. Ritter, M. Cameron, and D. H. Pollock, *Latin America to the Year 2000*. New York: Praeger.

Cavarozzi, M., 1994. "Politics: A Key for the Long Term in South America." In W. C. Smith, C. H. Acuña, and E. Gamarra, eds., *Latin American Political Economy in the Age of Neoliberal Reform*. New Brunswick, N.J.: Transaction Books.

Centeno, M. A., 1994. *Democracy Within Reason: Technocratic Revolution in Mexico*. University Park: Pennsylvania State University Press.

CEPAL (Comisión Económica para América Latina y el Caribe), 1988. "Equidad, transformación social y democracia en América Latina." Unpublished manuscript. Santiago.

CEPAL, 1989a. *Anuario Estadístico*. Santiago: United Nations.

CEPAL, 1989b. *Transformación ocupacional y crisis social en América Latina*. Santiago: United Nations.

CEPAL, 1990. *Magnitud de la pobreza en América Latina en los años ochenta*. Santiago: United Nations.

CEPAL, 1993. *Anuario Estadístico*. Santiago: United Nations.

CEPAL, 1996. *Panorama de la Inserción Internacional de América Latina y el Caribe*. Santiago: United Nations.

Chaudhry, K. A., 1993. "The Myths of the Market and the Common History of Late Developers." *Politics and Society* 21 (September).

Collier, D., ed., 1979. *The New Authoritarianism in Latin America*. Princeton: Princeton University Press.

Collier, R. B., and D. Collier, 1991. *Shaping the Political Arena*. Princeton: Princeton University Press.

Collier, D., and S. Levitsky, 1997. "Democracy with Adjectives: Conceptual Innovation in Comparative Research." *World Politics* 49 (April).

Cook, M. L., 1996. *Organizing Dissent: Unions, the State, and the Democratic Teachers' Movement in Mexico.* University Park: Pennsylvania State University Press.

Cook, M. L., K. J. Middlebrook, and J. Molinar, eds., 1994. *The Politics of Economic Restructuring: State-Society Relations and Regime Change in Mexico.* La Jolla: Center for U.S.-Mexican Studies, University of California, San Diego.

Córdova, A., 1992. "El PAN, partido gobernante." *Revista Mexicana de Sociología* 54 (July-September).

Cornelius, W. A., 1975. *Politics and the Migrant Poor in Mexico City.* Stanford: Stanford University Press.

Cornelius, W. A., J. Gentleman, and P. H. Smith, 1989. "Overview: The Dynamics of Political Change in Mexico." In W. A. Cornelius, J. Gentleman, and P. H. Smith, eds., *Mexico's Alternative Political Futures.* San Diego: Center of U.S.-Mexican Studies, University of California.

Corradi, J., P. Weiss Fagen, and M. A. Garretón, eds., 1992. *Fear at the Edge: State Terror and Resistance in Latin America.* Berkeley and Los Angeles: University of California Press.

Crespo, J. A., 1991. "La evolución del sistema de partidos en México." *Foro Internacional* 31 (April–June).

Crespo, J. A., 1992. "Crisis económica: Crisis de legitimidad." In C. Bazdrech, N. Bassai, N. Lustig, and S. Loaeza, eds., *México, auge, crisis y ajuste.* Mexico, D.F.: El Trimestre Económico, Fondo de Cultura Económica.

Cukierman, A., Z. Hercowitz, and L. Leiderman, eds., 1992. *Political Economy, Growth, and Business Cycles.* Cambridge: MIT Press.

Dahl, R., 1961. *Who Governs: Democracy and Power in an American City.* New Haven: Yale University Press.

Dahl, R., 1982. *Dilemmas of Pluralist Democracy.* New Haven: Yale University Press.

Damill, M., J. Frenkel, and R. Rozenwucel, 1993. "Crecimiento económico en América Latina: Experiencias recientes y perspectivas." *Desarrollo Económico,* no. 130.

De La Garza, E., 1989. "Para-estatales y corporativismo." *El Cotidiano,* no 28 (March–April).

Devlin, R., 1993. "Privatizations and Social Welfare." *CEPAL Review,* no. 49.

Deyo, F., ed., 1987. *The Political Economy of New Asian Industrialism.* Ithaca: Cornell University Press.

Diamond, L., 1992. "Economic Development and Democracy Reconsidered." In G. Marks and L. Diamond, eds., *Reexamining Democracy: Essays in Honor of Seymour Martin Lipset.* Newbury Park: Sage.

———. 1996. "Is the Third Wave Over?" *Journal of Democracy* 7 (3).

Díaz, A., 1991. "Nuevas tendencias en la estructura social chilena: Asalarización informal y pobreza en los ochenta." *Proposiciones,* no. 20.

———. 1993. "Nuevas tendencias de la industria en América Latina: Cadenas productivas, PYME y especialización flexible." *Proposiciones,* no. 23.

Díaz Alejandro, C., 1983. "Open Economy, Closed Polity?" In D. Tussie, ed., *Latin America in the World Economy.* Hampshire, Eng.: Gower.

Díaz Amador, M. del C., 1996. *La producción social de la ciudadanía política en México: Un estudio de caso: el movimiento urbano nacional del PRI.* Ph. D. dissertation, Centro de Estudios Sociológicos, El Colegio de México.

Dornbusch, R., and S. Edwards, eds., 1991. *The Macroeconomics of Populism in Latin America.* Chicago: University of Chicago Press.

Draibe, S., 1993. "As Políticas Sociais e o Neoliberalismo." *Revista USP*, no. 17 (March).

Dresser, D., 1994. "Bringing the Poor Back In: National Solidarity as a Strategy for Regime Legitimation." In W. Cornelius, A. Craig, and J. Fox, eds., *Transforming State-Society Relations in Mexico: The National Solidarity Strategy*. San Diego: Center for U.S.-Mexican Studies, University of California.

Ducatenzeiler, G., and P. Oxhorn, 1994. "Democracia, autoritarismo y el problema de la gobernabilidad en América Latina." *Desarrollo Económico* 34 (April–June).

Durand, V. M., J.-F. Prud'homme, and C. Márquez, 1990. *El Partido Revolucionario Institucional y la clase obrera: crisis y perspectiva de su relación*. Unpublished manuscript, Instituto Latinoamericano de Estudios Transnacionales, Mexico, D.F.

Eckstein, S., 1988. *The Poverty of Revolution: The State and the Urban Poor in Mexico*, 2d ed. Princeton: Princeton University Press.

ECLAC (Economic Commission for Latin America and the Caribbean), 1990. *Changing Production Patterns with Social Equity: The Prime Task of Latin America and the Caribbean Development in the 1990s*. Santiago: United Naitons.

———. 1992. *Social Equity and Changing Production Patterns: An Integrated Approach*. Santiago: United Nations.

———. 1994a. *Open Regionalism in Latin America and the Caribbean: Economic Integration as a Contribution to Changing Production Patterns with Social Equity*. Santiago: United Nations.

———. 1994b. *Social Panorama of Latin America*. Santiago: ECLAC.

———. 1996. *Readiness of Small Countries to Participate in the Free Trade Area of the Americas (FTAA)*. Mexico, D.F.: United Nations.

Edgren, G., 1990. "Employment Adjustment and the Unions: Case Studies of Enterprises in Asia." *International Labour Review* 29.

Edwards, S., and G. Tabellini, 1990. *Explaining Fiscal Policies and Inflation in Developing Countries*. Working paper no. 3493, October, National Bureau of Economic Research, Cambridge, Massachusetts.

Erickson, K., 1977. *The Brazilian Corporative State and the Working Class Politics*. Berkeley and Los Angeles: University of California Press.

Ethier, D., ed., 1990. *Democratic Transition and Consolidation in Southern Europe, Latin America, and Southeast Asia*. London: Macmillan.

Evans, P., 1995. *Embedded Autonomy: States and Industrial Transformation*. Princeton: Princeton University Press.

Faro, C. de, ed., 1990. *Plano Collor: Avaliações e Perspectivas*. São Paulo: Livros Técnicos e Científicos Editora.

Farrera, J., 1994. "El movimiento urbano popular, la organización de pobladores y la transición democrática en México." In V. M. Durand, ed., *La construción de la democracia en México*. Mexico, D.F.: Siglo XXI Editores.

Faucher, P., G. Ducatenzeiler, and J. Castro Rea, 1993. "A improvável estabilizaçao e o inconcebível capitalismo popular de mercado." In L. Sola, ed., *Estado, Mercado e Democracia*. São Paulo, Rio de Janeiro: Paz e Tera.

FIEL, 1989. *El control de cambios en la Argentina: Liberación cambiaria y crecimiento*. Buenos Aires: Manantial.

———. 1991. *La reforma económica 1989–91: Balance y perspectivas*. Buenos Aires: Manantial.

Fiori, J. L., 1994. "Los monederos falsos." *La Ciudad Futura*, no. 41.

Fox, J., 1994. "The Difficult Transition from Clientelism to Citizenship: Lessons from Mexico." *World Politics* 46 (January).

Frenkel, R., J. M. Fanelli, and G. Rozenwurcel, 1992. *Crítica al consenso de Washing-ton*. Working document no. 1, Lima, Fondad.

Frieden, J. A., 1991. "Invested Interests: The Politics of National Economic Policies in a World of Global Finance." *International Organization* 45 (autumn).

Frye, T., 1997. "A Politics of Institutional Choice: Post-Communist Presidencies." Paper presented at the conference, Economic and Political Liberalization, 28 February to 2 March, Duke University, Durham, North Carolina.

Fuchs, M., 1990. "Los programas de capitalización de la deuda externa argentina." Buenos Aires: ECLA.

Fukuyama, F., 1992. *The End of History and the Last Man*. New York: Free Press.

Garabito, R. A., 1991. "La COR: Recambio fallido." *Trabajo*, no 5–6 (winter-spring).

García, N., 1991. *Reestructuración, ahorro y mercado de trabajo*. Santiago: Programa Regional del Empleo pora América Latina de Naciones Unidas.

Garretón, M. A., 1984. *Dictaduras y democratización*. Santiago: Facultad Latino-americano de Ciencias Sociales.

———. 1989. *The Chilean Political Process*. Boston: Unwin Hyman.

———. 1994. "The Political Dimension of Processes of Transformation in Chile." In W. Smith, C. Acuña, and E. Gamarra, eds., *Democracy, Markets, and Structural Reform in Latin America: Argentina, Bolivia, Brazil, Chile, and Mexico*. Miami: University of Miami North-South Center.

———. 1995. "Redemocratization in Chile." *Journal of Democracy* 6 (January).

———. 1998. "Social and Economic Transformations in Latin America: The Emergence of a New Political Matrix?" In P. Oxhorn and P. K. Starr, eds., *Markets and Democracy in Latin America: Conflict or Convergence?* Boulder: Lynne Rienner.

Garrido, L. J., 1982. *El partido de la revolución institucionalizada*. México: Siglo XXI Editores.

———. 1993. *La ruptura*. Mexico, D.F.: Grijalbo.

Gay, R., 1990. "Popular Incorporation and Prospects for Democracy: Some Implications of the Brazilian Case." *Theory and Society* 19 (3).

Geddes, B., 1995. "The Politics of Economic Liberalization." *Latin American Research Review* 30 (2).

Gerchunoff, P., ed., 1992. *Las privatizaciones en la Argentina: Primera etapa*. Buenos Aires: Instituto Torcuato Di Tella.

Gerchunoff, P., and J. C. Torre, 1992. "What Role for the State in Latin America." In S. Teitel, ed., *Towards a New Development Strategy for Latin America: Pathways from Hirschman's Thought*. Washington: Inter-American Development Bank.

Gerchunoff, P., and J. L. Machinea, 1994. "Un ensayo sobre la política económica después de la estabilización." In P. Bustos, ed., *Más allá de la estabilidad*. Buenos Aires: Fundación Ebert.

Gereffi, G., and D. Wyman, eds., 1990. *Manufacturing Miracles: Paths of Industriali-zation in Latin America and East Asia*. Princeton: Princeton University Press.

Gibson, E. L., 1992. "Conservative Electoral Movements and Democratic Politics: Core Constituencies, Coalition Building, and the Latin American Electoral Right." In D. Chalmers, Maria do Carmo Campello de Souza, and A. Borón, eds., *The Right and Democracy in Latin America*. New York: Praeger.

Gourevitch, P., 1986. *Politics in Hard Times*. Ithaca: Cornell University Press.

Graham, C., 1992. "The Politics of Protecting the Poor During Adjustment: Bolivia's Emergency Social Fund." *World Development* 20 (9).

————. 1994. *Safety Nets, Politics, and the Poor: Transitions to Market Economies.* Washington, D.C.: Brookings Institution.

Grindle, M., and J. Thomas, 1991. *Public Choice and Policy Change.* Baltimore: John Hopkins University Press.

Grossman, G. M., 1990. "Promoting New Industrial Activities: A Survey of Recent Arguments and Evidence." *OECD Economic Studies*, no. 14.

Grossman, G. M., and E. Helpman, 1993. *Innovation and Growth.* Cambridge: MIT Press.

Guadarrama, G., 1987. "Entrepreneurs and Politics: Businessmen in Sonora and Nuevo León, July 1985." In A. Alvarado, ed., *Electoral Patterns and Perspectives in Mexico.* San Diego: Center for U.S.-Mexican Studies, University of California.

Guerra, F. X., 1985. *Le Mexique: De l'ancien régime à la revolution*, vol. 1. Paris: Editions L'Harmattan-Publications de la Sorbonne.

Gunther, R., H.-J. Puhle, and P. N. Diamandouros, eds., 1995. *The Politics of Democratic Consolidation: Southern Europe in Comparative Perspective.* Baltimore: Johns Hopkins University Press.

Haggard, S., 1990. *Pathways from the Periphery: The Politics of Growth in the Newly Industrializing Countries.* Ithaca: Cornell University Press.

Haggard, S., and R. Kaufman, 1992a. "Economic Adjustment and the Prospect for Democracy." In S. Haggard and R. Kaufman, eds., *The Politics of Economic Adjustment.* Princeton: Princeton University Press.

————, eds., 1992b. *The Politics of Economic Adjustment.* Princeton: Princeton University Press.

————. 1995. *The Political Economy of Democratic Transitions.* Princeton: Princeton University Press.

Haggard, S., and S. Maxfield, 1993. "Political Explanations of Financial Policy in Developing Countries." In S. Haggard, C. Lee, and S. Maxfield, eds., *The Politics of Finance in Developing Countries.* Ithaca: Cornell University Press.

Hagopian, F., 1990. "Democracy by Undemocratic Means: Elites, Political Pacts, and Regime Transition in Brazil." *Comparative Political Studies* 23 (July).

————. 1993. "After Regime Change: Authoritarian Legacies, Political Representation, and the Democratic Future of South America." *World Politics* 45 (April).

Hamilton, N., 1985. *The Limits of State Autonomy: Post Revolutionary Mexico.* Princeton: Princeton University Press.

Hankiss, E., 1991. *East European Alternatives: Are There Any?* Oxford: Oxford University Press.

Hansen, R. D., 1971. *The Politics of Mexican Development.* Baltimore: Johns Hopkins University Press.

Held, D., 1987. *Models of Democracy.* Stanford: Stanford University Press.

Helwege, A., 1995. "Poverty in Latin America: Back to the Abyss?" *Journal of Interamerican Studies and World Affairs* 37 (fall).

Henríquez, H., 1991. *Trabajadores de la industria de confecciones: Algunos aspectos de sus condiciones de trabajo.* Material de discusión, Centro de Estudios Sociales, Santiago.

Heredia, B., 1991. "The Political Economy of the Mexican Crisis." In Dharam Ghai, ed., *The IMF and the South: The Social Impact of Crisis and Adjustment.* London: Zed.

————. 1992. "Profits, Politics, and Size: The Political Transformation of Mexican Business." In D. Chalmers, Maria do Carmo Campello de Souza, and A. Borón, eds., *The Right and Democracy in Latin America.* New York: Praeger.

————. 1994. "Estructura económica y reforma económica: El caso de México." *Política y Gobierno* l (January-February).

Hermet, G., A. Rouquié, and J. Linz, 1982. *¿Para qué sirven las elecciones?* México: Fondo de Cultura Económica.

Hershberg, E., 1997. "Market-Oriented Development Strategies and State-Society Relations in New Democracies: Lessons from Contemporary Chile and Spain." In D. Chalmers, C. Vilas, K. Hite, S. Martin, K. Piester, and M. Segarra, eds., *The New Politics of Inequality in Latin America: Rethinking Participation and Representation*. Oxford: Oxford University Press.

Hirsch, F., and J. Goldthorpe, eds., 1978. *The Political Economy of Inflation*. London: Martin Robertson.

Hirschman, A., 1981a. The Social and Political Matrix of Inflation: Elaborations on the Latin American Experience. In *Essays in Trespassing*. Cambridge: Cambridge University Press.

————. 1981b. *Essays in Trespassing*. Cambridge: Cambridge University Press.

Hunter, W., 1995. "Politicians Against Soldiers: Contesting the Military in Postauthoritarian Brazil." *Comparative Politics* 27 (July).

Huntington, S., 1989. "No Exit: The Errors of Endism." *The National Interest* 17 (fall).

————. 1991. "Democracy's Third Wave." *Journal of Democracy* 2 (spring).

IBGE. *Anuário Estatístico*. Rio de Janeiro: Instituto Brasileiro de Geografia e Estatística.

IDB (Inter-American Development Bank), 1997. *Integration and Trade in the Americas*. Periodic note, Inter-American Development Bank, Washington, D.C.

IDB-ECLAC, 1993. *The Transition*. Summary of the Sixth Coloquium, 1–2 December, IDB/ECLAC Project, Washington, D.C.

IMF, 1995. "Editorial." *Bulletin* (September).

Immergut, E., 1992. "The Rules of the Game: The Logic of Health Policy-Making in France, Switzerland, and Sweden." In S. Steinmo, K. Thelen, and F. Longstreth, eds., *Structuring Politics: Historical Institutionalism in Comparative Analysis*. New York: Cambridge University Press.

Instituto de Economia do Setor Público. Various Issues. FUNDAP, Indicatores IESP.

Instituto Nacional de Estadísticas, Geografía e Información, 1992. *Cuadernos de información oportuna*, Mexico, D.F. (June).

IPEA, 1991a. *Boletim Conjuntural* (April).

IPEA, 1991b. *Perspectivas da Economia Brasileira, 1992*. IPEA: Brasilia.

IPEA, 1992. "A Crise Econômica e Social dos Ultimos 12 Anos." *Boletim Conjuntural* (October).

Karl, T. L., 1990. "Dilemmas of Democratization in Latin America." *Comparative Politics* 23 (October).

————. 1995. "The Hybrid Regimes of Central America." *Journal of Democracy* 6 (July).

Kaufman, R. R., 1988. *The Politics of Debt in Argentina, Brazil and Mexico*. Berkeley: Institute of International Studies, University of California.

Keohane, R., and H. Milner, eds., 1996. *Internationalization and Domestic Politics*. Cambridge: Cambridge University Press.

Kikery, S., J. Nellis, and M. Shirley, 1992. *Privatization. The Lessons of Experience*. Washington: World Bank.

Korzeniewicz, R., and W. C. Smith, 1997. "The Second Great Transformation: Institutional Discontinuities in Historical Perspective." Paper presented at the

Twentieth International Congress of the Latin American Studies Association, April, Guadalajara, Mexico.

Krugman, P., 1992. "Toward a Counter-Revolution in Development Theory." In *Proceedings of the World Bank Annual Conference on Development Economics*, Washington (Supplement to *World Bank Economic Review and World Bank Research Observer*).

Lindberg, L., and C. Maier, eds., 1985. *The Politics of Inflation and Economic Stagnation: Theoretical Approaches and International Case Studies*. Washington, D.C.: Brookings Institution.

Linz, J., 1987. *The Breakdown of Democratic Regimes: Crisis, Breakdown, and Reequilibration*. Baltimore: John Hopkins University Press.

———. 1990. "The Perils of Presidentialism." *Journal of Democracy* 1 (Winter): 51–69.

Linz, J., and A. Stepan, 1996a. "Toward Consolidated Democracies." *Journal of Democracy* 7 (April).

———. 1996b. *Problems of Democratic Transition and Consolidation: Southern Europe, South America, and Postcommunist Europe*. Baltimore: John Hopkins University Press.

Linz, J., and A. Valenzuela, 1994. *The Failure of Presidential Democracy*. Baltimore: Johns Hopkins University Press.

Lipset, S. M., 1959. "Some Social Requisites of Democracy: Economic Development and Political Legitimacy." *American Political Science Review* 53 (March).

———. 1994. "The Social Requisites of Democracy Revisited." *American Sociological Review* 59 (February).

Loaeza, S., 1992. "The Role of the Right in Political Change in Mexico." In D. Chalmers, Maria do Carmo Campello de Souza, and A. Borón, eds., *The Right and Democracy in Latin America*. New York: Praeger.

Lomnitz, L., 1977. *Networks and Marginality: Life in a Mexican Shantytown*. New York: Academic Press.

Lopes, F. L., 1984. "Inflação Inercial, Hiperinflação e Desinflação." *Revista da ANPEC*, no. 7.

Lustig, N., 1992. *Mexico: The Remaking of an Economy*. Washington, D.C.: The Brookings Institution.

Mahon, J., 1996. *Mobile Capital and Latin American Development*. University Park: Pennsylvania State University Press.

Mainwaring, S., and T. Scully, eds., 1995. *Building Democratic Institutions: Party Systems in Latin America*. Stanford: Stanford University Press.

Mainwaring, S., G. O'Donnell, and J. S. Valenzuela, eds., 1992. *Issues in Democratic Consolidation: The New South American Democracies in Comparative Perspective*. Notre Dame: Published for the Helen Kellogg Institute for International Studies by the University of Notre Dame Press.

Malloy, J., 1987. "The Politics of Transition." In J. Malloy and M. Seligson, eds., *Authoritarians and Democrats: Regime Transition in Latin America*. Pittsburgh: University of Pittsburgh Press.

———. 1991. "Parties, Economic Policymaking, and The Problem of Democratic Governance in the Central Andes." Paper presented at the Sixteenth International Congress of the Latin American Studies Association, April, Washington, D.C.

Mankiw, G., and D. Romer, eds., 1991. *New Keynesian Economics*. Cambridge: MIT Press.

Marsh, D., 1992. "British Industrial Relations Policy Transformed: The Thatcher Legacy." *Journal of Public Policy* 2 (3).

Mauceri, P., 1995. "State Reform, Coalitions, and the Neoliberal Autogolpe in Peru." *Latin American Research Review* 30 (1).

McIlroy, J., 1991. *The Permanent Revolution? Conservative Law and the Trade Unions.* Nottingham: Spokesman Press.

McKinnon, R., 1993. *The Order of Economic Liberalization.* Baltimore: Johns Hopkins University Press.

Meller, P., 1984. "Análisis del problema de la elevada tasa de desocupación chilena." *Colección Estudios CIEPLAN,* no. 4 (September).

——. 1992. *Adjustment and Equity in Chile.* Paris: Organization for Economic Development and Cooperation.

Mesa-Lago, C., 1978. *Social Security in Latin America: Pressure Groups, Stratification, and Inequality.* Pittsburgh: University of Pittsburgh Press.

Meyer, L., 1993. "El presidencialismo: Del populismo al neoliberalismo." *Revista Mexicana de Sociología* 54 (April–June).

Middlebrook, K., 1986. "Political Liberalization in an Authoritarian Regime: The Case of Mexico." In G. O'Donnell, P. C. Schmitter, and L. Whitehead, eds., *Transitions from Authoritarian Rule: Latin America.* Baltimore: Johns Hopkins University Press.

MIDEPLAN (Ministerio de Planificación Nacional), 1992. *Calidad de vida y desarrollo social.* Santiago: Ministerio de Planificación Nacional.

Millet, R., and M. Gold-Biss, eds., 1996. *Beyond Praetorianism: The Latin American Military in Transition.* Coral Gables: North-South Center Press, University of Miami.

Mizrahi, Y., 1994. *A New Conservative Opposition in Mexico: the Politics of Entrepreneurs in Chihuahua (1983–1993).* Ph.D. dissertation, University of California, Berkeley.

Molinar, J., 1991. *El tiempo de la legitimidad: Elecciones, autoritarismo y democracia en México.* Mexico, D.F.: Cal y Arena.

Moller, C., 1989. "Flexibilisation: The Impoverishment of Employees and the Reduction of Work Place Solidarity." In J. B. Agassi and S. Heycock, eds., *The Redesign of Working Time: Promise or Threat?* Germany: Edition Sigma.

Montiel, Y., 1991. *Proceso de trabajo, acción sindical y nuevas tecnologías en Volkswagen de México.* Mexico, D.F.: Centro de Investigaciones Superiores en Antropología Social (CIESAS).

Moore, M., and L. Hamalai, 1993. "Economic Liberalization, Political Pluralism, and Business Associations in Developing Countries." *World Development* 21 (12).

Moraes Filho, E., 1962. *O Sindicato Unico no Brazil.* Rio de Janeiro: Noite.

Morgan Bank, 1994. "Sustainability of Latin America's Debt." *Economic Research Notes* (February).

Mueller, D., 1976. "Public Choice: A Survey." *Journal of Economic Literature* 14 (2).

Murillo, M. V., 1997. "Union Politics, Market-Oriented Reforms, and the Reshaping of Argentine Corporatism." In D. Chalmers, C. Vilas, K. Hite, S. Martin, K. Piester, and M. Segarra, eds., *The New Politics of Inequality in Latin America: Rethinking Participation and Representation.* Oxford: Oxford University Press.

Naím, M., 1993. "Latin America: Post-Adjustment Blues." *Foreign Policy* 92 (fall).

Nakano, Y., 1990. "As fragilidades do Plano Collor de Estabilizacão." In C. de Faro, ed., *Plano Collor: Avaliações e Perspectivas.* São Paulo: Livros Técnicos e Científicos Editora.

Nelson, J., 1989. "The Politics of Pro-Poor Adjustment." In J. Nelson, ed., *Fragile Coalitions: The Politics of Economic Adjustment*. New Brunswick: Transaction Books.
———, ed., 1990. *Economic Crisis and Policy Choice*. Princeton: Princeton University Press.
Nelson, J., and contributors, J. Kochanowicz, K. Mizsei, and Oscar Muñoz, 1994. *Intricate Links: Democratization and Market Reforms in Latin America and Eastern Europe*. U.S.-Third World Policy Perspectives, no. 20. New Brunswick: Transaction Publishers.
Nogueiro da Costa, F., 1993. "Além da Hiper-Estagflação." *Estudos Especiais-CECON*, no. 4. Campinas: CECON-IE-UNICAMP.
Nordhaus, W., 1975. "The Political Business Cycle." *Review of Economic Studies* 42 (2).
North, D., 1981. *Structure and Change in Economic History*. New York: Norton.
North, D. C., 1990. *Institutions, Institutional Change, and Economic Performance*. Cambridge: Cambridge University Press.
Notermans, T., 1993. "The Abdication from National Policy Autonomy: Why the Macroeconomic Policy Regime Has Become So Unfavorable to Labor." *Politics and Society* 21 (June).
Noyola, J., 1956. "El desarrollo económico y la inflación en México y en otros países latinoamericanos." *Investigación Económica* 16: 4.
O'Donnell, G., 1972. *Modernización y autoritarismo*. Buenos Aires: Paidós.
———. 1978. "States and Alliances in Argentina, 1956–1976." *Journal of Development Studies* 15:1.
———. 1979. *Modernization and Bureaucratic Authoritarianism*. Berkeley: University of California Press.
———. 1982. *El Estado burocrático autoritario*. Buenos Aires: Ed. de Belgrano.
———. 1993. "On the State, Democratization, and Some Conceptual Problems: A Latin American View with Glances at Some Postcommunist Countries." *World Development* 21: 8.
———. 1994. "Delegative Democracy." *Journal of Democracy* 5 (January).
———. 1996a. "Illusions About Consolidation." *Journal of Democracy* 7 (April).
———. 1996b. "Illusions and Conceptual Flaws." *Journal of Democracy* 7 (October).
O'Donnell, G., and P. Schmitter, 1986. *Transitions from Authoritarian Rule: Tentative Conclusions About Uncertain Democracies*. Baltimore: Johns Hopkins University Press.
Olson, M., 1965. *The Logic of Collective Action*. Cambridge: Harvard University Press.
Oxhorn, P., 1991. "The Popular Sector Response to an Authoritarian Regime: Chilean Shantytown Organizations Since the Military Coup." *Latin American Perspectives* 18 (winter).
———. 1994. "Where Did All of the Protesters Go? Popular Mobilization, Transition to Democracy, and the New Democratic Regime in Chile." *Latin American Perspectives* 21 (summer).
———. 1995a. "From Controlled Inclusion to Reactionary Exclusion: The Struggle for Civil Society in Latin America." In J. Hall, ed., *Civil Society: Theory, History, and Comparison*. Cambridge: Polity Press.
———. 1995b. *Organizing Civil Society: Popular Organizations and the Struggle for Democracy in Chile*. University Park: Pennsylvania State University Press.
———. 1996. "Surviving the Return to 'Normalcy': Social Movements, Democratic Consolidation, and Economic Restructuring." *International Review of Sociology* 6: 1.

Oxhorn, P., and G. Ducatenzeiler, 1994. "Social Policies as Political Strategies: Processes of Inclusion and Exclusion." Paper presented at the Thirteenth International Congress of the Latin American Studies Association, 10–12 March, Atlanta.

———. 1998. "The Problematic Relationship Between Economic and Political Liberalization: Some Theoretical Considerations." In P. Oxhorn and P. K. Starr, eds., *Markets and Democracy in Latin America: Conflict or Convergence?* Boulder: Lynne Rienner.

Paiva, C., 1992. *The Collor Plan: Alternative Interpretations.* M.A. thesis, University of Illinois, Champaign.

Palermo, V., and M. Novaro, 1996. *Política y poder en el gobierno de Menem.* Buenos Aires: Facultad Latinoamericano de Ciencias Sociales -Norma.

Panebianco, A., 1990. *Modelos de partido.* Madrid: Alianza Universidad.

Pazos, F., 1972. *Chronic Inflation in Latin America.* New York: Praeger.

Peres, W., 1993. "The Internationalization of Latin American Industrial Firms." *CEPAL Review* 49 (April).

Pérez, G., and S. León, eds., 1987. *17 ángulos de un sexenio.* Mexico, D.F.: Plaza y Valdés.

Persson, T., and G. Tabellini, 1992. "Growth, Distribution, and Politics." *European Economic Review* 36 (April).

Petras, J., and F. Leiva, 1994. *Democracy and Poverty in Chile: The Limits to Electoral Politics.* Boulder: Westview Press.

Piester, K., 1994. "Targeting the Poor: The Politics of Social Welfare Reforms in Mexico." Paper presented at the conference, New Forms of Inequality and Popular Representation in Latin America, Columbia University, 3-6 March, New York.

Pinto, A., 1973. *Inflación: Raíces estructurales.* Lecturas, no. 3. Mexico: Fondo de Cultura.

Polanyi, K., 1944. *The Great Transformation: The Political and Economic Origins of Our Time.* Boston: Beacon Press.

Pollack, M., and A. Uthoff, 1990. *Pobreza y empleo: Un análisis del período 1969-1987 en el Gran Santiago.* Documento de Trabajo no. 348. Santiago: Programa Regional del Empleo pora América Latina de Naciones Unidas-OIT.

Portes, A., 1994. "By-passing the Rules: The Dialectics of Labour Standards and Informalization in Less Developed Countries." In N. Sensuberger and D. Cambell, eds., *International Labor Standards and Economic Interdependence.* Geneva: Institute for Labour Studies.

PREALC (Programa Regional del Empleo pora América Latina de Naciones Unidas), 1992. *Empleo y transformación productiva en América Latina y el Caribe.* Documento de Trabajo no. 369. Santiago: Programa Regional del Empleo pora América Latina de Naciones Unidas-OIT.

Prud'homme, J.-F., 1994. "Acción colectiva y lucha por la democracia en México y Chile." In *Transformaciones sociales y acciones colectivas: América Latina en el contexto internacional de los noventa.* Mexico, D.F.: El Colegio de México.

———. 1996. "La negociación de las reglas del juego: Tres reformas electorales (1988-1994)." *Política y gobierno* 3 (1).

Przeworski, A., 1985. *Capitalism and Social Democracy.* Cambridge: Cambridge University Press.

———. 1986. "Some Problems in the Study of the Transition to Democracy." In G. O'Donnell, P. C. Schmitter, and L. Whitehead, eds., *Transitions from Authoritarian Rule: Comparative Perspectives.* Baltimore: Johns Hopkins University Press.

————. 1991. *Democracy and the Market: Political and Economic Reforms in Eastern Europe and Latin America*. Cambridge: Cambridge University Press.

Przeworski, A., and F. Limongi, 1993. "Political Regimes and Economic Growth." *Journal of Economic Perspectives* 7 (summer).

Przeworski, A., and M. Wallerstein, 1985. "Material Interests, Class Compromise, and the State." In A. Przeworski, ed., *Capitalism and Social Democracy*. Cambridge: Cambridge University Press.

Putnam, R. D., 1993. *Making Democracy Work*. Princeton: Princeton University Press.

Quintero Ramírez, C., 1990. *The Unionization of the Tijuana Maquiladora*. Mexico, D.F.: National Council of Culture and the Arts.

————. 1991. "Conflictos laborales en Matamoros: 1970–1990, el caso de las maquiladoras." Unpublished manuscript, Mexico.

Rangel, I., 1963. *A Inflação Brasileira*. São Paulo: Brasiliense.

Razeto, L., 1993. "Ideas para un proyecto de desarrollo de un sector de economía popular de solidaridad y trabajo para superar la pobreza." In M. Velásquez, ed., *Economía y Trabajo en Chile, 1992–1993*. Santiago: Programa de Economía del Trabajo.

Rego, E. C. L., 1991. "Política Monetária em 90: Alterações e Limites." In F. A. de Olivera, ed., *A Economia Brasileira em Preto e Branco*. Campinas: Editora HUCITEC.

Remmer, K., 1989. *Military Rule in Latin America*. Boston: Unwin Hyman.

————. 1990. "Democracy and Economic Crisis: The Latin American Experience." *World Politics* 17 (April).

Reynolds, C., F. Thuomi, and R. Wettmann, 1993. *Case for Open Regionalism in the Andes: Policy Implications of Andean Integration in a Period of Hemisphere Liberalization and Structural Adjustment*. Report for the U.S. Agency for International Development, October.

Reynoso, V. M., 1993. "El Partido Acción Nacional: ¿la oposición hará gobierno?" *Revista Mexicana de Sociología* 55 (April–June).

Rezende, F., J. R. Afonso, R. Villela, and R. Varsano, 1989. "A Questão Fiscal." In *Perspectivas da Economia Brasileira* 1989. Rio de Janeiro: IPEA.

Roberts, K., 1995. "Neoliberalism and the Transformation of Populism in Latin America: The Peruvian Case." *World Politics* 48 (October).

Rodrigues, J. A., 1968. *Sindicato e Desenvolvimento no Brasil*. São Paulo: Difusão Européia do Livro.

Rodrigues, L. M., 1966. *Conflito e Sindicalismo no Brasil*. São Paulo: Difusão Européia do Livro.

Romer, P., 1989. "Capital Accumulation in the Theory of Long-Run Growth." In R. Barro, ed. *Modern Business Cycle Theory*. Cambridge: Harvard University Press.

Ros, J., 1992. "Ajuste macroeconómico, reformas estructurales y crecimiento." Unpublished manuscript. South Bend: Helen Kellogg Institute.

Rueschemeyer, D., E. Stephens, and J. Stephens, 1992. *Capitalist Development and Democracy*. Chicago: University of Chicago Press.

Ruiz-Tagle, J. 1986. *El sindicalismo chileno después del Plan Laboral*. Santiago: PET.

————. 1993. "Reducción de la pobreza y distribución de los ingresos en Chile." *Mensaje* 42 (December).

Sábato, J., and J. Schvarzer, 1988. "Trabas para la democracia: Funcionamiento de la economía y poder político en Argentina." In J. Sábato, ed., *La clase dominante en la Argentina moderna: Formación y características*. Buenos Aires: CISEA-GEL.

Sachs, J. D., 1989. "Social Conflict and Populist Policies in Latin America." In R. Brunetta and C. Dell-Arringa, eds., *Labor Relations and Economic Performance.* London: Macmillan.

———. 1994. "Life in the Economic Emergency Room." In J. Williamson, ed., *The Political Economy of Policy Reform.* Washington, D.C.: Institute for International Economics.

Sachs, J., A. Tornell, and A. Velasco, 1996. "The Collapse of the Mexican Peso: What Have We Learned?" In *Economic Policy: A European Forum*, no. 22 (April). London: Centre for Economic Policy Research, United Kingdom.

Sargent, T., and N. Wallace, 1981. "Some Unpleasant Monetarist Arithmetic." *Quarterly Review* 5.

Sartori, G., 1976. *Parties and Party System: A Framework for Analysis*, vol. 1. Cambridge: Cambridge University Press.

———. 1987. *The Theory of Democracy Revisited.* Chatham, N.J.: Chatham House Publishers.

Schmitter, P., 1971. *Interest Conflict and Political Change.* Stanford: Stanford University Press.

———. 1974. "Still the Century of Corporatism?" *Review of Politics* 36 (January).

———. 1983. "Democratic Theory and Neocorporatist Practice." *Social Research* 50 (winter).

———. 1991. "The Consolidation of Democracy and the Choice of Institutions." Working paper no. 7, East South System Transformations, Department of Political Science, University of Chicago.

———. 1995. "Organized Interest and Democratic Consolidation in Southern Europe." In R. Gunther, H.-J. Puhle, and P. N. Diamandouros, eds., *The Politics of Democratic Consolidation: Southern Europe in Comparative Perspective.* Baltimore: Johns Hopkins University Press.

Schneider, B. R., 1995. "Democratic Consolidations: Some Broad Comparisons and Sweeping Arguments." *Latin American Research Review* 30 (2).

Schumpeter, J., 1950. *Capitalism, Socialism, and Democracy.* New York: Harper and Row.

Schvarzer, J., 1984. "Dimensiones políticas de la deuda externa de la Argentina." *El Bimestre*, no. 14.

Schvarzer, J., 1986, *La política económica de Martínez de Hoz.* Buenos Aires: Hyspamérica.

———. 1993a. "Argentine 1989–1992: La restructuration de l'économie." In *Problèmes d'Amérique latine*, n.s., no. 8.

———. 1993b. "El proceso de privatizaciones en la Argentina. Implicaciones preliminares sobre sus efectos en la gobernalidad del sistema." *Realidad Económica*, no. 120.

———. 1993c. "Expansión, maduración y perspectivas de las ramas básicas de procesos en la industria Argentina: Una mirada ex post desde la economía política." *Desarrollo Económico*, no. 131.

Scully, T., 1996. "Chile: The Political Underpinnings of Economic Liberalization." In J. Domínquez and A. Lowenthal, eds., *Constructing Democratic Governance: South America in the 1990s.* Baltimore: Johns Hopkins University Press.

Shaiken, H., 1990. "Alta tecnología en México, el caso de la producción de motores automotrices." In J. Carrillo, ed., *La nueva era de la industria automotriz en México.* Tijuana, Mexico: El Colegio de la Frontera Norte.

Shaiken, H., and S. Herzenberg, 1987. *Automation and Global Production*. Monograph series no. 26. San Diego: Center for U.S.-Mexican Studies.

Sheahan J., 1980. "Market-oriented Economic Policies and Political Repression in Latin America." *Economic Development and Cultural Change* 28 (January).

Shulman, S., 1984. "Competition and Racial Discrimination: The Employment Effects of Reagan's Labor Market Reforms." *Review of Radical Political Economics* 16.

Silva, E., 1996. "From Dictatorship to Democracy: The Business-State Nexus in Chile's Economic Transformation 1975–1994." *Comparative Politics* 28 (April).

Simão, A., 1966, *Sindicato e Estado*. São Paulo: Dominus.

Simonsen, M. H., 1990. "Inflação-Interpretações Brasileiras." In *Inflação e Hiperinflação: Interpretações e Retórica*. São Paulo: Editora Bienal.

Skidmore, T., 1967. *Politics in Brazil, 1930–1964: An Experiment in Democracy*. New York: Oxford University Press.

———. 1977. "The Politics of Economic Stabilization in Postwar Latin America." In J. Malloy, ed., *Authoritarianism and Corporatism in Latin America*. Pittsburgh: University of Pittsburgh Press.

Smith, W.C., and R. Korzeniewicz, 1996. "Latin America and the Second Great Transformation." In W. C. Smith and R. Korzeniewicz, eds., *Politics, Social Change, and Economic Restructuring in Latin America*. Miami: North-South Center Press.

Smith, W., C. Acuña, and E. Gamarra, eds., 1994a. *Democracy, Markets, and Structural Reform in Latin America: Argentina, Bolivia, Brail, Chile, and Mexico*. Miami: Transaction Publishers, North-South Center, University of Miami, New Brunswick.

———, eds., 1994b. *Latin American Political Economy in the Age of Neoliberal Reform: Theoretical and Comparative Perspectives for the 1990s*. Miami: Transaction Publishers, North-South Center, University of Miami, New Brunswick.

Soh, B. H., 1986. "Political Business Cycle in Industrialized Democratic Countries." *Kyklos* 39 (1).

Sola, L., 1994. "Estado, Reforma Fiscal e Governabilidade Democrática: Qual Estado?" *Novos Estudos Cebrap*, no. 38 (March).

Solís, L., 1975. *La realidad económica mexicana: retrovisión y perspectivas*. Mexico, D.F.: Siglo XXI.

Sullivan, M. P., 1991. "Latin American Debt: Characteristics, Trends, and US Policy." In *Congressional Research Service*, 11 April. Washington, D.C.: Library of Congress.

Sunkel, O., 1960. "Inflation in China: An Unorthodox Approach." *International Economic Papers*, no. 10.

Tamayo, J., 1992. "El neocardenismo y el nuevo estado." In J. Alonso, A. Asiz, and J. Tamayo, eds., *El nuevo estado mexicano II: Estado y política*. Guadalajara, Mexico: Universidad de Guadalajara Nueva Imágen, CIESAS.

Tavares de Almeida, M. H., 1994. "Alem do corporatismo: Interesses organizados e democratizacão." Paper presented at the Eighteenth Congress of the Latin American Studies Association, 10–12 March, Atlanta.

Taylor, C., 1990. *Invoking Civil Society*. Working papers and proceedings of the Center for Psychosocial Studies, no. 31, Chicago.

Thorp, R., and L. Whitehead, eds., 1979. *Inflation and Stabilization in Latin America*. London: Macmillan.

Torre, J. C., 1991. "América Latina, el gobierno de la democracia en tiempos difíciles." Unpublished manuscript. Buenos Aires: Instituto Torcuato Di Tella.

United Nations (UN), 1993. *The Transnationalization of Service Industries: An Empirical Analysis of the Determinants of Foreign Direct Investment by Transnational Service Corporations.* New York: United Nations.

Valenzuela, J. S., 1992. Democratic Consolidation in Post-Transitional Settings: Notions, Process, and Facilitating Conditions." In S. Mainwaring, G. O'Donnell, and J. S. Valenzuela, eds., *Issues in Democratic Consolidation: The New South American Democracies in Comparative Perspective.* Notre Dame: University of Notre Dame Press.

Vellinga, M., 1979. *Industrialización, burguesía y clase obrera en México: El caso de Monterrey.* Mexico, D.F.: Siglo XXI Editores.

von Doellinger, C., 1991. "Reordenação do Sistema Financeiro." In *Perspectivas da Economia Brasileira, 1992.* Brasilia: IPEA.

Waisman, C., 1987. *Reversal of Development in Argentina.* Princeton: Princeton University Press.

Walzer, M., 1991. "A Better Vision: The Idea of Civil Society. A Path to Social Reconstruction." *DISSENT* 38 (spring).

Ward, Peter M., 1993. "Social Welfare Policy and Political Opening in Mexico." *Journal of Latin American Studies* 25 (October).

Waterbury, J., 1992. "The Heart of the Matter? Public Enterprise and the Adjustment Process." In S. Haggard and R. Kaufman, eds., *The Politics of Economic Adjustment.* Princeton: Princeton University Press.

Weffort, F., 1991. *America Astray.* Working paper no. 162, July, University of Notre Dame, Kellogg Institute for International Studies.

————. 1992. *Que Democracia?* São Paulo: Editora Companhia das letras.

Weldon, J., 1997. "Political Sources of *Presidentialismo* in Mexico." In S. Mainwaring and M. Shugart, eds., *Presidentialism and Democracy in Latin America.* Cambridge: Cambridge University Press.

Weyland, K., 1993. "The Rise and Fall of President Collor and Its Impact on Brazilian Democracy." *Journal of InterAmerican Studies and World Affairs* 35 (July).

————. 1996. "Neopopulism and Neoliberalism in Latin America: Unexpected Affinities." *Studies in Comparative International Development* 31 (fall).

Wiarda, H., 1982. *Politics and Social Change in Latin America: The Distinct Tradition,* 2nd ed. Amherst: University of Massachusetts Press.

————. 1990. *The Democratic Revolution in Latin America.* New York: Holmes and Meier.

Williamson, J., 1990. "The Progress of Policy Reform in Latin America." In J. Williamson, ed., *Latin American Adjustment: How Much Has Happened?* Washington, D.C.: Institute for International Economics.

————. 1993. "Democracy and the 'Washington Consensus.'" *World Development* 21 (August).

————, ed., 1994. *The Political Economy of Policy Reform.* Washington, D.C.: Institute for International Economics.

Williamson, J., and S. Haggard, 1994. "The Political Conditions for Economic Reform." In J. Williamson, ed., *The Political Economy of Policy Reform.* Washington, D.C.: Institute for International Economics.

World Bank, 1990. *World Development Report.* New York: Oxford University Press.

Zapata, F., 1987. *Relaciones laborales y negociación colectiva en el sector público mexicano.* Working documents of the Centro de Estudios Sociológicos, El Colegio de México, D.F.

————. 1990a. "La crisis del control sindical sobre el mercado de trabajo en México." In *México en el umbral del milenio*. Mexico, D.F.: El Colegio de México.

————. 1990b. "Los trabajadores y la política en México." *Revista Paraguaya de Sociología*, no. 75.

————. 1990c. "El empleo en el Estado en México." In A. Marshall, ed., *El empleo público frente a la crisis*. Geneva: Estudios sobre América Latina, Instituto Internacional de Estudios Laborales.

————. 1995a. *El sindicalismo mexicano frente a la restructuración*. Mexico, D.F.: El Colegio de México.

————. 1995b. "Labor relations, productivity, and enterprise competitiveness." Report prepared for the Labour Law and Labour Relations Branch of the International Labor Office (ILO), Geneva, Switzerland.

Zini Jr., A. A., 1992. "Monetary Reform, State Intervention, and the Collor Plan." In A. A. Zini Jr., ed., *Market and the State in Economic Development in the 1990s*. Amsterdam: North-Holland.

Index

Acuña, C., 39–40
Aerolíneas Argentinas, foreign debt and
    privatization of, 73, 77–79, 81
Agreement for Economic Recovery,
    Mexican peso crisis and, 187–89
Albina Garabito, Rosa, 158n.10
Alemann, R., 68n.7
Aleman (President), 173n.8
Alesina, A., 28
Alfonsín, Raúl, 65–66, 222
Alianza Popular Revolucionaria Americana,
    225
Alliance for Growth, 172n.7
Alsogaray, Alvaro, 63, 68–69, 73–74
Alsogaray, María Julia, 63, 73–76, 79
Andean Group, 44–45
Andean Pact, 51
Andrés Pérez, 143
antidumping duties, "shallow" integration
    and, 53
apathy, neopluralism and, 211–13
Argentina: corporatism in, 156, 213–14;
    democratic transition in, 212n.27, 219;
    economic reform in, 15, 62–88, 231;
    exchange-rate variations with Brazil, 50;
    external debt problems and, 70–73;
    hyperinflation crisis in, 32, 67–69, 88;
    international financial capital influx in,
    79–83; labor movement and Peronism,
    199n.4; peso revaluation in, 83–86;
    popular sector in, 143; populism in, 210,
    217; privatization and foreign debt
    payment, 73–79; socioeconomic
    inequality in, 224
Argentine Council for Foreign Relations
    (CARI), 73

Argentine External Finances in the Decade
    of the 1990s, 73
Aujac, H., 27
authoritarian regimes: corporatism and,
    213–14; democratic regimes with
    elements of, 234–39; institutionalization
    of, 7; leadership styles and, 222–23;
    Mexican interest representation and,
    175–80; missing-social-contract
    hypothesis and, 38–41; neopluralism and,
    200–208, 213n.29, 214–17; organized
    labor and, 216n.33; role of, in economic
    reform, 4–6, 170
automotive sector in Mexico, union
    organization in, 157n.8
Aylwin, Patricio (President), 149, 222

Bachrach, P., 208
Baer, Werner, 15–16, 89–126, 232–33, 238
Baker Plan, Argentinian foreign debt and,
    72–73
Balbin, R., 65n.4
bankruptcies, economic reform and,
    203n.11
Barcelona negotiations, 185–86
Barrera, Manuel, 16–17, 127–49, 231–34
Bell Atlantic, 76
Bolivia: corporatist actors in, 156n.5;
    Emergency Social Fund in, 35n.19;
    hyperinflation crisis in, 32; hyper-
    presidentialism in, 207n.21; popular
    sector in, 143; targeted-assistance
    programs in, 34–35
bond issues: Argentinian economic reform
    and foreign capital, 80–83; Collor II
    reforms in Brazil and, 102–108

bourgeoisie: neopluralism and, 203–208
Brady Plan: Argentinian foreign debt and,
72–73, 78, 80, 84n.26
Brazil: absence of fiscal adjustment in,
118–20; Bresser Plan, 93–94; Collor I
reforms, 97–102; Collor II reforms,
102–108; *Comunidade Solidária*
program, 35n.18; Constitution of 1988,
96–97; corporatism in, 156, 213–14;
democratic transition in, 212n.27, 219;
economic reform in, 15–16; exchange-
rate variations with Argentina, 50; fight
for shares crisis, 115–20; gradualism *vs.*
policy shocks, 94–96; hybrid regime in,
220–21; inflation and economic policy in,
30–32, 89–126; Itamar Franco inter-
regnum and, 108–110; missing-social-
contract hypothesis and political pacts
in, 39; neopluralism in, 202n.9, 214,
216–17; Plano Real of, 120–24; policy
makers and policies in, 90; populist
government in, 210; socioeconomic
inequality in, 223–24; stabilization and
adjustment patterns in, 51; stagflation of
1987–1993, 115–20; targeted social
policies in, 35
Bresser Pereira, Luiz Carlos, 4, 13–14,
21–41, 94, 100n.19, 231, 233–34
Bresser Plan, Brazilian economic reform
and, 93–94
Buchanan, James, 24
Buchanan, Paul, 37, 38n.23
business community: growing influence of,
in Latin America, 231–34; Mexican peso
crisis and, 186–89; state economic
policies and, 6n.3

Canitrot, A., 27
capitalism: Argentinian economic reform
and return of, 79–83; neoliberal
economic reform and, 229–34
Capitalism, Socialism and Democracy, 237
Cárdenas, Cuauhtémoc, 155, 162n.12, 178
Cárdenas, Lázaro, 17, 210; Mexico
corporatism and, 153–61; Mexico labor
movement and, 162n.12
cardenista movement, 178–80
Cardoso, Fernando Henrique, 39, 109–110,
120, 209n.9
Cardoso de Melo, Zélia, 102–104

cash-flow controls, Brazilian economic
reform and, 94–96, 103–108
Catholic Church, Latin American economic
reform and, 231n.4
caudillismo, 236
Cavallo, Domingo, 15, 63–64
*Cementos Mexicanos, Ingenieros Civiles
Asociados,* 163
Central American Common Market, 44–45,
51
Central Bank of Argentina, 63–64; peso
revaluation, 83–86; return of foreign
capital and, 80–83
Central Bank of Brazil: Collor II reforms
and, 102–108; "Immediate Action Plan"
and, 110; independence of, 126
Central Unitaria de Trabajadores (CUT),
148–49
"centrifugal diversification," Mexican
political and economic reform and,
179–80, 190–92
Chiapas revolt, 155–56, 164, 186, 190,
211n.26
Chile: business interests in, 231–34; collapse of democracy in, 227; corporatist
actors in, 156n.5; employment patterns,
131–34, 232; financial guarantees for
military in, 232n.5; financial market
regulation in, 230n.3; labor relations
during adjustment, 137–42; macroeconomic adjustment in, 127–49;
neoliberal economic reform in, 4, 6n.3,
16–17, 204n.15, 234; neopluralism and
democratic regime in, 207–208, 213–14,
216–17; poverty levels in, 136–37,
210n.23, 214n.30; repression and
economic reform in, 7n.5; "shallow"
integration and, 54; social and political
inclusion in popular sector, 142–46;
social policy reforms in, 205n.17;
stabilization and adjustment patterns in,
51; state fiscal crisis resolved, 213n.28;
targeted assistance programs in, 34–35,
211; wage patterns, 134–37
Citibank: Argentinian economic reform and,
82–83
Citicorp Equity Investment (CEI):
Argentinian economic reform and, 82–83
citizenship: neopluralism and, 212–13;
quality of democracy and, 11

civil society: Chilean popular sector and,
146–49; corporatism and, 195–96;
democratic autonomy and, 11; economic
reform and, 5–7, 12; Mexican political
reform and, 191–92; missing-social-
contract hypothesis and, 38–41; neopluralism and resurrection of, 208,
211–13, 215–17; predatory capitalism
and, 233–34, 239n.13
class structure: class coalitions in Latin
America, 22; corporatist imperative and,
198–200; import-substituting industrialization and, 203–208; missing-social-
contract hypothesis and, 38–41; neopluralism and, 200–208; politics of power
and neopluralism and, 209–213
clientelism: Mexican interest representation
and, 175n.13; neopluralism and, 200–208,
212–13
*Código Federal de Instituciones y Procesos
Electorales (COFIPE),* 184n.33
Código Federal Electoral, 183n.33
Coercion, Mexican model of cooperation
and, 173n.10
COFINS tax, Collor II reforms in Brazil and,
107
cold war, Latin American economic reform
and, 231n.4
Colegio de Profesores, 149
Colegio Medico, 149
collective action, Mexican interest
representation and, 175n.13
collective bargaining: absence of, in
Mexico, 157–61; neopluralism and, 216
Collier, D., 239n.13
Collor de Mello, Fernando (President),
89–91, 97–108, 202n.9, 207n.21, 208n.22,
238
Colombia, threats to democracy in, 227
Colosio, Luis, 158n.10
Common External Tariff (CET): "shallow"
integration and, 53–54
Comunidade Solidária program, 35n.18
Concertation, Mexican political reform and,
161–66, 183n.32
Confederation of Mexican Workers (CTM),
153–61, 165n.14
Confederation of Revolutionary Workers
(COR): Mexican corporatism and,
158–61

Constitution of 1988: Brazilian economic
reform and, 96–97; fight for shares and,
117–20; hybrid regime and, 221
consumer price index: Brazilian economic
reform and, 96n.8
continuismo: Latin American leadership and
political structure and, 221–23
controlled inclusion: corporatist imperative
and ISI, 198–200; organized labor and,
205–208
Convertibility Plan, Argentina's economic
reform and, 64, 80, 83–86
cooperation, model of, 173n.10; Mexican
hegemonic party system, 181–86, 190–92;
Mexican interest representation and party
system, 171–80
*Coordinadora Intersindical Primero de
Mayo,* 155
corporatism: characteristics of, 197–200;
end of, 195–217; import-substituting
industrialization (ISI) and, 197–200;
Mexican economic reform and, 17;
Mexican political reform and, 161–67,
175–80, 231; Mexican trade unions and,
151–67; neopluralism and, 200–208;
organized labor and, 204–208; political
reform and, 214–17; populist movements and, 210; social stability and,
213–14
Costa Rica: Latin American economic
integration and, 52; targeted-assistance
programs in, 34–35
Credit, Collor I reform period in Brazil and
impact on, 99–102
creditor banks: Argentinian economic
reform and flow of foreign capital,
81–82
Cruzado Plan, 39, 89–92
Cuba, 227
Cukierman, A. Z., 28
currency exchange: Argentina's foreign
debt and, 71–73; Argentina's peso
revaluation and, 83–86; Brazilian
economic reform and, 114–15;
Collor I period reforms in Brazil,
97–102; fight for shares in Brazil,
119–20; Plano Real in Brazil and,
121–24
cyclical economic crises: political origins
hypothesis and, 26–27

Dahl, Robert, 208–209, 223, 236
debt certificates: privatization of
    Argentinian companies and, 75–79
debt crisis, corporatist imperative and,
    199–200
decritismo, 237
de facto market integration, 14, 57
de la Madrid regime, Mexican political
    reform and, 176–80, 183n.33
"delegative democracy," 207, 226, 235–39
"democratic autonomy" concept, 11
democratic consolidation, economic reform
    and, 11–12, 226, 228–39
Democratic Current, split with Mexican PRI,
    178–80
democratic norms, neopluralism and, 209–13
democratic regimes: Argentinian economic
    reform and, 65–69; authoritarian elements
    in, 234–39; authoritarianism institution-
    alized in, 7–8; Brazilian stagnation and
    inflation and, 89–126; Chilean labor
    movement and, 148–49; continuismo and
    conversion in, 221–23; definitions of, 7–8;
    economic crises and, 219–26; economic
    reform under, 4–5; hybrid regimes,
    220–21; Mexican interest representation
    and partisan politics, 169–72; minimalist
    conception of, 224–25, 237–39; neo-
    pluralism and, 200–213; quality of,
    economic reforms and, 10–11; social
    inequalities and, 223–25
Democratic Revolutionary Party (PRD): as
    center-left political force, 171n.4; interest
    representation and, 172–86; Mexican
    economic developmental models and,
    17–18; Mexican hegemonic party system,
    182–86; Mexican peso crisis and, 187–89;
    Mexican political reform and, 162–66,
    192–93; wins Mexico City mayoral race,
    235n.7
developmental models: corporatist impera-
    tive and, 197–200; import-substituting
    industrialization and, 196–97; interest
    intermediation and, 17–18; Mexican
    interest representation and party system,
    169–80, 189–92; Mexican peso crisis and,
    187–89; missing-social-contract theory
    and, 39–41; outward-looking develop-
    ment models, 4, 16–17; socioeconomic
    inequality and democracy in, 224–25

Díaz Ordaz administration, 173n.8
"dominant-party systems," Mexican interest
    representation and, 170n.2
Dornbusch, R., 28
Draibe, S., 35
Dresser, D., 207n.19
Ducatenzeiler, Graciela, 3–19, 33, 227–39

Eastern Europe, parallels with Latin
    America, 222–23, 238n.12
economic crises, Latin American
    democracies and, 219–26
Economic Emergency Law, 69
economic integration: emergence of, in
    Latin America, 43–47; obstacles to, 49–56;
    open regionalism and, 47–49; "shallow"
    integration, 52–54; stabilization and
    adjustment patterns, 50–52
economic reform: in Argentina, 61–88; in
    Brazil, 91–126; Chilean macroeconomic
    adjustment, 127–49; democratization in
    Latin America and, 3–19; Mexican interest
    representation and, 172–80, 190–92;
    political origins of, 21–41; regime type
    and success of, 4–6, 235n.8
economic systems: rational-choice theory
    and role of, 25–27
Ecuador: hyper-presidentialism in, 207n.21,
    215n.31; populism in, 217
education: corporatist imperative and,
    199–200; neopluralism and, 211–213
Edwards, S., 28
El Barzón movement, 187
electoral democracy, *vs.* liberal democracy,
    237n.10
electoral politics: hegemonic Mexican party
    system and, 180–86; Mexican corporatism
    and, 155–61, 165–67; Mexican interest
    representation and, 172–80; Mexican
    peso crisis and, 187–89; neopluralism
    and, 202–208
El Salvador, Latin American economic
    integration and, 52
Emergency Social Fund (Bolivia), 35n.19
employment patterns: Brazilian economic
    reform and, 113–15; Chilean macro-
    economics and, 128–31; Chilean popular
    sector insertion, 131–34; market forces in
    Latin America and, 232
Engel Company, 63

Entel, Argentine foreign debt and privatization of, 73–79
equity among nations, open regionalism and, 54–56
Estado Novo dictatorship (Brazil), 221
exchange-rate anchor: hyperinflation control, 32n.16; Plano Real, 122–24
exports: Brazilian economic reform and, 113–15; intraregional trade and investment, 45–46; Mexican political reform and, 163–64

Federal Work Law (LFT) (Mexico), 153–54
Federation of Unions of State Workers (FSTSE), 160–61
Federation of Workers in Goods and Services (FESEBES), 158–61
financial movements tax, Brazilian economic reform and, 109–110
FINSOCIAL tax, Collor II reforms in Brazil and, 107
fiscal adjustment measures: absence of, in Brazil, 118–20; Plano Real, 120–24
Ford Motor Company: Mexican corporatist sector and, 156–57
foreign debt: Argentine privatization and, 73–79; Argentinian economic reform and payment of, 70–73; financial recycling of, in Argentina, 86–88
Foro El Sindicalism ante la Nación, 155
Fox, J., 207n.19
Free Trade Area for the Americas (FTAA), 43, 50, 54–56
Frei, President, 149
Frieden, Jeffrey, 88
Fuentes, Juan Alberto, 14–15, 43–57
Fujimori, Alberto, 200, 207n.21, 208n.22, 215n.31, 238
Fukuyama, Francis, 7
Funaro, Dilson, 94

game theory: political support hypothesis and, 28
Geddes, B., 4–5, 9
General Agreement on Tariffs and Trade (GATT): Mexican political reform and, 163–66
Gini coefficient: Chilean income distribution, 137
Goldthrope, J., 28

González Fraga, J., 80n.20
governability: consolidation of democracy and, 226; economic reforms and, 22–41; Mexican interest representation and, 170n.2; missing-social-contract hypothesis and, 36–41
government deficits: Argentina's peso revaluation and, 85–86; Brazilian economic reform and, 92–126; Collor I reform period in Brazil and impact on, 99–102
gradual adjustment process, Latin American open regionalism and, 48–49
gradualism: in Brazilian economic reform, 94–96; Mexican hegemonic party system and, 182n.30
Graham, Carol, 35
Green Environmentalist Party of Mexico (PVEM): Mexican political reform and, 162–66
Grindle, M., 29
gross domestic product (GDP): in Brazil, investment as portion of, 111–15; Chilean employment statistics, 128–31; Chilean wage patterns and, 134–37; Collor Plan growth rates in Brazil and, 101–102; corporatist imperative and, 199–200; Mexican peso crisis, 186–89
Group of Rio, 49
Guatemala: democratic transition in, 219–20; socioeconomic inequality in, 223–24
Guimaraes, Ulysses, 222

Haggard, S., 28
Haiti, political instability in, 228
Haya de la Torre, 225
hegemonic party system, Mexican political reform, 180–86
Held, D., 11
Hernández Juárez, Francisco, 153–54, 158
heterodox mechanisms, inflation control with, 32
Hirsch, F., 28
Hirschman, A., 27–28
Hobbes, Thomas, missing-social-contract hypothesis and, 36–37
Hojalata y Lámina (HYLSA), 159
hybrid regimes: emergence of, 220–21; hyper-presidentialism and, 238–39; Latin American democracies as, 18–19, 235n.9

hyperinflation: Argentinian economic
reforms and, 35, 67–69, 88; Brazil's fight
for shares and, 16, 115–20; economic
policy making and, 31–32
hyper-presidentialism, 207, 236–39

"Immediate Action Plan" Brazilian
economic reform and, 109–110
imports: Argentina's peso revaluation and,
84–86; Latin American economic integration and, 46–47
import-substituting industrialization (ISI):
corporatist imperative and, 197–200;
developmental models and, 18, 196–97;
Mexican interest representation and,
174–80; neopluralism and, 200–208;
organized labor and, 203–205; politics of
power and, 209–213
income distribution: Brazilian economic
reform and, 112–15; Chilean wage
patterns and, 134–37; job growth and,
232; Latin American civil society and, 22;
Mexican interest representation and party
system, 171n.5; missing-social-contract
hypothesis and, 37–41; Plano Real in
Brazil and, 122–24; political support
hypothesis and, 28; predatory capitalism
and, 232–34; social compensation
strategies and, 34–36
indexation: Collor II reforms in Brazil and,
102–108; Plano Real and, 120–24
inflation: Argentinian economic reform and,
67–71; Brazilian stagnation and, 89–126;
Bresser Plan and, 93–94; Collor I reform
period in Brazil and impact on, 98–102;
Collor II reforms in Brazil and, 102–108;
fight for shares in Brazil and, 115–20;
gradualism vs. shock policies in Brazil,
94–96; "Immediate Action Plan" in Brazil,
109–110; Mexican interest representation
and, 174–80; Mexican political reform
and, 163–66; political economy and,
30–32; political support hypothesis,
27–30
Institute for the Promotion of Housing for
Workers, 153
institutional flexibility, Latin American open
regionalism and, 48–49
"institutionalization of uncertainty,"
democratic regimes and, 223–26

institutional requirements, open
regionalism and, 54–56
Institutional Revolutionary Party (PRI,
Partido Revolucionario Institucional):
economic developmental models and,
17–18, 172; electoral politics, 155–61,
158n.10; hegemonic party system, 181–86;
interest representation and, 172–92; labor
movement's allegiance to, 199n.4; loses
majority in 1997, 235n.7; Mexican political
reform and, 162–66, 192–93; neopluralism
and, 201–208; peso crisis and, 187–89;
socioeconomic inequalities and, 225
intellectual property, "shallow" integration
and, 53–54
Inter-American Development Bank (IADB):
open regionalism and, 56
interest rates: Brazilian stagnation and inflation and, 92–93; Collor II reforms in Brazil
and, 105–108; Mexican peso crisis and,
187–89; Plano Real in Brazil and, 121–24
interest representation: Mexican developmental model and, 172–80; Mexican
party system and, 189–92
international factors in economic reform,
231n.4, 235.8
international financial flows, Argentinian
economic reform and, 79–83
International Monetary Fund (IMF):
Brazilian inflation crisis and, 31n.15, 35;
Chilean macroeconomics, 130
intraregional trade and investment: free
trade agreements and, 46–47; Latin
American expansion of, 45–46; "shallow"
integration and, 53–54
investments: intraregional trade and investment, 45–46; as portion of Brazilian GDP,
111–15; "shallow" integration and, 53–54
Israel, inflation crises in, 32
Itamar Franco, M. (President), 91, 107–110

Kalecki, Michael, 27
Keynes, John Meynard, 234
Keynesian economics, political factors in,
30–32
Korzeniewicz, R., 233

labor forces. See also organized labor:
Chilean adjustment period, 137–42;
corporatist imperative and, 198–200;

macroeconomics and, 128–31; Mexican corporatism, 152–61, 166–67; Mexican political reform and, 161–66; neo-pluralism and, 202–208, 216–17; popular sector insertion, 131–46; social and political inclusion in Chilean popular sectors, 143–46
Lagos, Ricardo, 222
Latin American Integration Association (ALADI), 51–52
Latin American structuralist theory: corporatism and, 196–217; political support hypothesis and, 27
Leadership, role of, in Latin American democratic reforms, 222–23
Leiderman, 28
Levitsky, S., 239n.13
liberal democracy, *vs.* electoral democracy, 237n.10
liberalism: economic reform and, 7–8
liberal Right, neopluralism and, 203–208
Lindberg, L., 28
Lipset, S. M., 9n.6, 223
Lombardo Toledano, Vicente, 153
"low-intensity citizenship," 212
Lula da Silva, Luiz Inacio, 222

macroeconomics: Argentina's foreign debt and, 71–73; Chilean economic reforms and, 127–49; Latin American economic integration and, 50–52; Mexican interest representation and, 172n.7, 173–80; political structure and, 30–31; political support hypothesis and, 28
Mailson de Nobrega, 94–96
Mainwaring, S., 180
Mancur Olson, 24
Manoïlesco, Mihaïl, 195, 201n.7, 215
Manufacturer's Hanover Bank, 76
manufacturing sector, Brazilian economic reform and, 111–15
maquiladoras, Mexican corporatism and, 159–61
market forces: absence of fiscal adjustment in Brazil and, 119–20; Argentinian foreign debt and, 72–73; consolidation of democracy and, 228–39; integration of, 14–15; Mexican interest representation and partisan politics, 169–70; neoliberal economic reform and, 8; neopluralism

and, 206–208, 215–17; outward-looking development models and, 4; political-origin hypothesis and, 23–27; predatory forms of, 19; state institutions and, 229–34
Martínez de Hoz, J. A., 65
Marx, Karl, 234
Marxist economics, political support hypothesis, 27–30
McKinnon, R., 87
Means, Gardiner, 27
Menem, Carlos, 15, 62–63, 65, 68, 207n.21, 222, 238; privatization initiatives and foreign debt payment, 73–79
Mercosur: exchange-rate variations and, 50; formation of, 44–45, 56–57; institutional strategies of, 58; Latin American economic integration and, 52
Mexican Social Security Institute (IMSS), 153–54
Mexico: "classic period" in, 173n.8; concertation and political reform in, 161–66; corporatism in, 151–67, 214; democratic transition in, 212n.27, 227; economic crisis of 1994–95, 186–89, 234n.7; economic reform in, 17–18; hyper-presidentialism in, 207n.21; inflation crises in, 32; interest representation and party system in, 169–92; neopluralism and, 214, 216–17; organized labor in, 205n.16; peso crisis in, 50, 86n.28, 186–89, 234n.7; popular sector in, 143; populist government in, 210; presidential elections in, 155–61; "shallow" integration and, 54; stabilization and adjustment patterns in, 51; targeted assistance programs in, 206–208, 211; union organization in, 151–67; wage controls in, 204n.14
Mexico-Chile Free Trade Agreement, 164n.13
Miami Summit of 1994, 50
military regimes. *See also* authoritarian regimes; discrediting of, 232n.4; as power brokers, 215n.31
Mill, John Stewart, 11
minimum wage, in Chile, 136
Ministry of Labor and Social Security (Mexico), 159
missing-social-contract hypothesis, 21, 36–41

modernization, political structure and, 209–213
modernization from above theory, corporatist imperative and, 198–200
money supply: Collor I reform period in Brazil and impact on, 98–102; Collor II reforms in Brazil and impact on, 104–108; Plano Real in Brazil and, 121–24
Montoro administration, 35
Montreal conference, 11–13
Morgan Bank, Argentinian economic reform and, 81, 86
multilateral rules, Latin American open regionalism and, 48
Muñoz Ledo, Porfirio, 162, 188n.37

Naim, M., 56
Nakano, Yoshiaki, 4, 13–14, 21–41, 231, 233–34
National Action Party (PAN, *Partido de Acción Nacional*); as center-right political force, 171n.4; economic developmental models and, 17–18; interest representation and, 172–80; Mexican hegemonic party system, 181–86; Mexican peso crisis and, 188–89; Mexican political reform and, 162–66
National Business Chamber, 153n.2
National Commission on Minimum Wages, 153
National Coordination of Educational Workers (Mexico), 160–61
National Political Accord, 187–89
National Solidarity Program (PRONASOL), 34–35; disbanding of, 207n.20; Mexican political reform and, 164–66; neopluralism and, 207–208, 211
National Union of Educational Workers (SNTE) (Mexico), 160–61
Nelson, Joan, 34
neoclassical economics: missing-social-contract hypothesis and, 36–41; political-origins hypothesis, 24–27
neoliberal economic reform: in Chile, 4, 6; Chilean labor relations and, 137–42; consolidation of democracy and, 228–39; corporatism and, 196–97; market role in, 8; organized labor and, 204; political origins hypothesis and, 26–27; politics of power and, 209–213; regime type and,

10–19, 235n.8; state's role in, 229n.2; Washington consensus bias towards, 33
neopluralism: developmental models and, 18; emergence of, 196–97; hyper-presidentialism and predatory capitalism and, 238–39; Mexican PRONASOL program and, 207; politics of power and, 208–213; state corporatism and, 200–208
neopopulism: emergence of, 217; hyper-presidentialism and, 238
net transition costs, political support hypothesis and, 29
Nicaragua, Latin American economic integration and, 52
Niskanen, William, 24
Nissan Mexicana, 157n.8
nonagricultural employment, Chilean labor relations, 140–42
nonreciprocity: open regionalism and, 55–56
North American Free Trade Agreement (NAFTA): Latin American economic integration and, 51–52; Mexican political reform and, 163–66
Noyola, J., 27

O'Donnell, G., 27, 65, 207–208, 224, 235–36
oil shocks, Brazilian fight for shares and, 117–20
oil workers union, Mexican political reform and, 178–80
open regionalism: characteristics of, 47–48; national equity and institutional requirements, 54–56; prospects for, in Latin America, 43, 47–57
Organization of American States (OAS), open regionalism and, 56
organized labor: adjustment period in Chile, 138–42; Chilean labor patterns, 133–34; Chilean popular sector and, 147–49; corporatism and, 151–67; democratic instability and, 210–213; economic reform and, 6–7, 12, 16–17, 17; interest representation and Mexican political reform, 178–80; liberal Right and, 203–204; membership in Chile, 139–42; Mexican automotive sector, 157n.8; military regimes and, 216n.33; neo-pluralism and, 216–17; political reform and, 161–66, 178–80; split between rank and file and elites, 205, 216–17

orthodox shock policies, inflation control and, 32
outward-looking development models, 4, 16–17
overnight markets, Brazilian economic reform and, 109–10, 118–20
Oxhorn, Philip, 3–19, 33, 195–217, 227–39

Pact for Stability and Economic Growth (PECE), 17; concertation and political reform in Mexico and, 161–66; Mexican labor movement and, 152–53, 158–61
Pacto de Los Pinos, 183
Pacto de Solidaridad Económica, 176–80
Paiva, Claudia, 15–16, 89–126, 232–33, 238
partisan politics: hegemony of, in Mexico, 180–86; Mexican interest representation and, 169–92; neopluralism and, 214–17; peso crisis and, 187–89
Party of Work (PT): Mexican political reform and, 162–66, 185–86
Paz Estensoro administration, 35n.19
Pérez, José Jesús, 158n.10
Perón, Isabel, 65n.4
Perón, Juan, statist policies of, 63–64, 210, 225
Peronism: Argentinian economic reforms and, 63–67; labor movement allegiance to, 199n.4
Peru: corporatist actors in, 156n.5; democratic transition in, 219–20, 228; hyperinflation crisis in, 32; neopluralism in, 202n.9, 215n.31, 217; socioeconomic inequality in, 223–25
peso revaluation: Argentinian economic reform and, 83–86; Mexican peso crisis, 186–89
Pinochet regime: Chilean macroeconomics and, 127–28, 166; as hyper-presidentialism, 238; neoliberal economic reforms of, 4; social welfare policies of, 205n.17, 211
Pinto, A., 27
Plan Laboral, 138–42
Plano Real (Brazil), 16, 39, 120–24
Plano Verão, 95–96
Pluralism, neopluralism and, 201–213
Poland, hyperinflation crisis in, 32
Polanyi, Karl, 233–34
policy consensus, economic recession and, 3–4, 13–14

policy-driven market integration, 14–15, 57
policy-making elites: economic reform and, 5–6; political support hypothesis and, 29–30
political alliances: Argentinian economic reform and, 64–69; missing-social-contract hypothesis and, 38–41
political-business-cycle theory, political support hypothesis and, 29–30
political class, Mexican creation of, 184–86
political economy, defined, 24
political-origin hypothesis, economic reform and, 23–27
political structure. See also democratic regimes: Brazilian fight for shares and, 115–20; Brazilian stabilization efforts and, 124–26; Chilean macroeconomic adjustment and, 127–49; Chilean popular sectors, 142–46; corporatism and, 153–61; economic reform and, 6–7, 9–19; hegemonic party system in Mexico and, 180–86; interest representation and, 172–80; leadership continuismo and conversion and, 221–23; Mexican concertation and reform of, 161–66; Mexican peso crisis, 186–89; missing-social-contract hypothesis and, 36–41; neopluralism and, 200–208; role of, in economic reform, 4–5, 21–41; socioeconomic modernization of, 209–213
political support hypothesis, economic reform and, 27–30
popular sector: Brazilian stagnation and inflation and, 89–92; Bresser Plan and, 93–94; Chilean labor market and, 131–42, 231; Collor I reform period in Brazil and impact on, 98–102; Collor II reforms in Brazil and, 103–108; Constitution of 1988, 96–97; democratic instability and, 210–213; economic reform and, 16–17; employment patterns in Chile, 131–34; macroeconomic adjustment in Chile and, 127–49; Mexican corporatism and, 153–61; neopluralism and, 202–208, 213, 231; organized labor and, 205–208; Plano Real and, 120–24; politics of, in Chile, 146–49; remuneration patterns, 134–37; social and political inclusion in Chile and, 142–46

populism: breakdown of democracy and, 210–213; corporatist imperative and ISI, 198–200; inflation and, 27–28; Mexican political reform and, 178–80; missing-social-contract hypothesis and, 38–41; socioeconomic inequality and, 225
Porfirio Díaz regime, 175n.15
poverty levels: market forces and, 232–34; percentage of Chilean households in, 136–37, 210n.23, 214n.30; social compensation strategies and, 32–41, 131
power relations: Argentinian economic reform and, 64–69; business interests and, 231–34; democratic regimes and, 234–39; military as brokers in, 215n.31; neopluralism and, 208–213; political-origins hypothesis and, 23–27
predatory capitalism, economic reform in Latin America and, 232–34
preventive price adjustments, Brazilian economic reform and, 95–96
price controls: Argentinian peso revaluation and, 84–86; Brazilian Bresser plan and, 94; Brazilian political structure and, 124–26; Collor I reform period in Brazil and, 97–102; Collor II reforms in Brazil and, 104–108; fight for shares and, 119–20; inflation management with, 32n.16; Mexican corporatism and, 156–61
priísta peace period, Mexican interest representation and, 175–76, 184n.34
privatization: Argentine foreign debt and, 73–79; consensus on, 4; consolidation of democracy and, 229; Latin American economic integration and, 47; Plano Real and, 123–24
protectionism, Mexican import-substitution industrialization (ISI) and, 174–80
Prud'homme, Jean-François, 17–18, 169–92
Przeworski, A., 4, 37
public-choice theory: political origin hypothesis and, 24
Putnam, R. D., 37

Radical Party of Argentina: economic reforms and, 66–68
Rangel, I., 27
rational-choice theory: political origin hypothesis and, 24–25
Razeto, L., 143

Real Plan of 1993. *See* Plano Real
reciprocal agreements: Latin American free trade agreements and, 45; "shallow" integration and, 53–54
Reform of the State Law, 69
Regional Confederation of Mexican Workers (CROM), 159–61
representative democracy, 235
repression: Chilean labor relations and, 137–42, 204–205; economic reform and, 7n.5, 9–10; neopluralism and, 215–17; of organized labor, 216n.33
Revolutionary Confederation of Workers and Peasants, 158–61
"rice with beans" strategy: Brazilian economic reform, 95–96
Robinson, Joan, 27
Ros, Jaime, 177
Ruiz Guinazú, Magdalena, 68n.9

Sachs, J. D., 28
Salinas de Gotari (President), 164, 181, 183n.33, 187, 207n.20, 211
Sarney, José, 90–91, 94–96
Sartori, G., 180
scale and specialization, Latin American open regionalism and, 47–48
Schmitter, Philippe, 195–99, 203, 208, 214, 220
Schumpeter, Joseph, 237
Schvarzer, Jorge, 15, 61–88, 231–32, 238
Scully, T., 180
Secretaría de Governación, 180
sectoral agreements: Latin American free trade agreements and, 44–45; Latin American open regionalism and, 48–49; "shallow" integration and, 53–54
sectoral employment distribution, Chilean statistics, 132–34
self-employment, Chilean rates of, 133–34
service sector: Latin American free trade agreements and, 45; "shallow" integration and, 53–54
sexenio regime of de la Madrid, Mexican political reform and, 176–80, 183–86
shock policies: Brazilian economic reform and, 94–96; inflation and, 31–32
Silva, E., 6n.3
Simonsen, Mario H., 117–18
Smith, W. C., 39–40, 233

social accords, Brazilian economic reform
and, 95–96
social compensation strategy, economic
reform and, 32–40, 231
social contract: Chilean popular sectors,
142–46; government legitimacy and,
21–41; Mexican interest representation
and, 174–80
Social Emergency Fund (*Fundo Social de
Emergência*), Plano Real and, 120–24
social mobility: corporatist imperative and,
198–200; neopluralism and, 210–211
social security taxes, Collor II reforms in
Brazil and, 107–108
social welfare, neopluralism and, 205–208,
211–13, 216–17
societal corporatism, characteristics of, 197
society-centered theories, Mexican
economic reform and, 170–72, 189–92
socioeconomic inequality: Argentinian
economic reform and, 68–69; Chilean
labor relations and, 138–42, 147–49;
consensus on economic reform and,
13–14; corporatist imperative and ISI,
198–200; democratic regimes and,
223–25; hyper-presidentialism and,
238–39; Latin American democracies and,
19; market forces and, 232–34; Mexican
targeted assistance programs, 206–208;
neopluralism and, 201–208, 215–17;
politics of power and, 208–213; predatory
capitalism and, 233–34, 238–39; quality of
democracy and, 11
Sola, L., 36
South East Asian newly industrialized
countries, economic reforms in, 6n.4
stabilization policies: Brazilian political
structure and, 124–26; differing patterns
of, 50–52; governability linked to, 39–41;
Latin American open regionalism and, 48
stagflation, Brazilian economic reform and,
115–20
stagnation, Brazilian economic reform and,
110–15, 118
state-centered theories: Mexican economic
reform and, 170–72, 189–92
State Employees Social Security Institute,
154
state institutions: Argentina's privatization
initiatives and, 76–79; crisis of, in 1980s,

22–23; economic development strategies
and, 6–7; hybrid regimes, 220–21;
Mexican corporatism and, 153–61;
missing-social-contract hypothesis and,
36–41; neopluralism and, 205–208,
213–17; rational-choice theory and role
of, 25–27; reduced role of, 229–34; role
of, in economic reform, 18–19
stock market, Argentinian economic reform
and foreign capital, 80–81
"successful" economic reform, definitions
of, 4–5
supranational institutions, Latin American
free trade agreements and, 45

targeted assistance programs: neopluralism
and, 205–208, 211–213, 215–17; social
compensation strategies and, 33–36, 231
tariff reductions: Collor I reforms in Brazil
and, 100–102; Collor II reforms in Brazil
and, 104–108; Latin American free trade
agreements and, 44; Latin American open
regionalism and, 48
Taxa Referêncial (Brazil), 103
tax reform: Brazilian economic reform and,
109–110; Plano Real, 120–24
technocratic groups: Argentinian economic
reform and, 64–69; economic reform and,
31–32; neopluralism and, 201–208
telephone companies, Argentinian
economic reform and, 81–83
Telephone Workers Union, 153–54
third–party competitors, Latin American
open regionalism and, 48
Thorp, R., 28
Tocqueville, Alexis de, 224–25
trade agreements: Latin American economic
integration and, 44–46; policy consensus
on, 4; "shallow" integration and, 52–54
transaction costs, Latin American open
regionalism and, 48–49
transnational corporations, Mexican
political reform and, 164
Tullock, Gordon, 24

unemployment: in Chile, wage structure
and, 129–31; Chilean national rates of,
132–34; demise of organized labor and,
204
unions. See labor forces; organized labor

United Nations Economic Commission
for Latin American and the Caribbean
(ECLAC), 43; open regionalism
and, 56
Unit of Real Value (URV, *Unidade Real de
Valor*), 120–24
urban popular movement, Mexican political
reform and, 178–80
Uruguay, collapse of democracy in, 227
Uruguay Round of Multilateral Trade
Negotiations: open regionalism and, 54

Vargas, Getúlio (President), 210, 225
Velasco Alvarado, General, 225
Velásquez, Fidel, 153n.3, 155
Venezuela: popular sector in, 143; threats to
democracy in, 227
VITRO company, 163
Volkswagen of Mexico, 157n.8, 158n.9

wage controls: Brazilian Bresser Plan and,
94; Collor I reform period in Brazil and,
97–102; Collor II reforms in Brazil and,
103–108; economic competitiveness and,
204; fight for shares and, 119–20;
Mexican corporatism and, 156–61,
204n.14

wage statistics: Brazilian economic reform
and, 113–15; Chilean index of real wages,
137; Chilean minimum wage, 136; Chilean
popular sector employment, 134–37;
Chilean unemployment and, 129–31
Ward, Peter M., 207n.19
Washington consensus: NAFTA provisions
and, 51; social compensation strategy
and, 33, 35
Weber, Max, 234
Weffort, Francisco, 18–19, 219–26, 233,
235n.10, 238–39
"white unionism": Mexican corporatism
and, 159–61
*Who Governs: Democracy and Power in an
American City*, 208–9
Williamson, John, 4, 28, 68, 202
World Bank, 4; Argentina's privatization
initiatives and, 78–79; Chilean macroeconomics, 130; social compensation
strategies and, 33–34
World Trade Organization (WTO): open
regionalism and, 54

Zapata, Francisco, 17, 151–67, 231
Zedillo, Ernesto (President), 162, 164,
184n.33, 186